Why JESUS *the*
MESSIAH

Why JESUS *the* MESSIAH

GOD'S PURPOSE *for sending*
ISA AL MASIH
according to the HOLY GOSPEL

JIM DUDDLESTON

This book is written for
all who are eager to learn more about Jesus the Messiah
and why he was sent,
but who may have reservations about the Christian religion;
Abdullah, Mohammed, Omar,
and numerous other international students
my wife and I have had the privilege
of welcoming to our home in Philadelphia; and
all who long for justice and peace
to be established
in our unjust, battered world.

Of the Messiah it was written:
In faithfulness he will bring forth justice;
he will not falter or be discouraged
till he establishes justice on earth. (Isaiah 42:3)

CONTENTS

TOPICS OF SPECIAL INTEREST

PREFACE

A number of years ago I came to realize that believing in Christianity is not the same as submitting to God and following the path he revealed to Jesus the Messiah (Isa al-Masih). I remember writing down in bold capital letters: **IF GOD DID NOT SEND JESUS THE MESSIAH TO START A NEW RELIGION CALLED CHRISTIANITY, THEN WHY DID HE SEND HIM?** I desperately wanted to answer this question. As I began to read the Gospel (*Injil* in Arabic) with new eyes, I observed that the Prophet Jesus never asked anyone to become a Christian, but he invited everyone to be part of the kingdom of God.

New and exciting questions flooded my mind: What did Jesus mean by the kingdom of God? Why were people so excited about it? How could a person be part of it? What would it look like to participate in the kingdom of God?

It is sad that most people equate Christianity, with its imperfect past; with the message God gave Jesus about his kingdom. This misunderstanding can lead people to reject the Messiah Jesus and the message God gave him without ever reading the Gospel. While I believed there was much good in Christianity and knew many humble, loving Christians, I had become increasingly uncomfortable with some of the religion's teachings and practices. How would I respond to my discomfort, my dilemma? Could I believe that Jesus was God's Messiah and seek to practice the way of life he taught, the kingdom of God, without calling myself a Christian?

I will never forget when a friend pointed out to me that Jesus had never asked anyone to become a Christian. I decided I would carefully study the Gospel (as recorded by Luke) for myself to understand the message God gave the Messiah Jesus. Instead of unquestioningly accepting what others had taught me, I would try to find out for myself why God sent Jesus as his Messiah. So I spent more than four years studying the Gospel. I had read it many times before this, but I had often read into it the beliefs I had been taught by Christian teachers.

This has been a hard but enriching journey. There is great joy in discovering truth from God for yourself. But it is not easy to question your beliefs. Daring to question some of what you have been taught, and being open to new ways of understanding, can cause stress within you and create conflict with those around you—even those closest to you. Nonetheless, the rewards of seeking after the truth are worth it. By reading the Gospel carefully for myself, I have come to know and love God more. And my love for God's Servant Jesus has greatly increased, as I have better understood the great cost of his love and obedience to God.

INTRODUCTION

The purpose of this book is to assist readers in understanding why God sent Jesus as his Messiah and what that can mean for their lives and the world around them. After extensive study and reflection on each passage of the Gospel, I have retold the story, weaving in my own understanding of its meaning and significance.

It may be good right from the beginning to say in brief what the Gospel is. The Gospel is first and foremost the good news of what God accomplished by sending Jesus as his Messiah. It is the story of what God has accomplished *through* his Servant Jesus; in other words, everything Jesus said and did is the good news, the Gospel from God. Secondly, it is the written account of this message. There are four witnesses to this good news—Matthew, Mark, Luke, and John—and each of their accounts is in itself *a* Gospel, a witness to the good news of *the* Gospel.[1] My study is based on the Gospel as recorded by Luke. And unless otherwise indicated, all Scriptural quotations are from the Gospel as recorded by Luke.

The Gospel is not a random collection of stories and teachings but an orderly account of One Story that changed the course of history. Because every passage contributes in some way to *The Story* of why God sent his Messiah, I attempt to show not only the meaning of each passage but also how it contributes to the whole story of the Gospel. Why, for example, when Jesus tells a story illustrating God's love, does he make the hero a Samaritan—an enemy of the Jewish people? What does that teach us about why God sent Jesus?

While this book is not a technical commentary addressing every possible question of interpretation, I have thought deeply and worked hard to arrive at a correct understanding of each passage. Of course, every retelling is someone's interpretation of a story, and this book is

---

1. Scot McKnight, *The King Jesus Gospel* (Grand Rapids, MI: Zondervan, 2011), 82.

no exception. When there is uncertainty among scholars about how to understand a particular passage, I usually point this out. Because my aim has been to show the unity of the story of the Gospel and to keep the story moving—as it naturally does when it is read without comments—I have not usually included extensive support for my understanding of a passage. Support can be found, however, in the books I cite as sources.

When I first began this book, I was determined to be ruthlessly, radically, thoroughly objective in my research and writing so as to present Jesus as he is revealed to be in the Gospel. To a large degree one can be objective in the study of the Gospel. We are, after all, dealing with words and their meanings in a particular context that can be carefully studied. So I carefully studied for myself and read scholars who have sought to be impartial in their understanding of the Greek words and the meanings of those words in the first-century Palestinian Roman world in which they were written. Convinced that Christianity does not "own" Jesus, but that he is for the whole world, I wanted to objectively, dispassionately write of why God sent him according to the words of the Gospel.

But I was naïve. I soon realized that, while one can objectively study the meaning of the Gospel, it would be impossible for me to write dispassionately about God and his obedient Servant Jesus. I could have tried to hide my love and high esteem for the greatness of God and the great obedience of his Servant Jesus, but would I be able to? Even if I could, should I? Love and passion need not distort the truth of what one sees. After all, the pulsating love and power of God revealed in his Servant Jesus are intended to move us. So while I have sought to be impartial in my study and understanding of what the Gospel says, my love and high esteem for God and his servant Jesus will be evident throughout this book.

I have written primarily for those who are not acquainted with the Gospel and are perhaps reading it for the first time. At the same time, I have assumed that readers believe in (or at least are open to) the existence of God, a God who cares about our damaged, divided world and has intervened with his great power and mercy to restore it and bring peace. Thus I assume that the reader is open to God revealing his will for humanity through prophets, visions, angels, miracles, and above all, his Messiah.

Because hundreds of millions of people know the Arabic word for God's honorable prophets, I have included the Arabic name in parenthesis when I first mention some of the prophets. While Allah is the Arabic name used by Arab Muslims and Christians, I use the name God because this book is based on an English translation.

While I have written primarily for those who do not call themselves Christians, I believe Christians who read this book and the Gospel with new eyes will find new insights. In fact, I have often stressed what I believe many Christians have overlooked or misunderstood in the life and teachings of Jesus. While some of what I write may seem new for those who have grown up with Christianity, I can assure you that nothing I have written is novel. My interpretations are in agreement with leading scholars of the Bible. So I encourage all readers, whatever their religious background or beliefs, to be open-minded and discover for themselves why God sent Jesus as his Messiah.

Please do not simply read the results of my study. Before reading my retelling of each passage, I encourage you to first read the Gospel itself and reflect on what it says. It is always good to pray for understanding while we read. And we can better learn and practice the message God gave his Messiah if we discuss our questions and share our insights with a few friends. Why not set aside a few minutes each day to read the Gospel along with this book as an aid in understanding it? Learn the joy of God speaking directly to you as you pray and read his words.

As we read through the Gospel story it can be helpful to jot down any questions and insights that come to mind. You may want to ask such questions as:

- Why does the Gospel say God sent Jesus?
- Who does the Gospel say Jesus is? Why do people have difficulty understanding who he is?
- How do Jesus' actions and teaching reveal the nature of God's kingdom?
- How do people respond to Jesus? What would it look like to put his teachings into practice?

One of the biggest challenges in reading the Gospel is to understand the different titles used for Jesus. The most common title used for him is Messiah (Al-Masih). While there are other honorable titles used for Jesus in the Gospel, he is above all portrayed as God's Messiah-Servant-Prophet (Al-Masih- 'Abd - Al-Nabi). I have observed in reading the Noble Quran that it also emphasizes that Jesus, son of Mary, is the Messiah, Servant and Prophet sent by God. Could a focus on understanding these

titles for Jesus help build bridges of understanding between Muslims and
Christians? That is my hope in writing this book.

I have also observed that many Christians do not understand what
it means for Jesus to be God's Messiah. In addition, while Muslims also
believe that Jesus is the Messiah (which he is called eleven times in the
Noble Quran), I have found that many of my Muslims friends do not fully
understand this title either. For these reasons, I give special attention to
what it means for Jesus to be God's Messiah and explain how other titles,
such as Son of Man and Son of God, elucidate the meaning of the primary
title, Messiah.

While the Gospel stresses that the man Jesus from a village in
Northern Palestine is God's Messiah-Servant-Prophet whom God raised
to his presence as Lord,[2] this does not mean that these titles exhaust our
understanding of who Jesus is. Jesus is not bound by a title. He is who he
is, what he says and what he does. And as the Gospel draws to a close, we
sense along with Jesus' disciples that there may be more to the Prophet
Jesus than we first realized. Other parts of the Holy Scriptures provide
us with a fuller understanding. I write of Jesus as he is presented in the
Gospel of Luke, a good place to start.

Our different religious traditions refer to Jesus in different ways. For
example, when the Muslim community speaks of Jesus, they most often
add "Peace Be Upon Him" (PBUH) to express respect for him as a great
prophet. Christians may speak of him simply as Jesus, Jesus Christ, or the
Lord Jesus Christ. Most others simply speak and write of Jesus. Because
I have written this book for people of different religious backgrounds, I
most often refer to Jesus simply as Jesus or the Prophet Jesus. For most
of the Gospel story, the crowds who see Jesus heal and hear him teach
believe that he is a great prophet sent by God to help his people. In time,
midway through the Gospel, Jesus' closest disciples come to see that he is
also God's promised Messiah. After that point I increasingly refer to Jesus
as the Messiah. But as readers, we must keep in mind that at that stage
only the closest disciples knew who he was.

---

2.   Darrell L. Bock, "Luke, Gospel of," in *Dictionary of Jesus and the Gospels: A
Compendium of Contemporary Biblical Scholarship*, ed. Joel B. Green, Scot McKnight,
and I. Howard Marshall (Downers Grove, IL: InterVarsity Press, 1992), 504.

Early in my studies of the Gospel, a friend who is a scholar pointed out to me that as we read the Gospel we need to keep in mind *who knows what* about Jesus and his mission in the story. For example, Mary (Maryam), the mother of Jesus, knows what the crowds don't know. Evil spirits know Jesus' identity as the Messiah long before Jesus' closest disciples do. And his disciples do not truly begin to understand who Jesus is until God raises him up to heaven. So if we want to join the disciples in their discovery of Jesus' identity and mission, then we as readers must put aside any preconceptions (whether right or wrong) and be alert to what the Gospel actually says about Jesus and to what the various characters know about him at any given point in the narrative.

When I write about Jesus, I do not intend any disrespect by not adding "Peace Be Upon Him" or by not addressing him as the Lord Jesus Christ. I simply want us to know the joy of learning about him as his identity and mission unfold in the Gospel story. If we are to understand and revere Jesus as his first disciples did, we must learn to see him as they first saw him: a man who appeared from the countryside of Galilee, a man healing and teaching with a unique authority from God, a man the crowds soon believed to be a great prophet sent by God, and a man his closest disciples came to believe was the Messiah sent by God to remake our broken world.

If we really believe that God sent Jesus, it only makes sense for us to carefully read the message God gave him. Jesus called this message good news—the Gospel! The good news was that God's kingdom, his good and just will for divided, broken humanity, was coming to earth through his Messiah in a new and powerful way. The message God gave the Prophet Jesus to proclaim and enact was such good news that those who first heard it sang, danced, and wrote poetry when they encountered it. Whether they were out in their fields working, at home eating with family and friends, or at a place of prayer, they would stop what they were doing and praise God for the powerful words and the wonderful deeds of Jesus, God's Messiah.

I often ask myself if perhaps we do not understand or experience much of what the first followers of Jesus experienced and came to understand. Perhaps if we can experience and understand what they did, we too will begin to sing, dance, and write poetry to God. And perhaps the world around us will also change.

A VERY BRIEF BACKGROUND
TO THE GOSPEL STORY

The story of the Gospel takes place over two thousand years ago, when the Jews in Palestine lived under the oppressive rule of the powerful Roman Empire. Roman soldiers were present everywhere to collect Roman taxes and suppress any thought of revolt. Their presence was a constant reminder that the Jewish people were in bondage to a godless foreign ruler. When the Gospel story begins, Augustus Caesar, emperor of the vast Roman Empire, was at the height of his power (Luke 2:1). Many in the eastern part of the Empire worshipped Augustus as a son of God. Augustus claimed he ruled the Empire for the Supreme God!

Roman rule was corrupt and oppressive. The few rich had lives of ease while the masses were poor and oppressed. What gave the Jewish people hope in the midst of this oppression were the promises of God. God had promised them he would send a Deliverer, a Messiah. This Messiah would come, set God's people free, establish God's kingdom, and bring peace to all the people on the earth.

The Jewish people were longing for the fulfillment of these promises, for the coming of the Messiah-King, someone like Moses (Musa) whom God would raise up to deliver them from their oppressors. The oppression and the longing grew so intense that some of the people revolted. Self-appointed leaders proclaiming themselves to be Israel's promised Messiah-King gathered armies to fight against the Romans. The retaliation was severe: On one occasion a Roman commander from Syria came to Jerusalem (al-Quds) to break up a Jewish revolt. There he crucified approximately two thousand Jewish rebels.

Since Palestine was considered a troublesome area, six Roman legions surrounded it. A legion consisted of three to six thousand soldiers. Four of the legions were placed in Syria and two in Egypt. These troops were ready to suppress any further revolts from the Jewish people. This was the political climate Jesus grew up in. It was in this climate that he proclaimed the arrival of God's kingdom, which would displace the kingdom of Rome!

Jesus grew up and spent most of his life in the region called Galilee in the northern part of Palestine (roughly equivalent today to the area north of the West Bank and south of Lebanon and Syria). Josephus, a historian at the time, wrote that there were 204 villages scattered throughout Galilee. The region was so small that walking from one village to another (the main form of transportation) would take less than a day.

The majority of the several hundred thousand people who lived in Galilee were poor farmers. They either rented land from wealthy landlords or hired themselves out to work in the fields as day laborers. Wealth was unevenly distributed. This was another factor that led to unrest in Palestine in Jesus' day. Even though the Galileans were poor farmers, they were fearless and inflexible. Galilee was rich soil for revolutionaries. Would the Prophet Jesus fulfill the revolutionary expectations of his people?

Jesus himself grew up in the village of Nazareth, a farming community of around 480 people in the hill country. While Nazareth was small, it was only six miles from Sepphoris, the capital of Galilee, and close to the major international roads. About the time of Jesus' birth, Sepphoris had been burned to the ground and its inhabitants enslaved for revolting against the Romans.[3] Jesus grew up in Nazareth hearing stories of brutal suppression.

There are five major parts to the Gospel story: (1) The births of John the Baptist (Al-Nabi Yahya) and Jesus in chapters 1 and 2 are followed by (2) a short section that prepares us for the ministry of Jesus (3:1–4:13). (3) We then read of Jesus announcing and enacting the good news of the kingdom of God in Galilee. In this section we read of many of his miracles and how some of the leaders of Israel begin to oppose him (4:14–9:50). (4) After this follows the longest section in the Gospel, Jesus' journey to Jerusalem with his disciples (9:51–19:44). Because he knows he will leave the disciples from Jerusalem to go to be with God, Jesus devotes much time on the way there preparing them for his departure. Thus this section contains very few miracles and many more stories (parables) through which Jesus teaches them about the kingdom of God. (5) The last part of the Gospel covers a period of only one week and vividly records Jesus' ministry in Jerusalem. The Gospel ends with Jesus' exaltation to God's presence after he instructs the disciples in what they should now do (19:28–24:53).

---

3. Richard A. Horsley, *Galilee: History, Politics, People* (Valley Forge, PA: Trinity Press International, 1995), 165.

PART ONE

THE BIRTHS OF JOHN AND JESUS (1:5–2:52)

The first part of the Gospel story begins with God sending angels, giving visions, and filling people with his Spirit. It is clear that God is powerfully working in a new way. The people respond with joy and amazement and give thanks to God. They believe God is finally fulfilling the promises he gave through the prophets to send his chosen Messiah to deliver them from their oppression under the Romans.

When one godly man sees the infant Jesus, he speaks out in praise: "The Lord has raised up a powerful sign of liberation for us from among the descendants of God's servant, King David (Dawud). As was prophesied through the mouths of his holy prophets in ancient times: God will liberate us from our enemies and from the hand of our oppressors!" (1:69–71; Voice).

The first chapters of the Gospel story show us that the people of Israel believed God had sent the Messiah to deliver them. They believed the Messiah would be a spiritual/political Warrior-King come to rescue them from their Roman enemies. Is this what God planned to do? Is this why he had sent his Messiah?

The first two chapters introduce the two key persons in the Gospel story— first the Prophet John (Al-Nabi Yahya), and then the Prophet and Messiah Jesus (Isa al-Masih). John is introduced first because he is born first. He also appears in public first, preaching God's word. His task is to prepare the people to receive God's promised Messiah. God raises up the Prophet John to tell his people to turn back to him, to love and obey him fully from their hearts. By turning back to God they will be ready to receive the Messiah when he appears. And once the Messiah appears, the Prophet John quickly disappears from the scene.

The Gospel begins with the dramatic appearance of the angel Gabriel (Gibril) to two humble, godly, but quite different couples. First he announces the birth of John to Zechariah (Zakariyya) and Elizabeth, and then that of Jesus to Joseph (Yusuf) and Mary (Maryam). After these announcements we read of the births themselves (1:57–2:20). The stories in the first part of the Gospel draw our attention to how people respond to the good news that God now fulfils his promise to send his Messiah. The years of longing, suffering, and despair now turn to joy through the expectation of deliverance from oppression, suffering, and humiliation. God now fulfils what he promised through the prophets— the Messiah is born!

The first part of the Gospel ends by saying that the twelve-year-old boy Jesus "grew in wisdom and stature, and in favor with God and man" (2:52). In the following part (3:1–4:13), we will read of how the Prophet Jesus begins his ministry as a thirty-year-old man.

THE INTRODUCTION TO THE GOSPEL (1:1–4)

The Gospel begins with a short introduction to assure us that it is true and trustworthy in all it records. This Gospel was written thirty to forty years after the Messiah Jesus proclaimed God's word in Palestine and was raised up to be with God. With the passing of time, the good news about what God accomplished by sending his Messiah was in danger of being distorted.

This Gospel was written to a prominent citizen in Rome who is addressed as "most excellent Theophilus." Theophilus had come to believe and pattern his life on the life and teachings of Jesus. But he may have received conflicting reports about who Jesus was and why God had sent him. Before Theophilus spread the good news of the Gospel to others in Rome, he wanted to be certain about what he had been taught about Jesus, who his disciples believed was God's Messiah.

Note how Luke seeks to assure Theophilus (and now us) that what is recorded in the Gospel is true and reliable. He says that he has met with the first disciples who "were eyewitnesses" of all that Jesus said and did. He also writes of having access to other "accounts of the things that have been fulfilled among us." The other accounts he researched to write his Gospel were both written and oral.[1]

---

1.   Darrell L. Bock, *Luke,* The NIV Application Commentary (Grand Rapids, MI: Zondervan, 1996), 41.

As part of their tradition the Jewish people carefully memorized what took place at important events. They would certainly memorize what happened and what was said when such a prominent person as the Prophet Jesus visited their town or village. In fact, at the time of Jesus the villages of Palestine had official storytellers whose accounts of an event were considered more reliable than written sources! "They wouldn't change the story or modify it; if they did, people would notice and set them straight."[2] The writer of this Gospel has "carefully investigated" both the written and the oral sources of all Jesus said and did in order "to write an orderly account." He wants Theophilus and others who read the Gospel to "know the certainty of the things" they have been taught.

The early disciples of the Prophet Jesus believed that God had inspired a doctor by the name of Luke to record the events in this Gospel. I like to imagine Luke walking from village to village in Palestine where Jesus had healed and taught. He would meet with the official storyteller of each village, who had carefully memorized what had happened when Jesus visited their village with his disciples. Luke would compare what they had memorized with the written accounts of all that Jesus said and did.

By "carefully investigating everything from the beginning," Luke could then write his own orderly account so that Theophilus (and now we) could be certain that what he read was reliable and true. Since Luke and all the early disciples "believed that the things that had actually happened—what we would call the historical facts—had changed the course of the world, it was vital that they be presented as clearly and unambiguously as possible."[3]

A FOCUS ON THE GOSPEL AS "AN ORDERLY ACCOUNT"

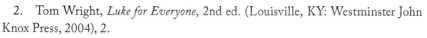

When Luke says that he writes "an orderly account" of the Gospel, he does not mean he records an exact chronological order of events. He means that he records the events logically to show how the

---

2. Tom Wright, *Luke for Everyone*, 2nd ed. (Louisville, KY: Westminster John Knox Press, 2004), 2.

3. Ibid., 4.

events are related.[4] As you read the Gospel, try to see how the words and deeds of the Prophet Jesus fit together by way of cause and effect, contrasts, and stories illustrating what Jesus taught.

By comparing all four witnesses to the Gospel—Matthew, Mark, Luke, and John—we learn that the authors were not overly concerned with recording the exact words of Jesus; instead, they wanted to show the *exact meaning* of his words, and each writer highlights different themes for different purposes. Similarly, the Gospel writers were not overly concerned with *when* an event had happened. They were concerned with the *significance* of what had happened.[5] They wanted their readers to see that God had changed the course of the world by sending his Messiah. They sought to persuade their readers to be part of the new way of living that God had so powerfully revealed in Jesus.

THE ANNOUNCEMENT OF JOHN THE BAPTIST'S BIRTH (1:5–25)

The story of the Gospel begins with an older couple living in the hills outside of Jerusalem (al-Quds). Zechariah and Elizabeth are good people who obey all the Lord's commandments and regulations blamelessly. They continue to be devoted to God in spite of a major sorrow: they have never been able to have a child. This is an unanswered prayer in their lives. In this time and culture, women who have not had children are mocked. But in spite of their old age, Zechariah and Elizabeth keep praying to God to give them a child. God is pleased with their faith.

The answer to their prayers comes in a dramatic way. As a priest—that is, a religious leader who performs certain duties for God—Zechariah has traveled from his country home to serve at the temple in Jerusalem for two weeks. He has received the once-in-a-lifetime honor of going into the temple alone to officiate the laws of God. As he burns incense at the altar, thinking he is by himself in the dark inner chamber of the temple, an angel suddenly stands before him! God has sent Gabriel to give a message to Zechariah.

4.   Steve Taylor, personal conversation, April 15, 2013.
5.   Joel B. Green, *The Gospel of Luke* (Grand Rapids, MI: Eerdmans, 1997), 36.

God has heard Zechariah and Elizabeth's many years of prayer for a child. In spite of their old age, they will now receive a son. But their son will not just be any son. Elizabeth will give birth to the great prophet who will prepare the people of Israel to receive God's Messiah. His name will be John.

Gabriel tells Zechariah that their son "will be great in the sight of the Lord . . . to make ready a people prepared for the Lord" (vv. 15–17). The Gospel, like the Noble Quran, uses many titles for the Prophet Jesus. In 1:16–17 the Messiah is also called the Lord. The title "lord" was used broadly at the time to refer to a ruler, superior, or authority figure. For example, a servant would use it to address his master. God was also addressed as Lord. Since the Messiah would be God's chosen King over Israel, Zechariah likely understood the title "lord" in this kingly sense.

Zechariah, hearing the promise, shows his weakness as a human being by questioning the message from God. He asks for a sign to help him believe. God grants him a sign—but a sign in the form of discipline. Zechariah will not be able to speak (or hear, it seems) until the baby is born.

After Zechariah's time of service in the temple is completed, he returns home to fulfill his duties as a leader and teacher of God's ways in his village. Soon his wife, Elizabeth, becomes pregnant and gives thanks to God for taking away her disgrace. God has completely reversed her situation. Not only will she give birth to a son, but their son will become a great prophet before God.

Unlike his father, John will not serve God through the temple establishment. He will proclaim the words of God in the countryside outside of Jerusalem. He will tell the people of Israel not to trust in their Jewish ethnicity for their salvation. They must turn in humility to God and obey him from their hearts. By preaching this message John will prepare the people to receive God's Messiah.

THE ANNOUNCEMENT OF THE BIRTH OF JESUS (1:26–38)

The announcement of the birth of Jesus the Messiah follows the announcement of the birth of his forerunner and cousin, John the Baptist. Mary's story is like that of Zechariah and Elizabeth in that God sends his angel

Gabriel to announce to her that she is to have a baby boy. Being a virgin, her pregnancy will be a miracle. God continues to orchestrate the events to prepare people for the message he gives his Servant Jesus.

While these stories have clear parallels, their differences are significant. First, the location is different. The story shifts from Jerusalem, the center of the Jewish religion, to Nazareth, a remote, insignificant village in Galilee. In the previous account Gabriel visits an older man, a priest performing his duties in the temple in Jerusalem. But Mary is a fourteen- or fifteen-year-old girl in a farming community far north of Jerusalem, surrounded by non-Jewish people. In addition, while Elizabeth's conception is miraculous because of her old age, Mary's is even more miraculous because she conceives the boy Jesus as a virgin.

Mary is going to be married to a man named Joseph, a descendent of David, a famous king and prophet in Israel's history who was highly regarded by the people. Joseph's being a descendant of David is important because the prophets said that the coming Messiah would be born in the family of David. Even though Joseph is not Jesus' biological father, he is his legal father. In this way, Jesus the Messiah is a descendent of David.

The big surprise in the story is that Mary will conceive as a virgin. She herself asks the angel Gabriel, "How is this possible?" Elizabeth is a barren older woman, so her pregnancy is a miracle, but Mary's is an even greater act of God. Zechariah and Elizabeth come together as husband and wife, and Elizabeth becomes pregnant. Mary, on the other hand, becomes pregnant by the miraculous power of God—nothing is impossible for God!

A FOCUS ON THE MEANING OF THE TITLE SON OF GOD

The Gospel and the Noble Quran are in harmony on this point. The Noble Quran is correct in denying that Jesus is God's Son in a biological sense. To suggest that Jesus is born from God having physical relations is blasphemous to God and to all who believe in the One True God. But if Jesus is not the Son of God in a physical sense, why is he called the Son of God?

First, it must be said that the Jews used this title metaphorically, not literally. It was a way of referring to the person for whom

God would have special love and a special purpose: the coming Messiah. To understand its meaning, as well as the meaning of other titles—like Servant of God, Son of Man, King of Israel, and Chosen One—we must try to understand it from the prophets who spoke beforehand about the Messiah.

Hundreds of years earlier, God had promised through the mouth of his prophets that he would appoint a descendent of King David to rule over his people as his King. "I will raise up your offspring to succeed you, who will come from your own body, and I will establish his kingdom. . . . I will be his father and he will be my son" (2 Samuel 7:12,14). Elsewhere God said, "I will be his father, and he will be my son. I will never take my love away from him" (1 Chronicles 17:13). From these wonderful words of God, we discover that God would care for the future Messiah-King like a father; therefore, the Messiah would be called God's Son.

With this background in the Scriptures, the people of Israel used the title Son of God as another way to refer to the promised and coming Messiah-King.

The context of the surrounding cultures also sheds light on this. It was very common throughout the Ancient Near East to call a king over a nation "Son of God." For example, the Romans called their emperor, Augustus, "the Son of God." They also called their emperor "the Father of the nation." In this light, "the relationship between a great king and his subject kings, who ruled by his authority and owed him allegiance, was expressed not only by the words 'lord' and 'servant' but also by 'father' and 'son.'"[6] In the Torah and Psalms (Tawrat and Zabur), God's angels and the people of Israel are also referred to as "sons of God." Again, this term was used in a metaphorical sense.

Over time, after God's historic promise to King David, the title "Son of God" came to be used especially for the descendent of David to whom God would give ultimate authority to set up God's kingdom over all the earth.

---

6. Kenneth L. Barker, *The NIV Study Bible* (Grand Rapids, MI: Zondervan, 1995), 1016, note on Ps. 2:7.

Now you understand the meaning of the angel Gabriel's words when he tells Mary that she will give birth to a son who "will be called the Son of God" (v. 35). This does not mean that Jesus is a physical son of God; it means that Jesus will have a unique relationship with God and will be the promised Messiah.

Thus, Luke, the writer of this Gospel story, uses the title Son of God synonymously with the title Messiah. The title emphasizes the special love God will have for Jesus—the kind of love that the very best of fathers would have for an only son.

The title Son of God also shows us that Jesus will be able to depend on God, his Father, to provide strength and protection and to be near him. God will care for him like a loyal father as Jesus obeys God in carrying out his mission.

Gabriel's announcement to Mary contains two statements that highlight two major themes in the Gospel. First, he says that Jesus will be the Messiah, the one who establishes God's kingdom on the earth. Second, he tells her that her son will be given a kingdom that will never end (v. 33). It is this kingdom that Jesus will speak of numerous times throughout the Gospel. Everything Jesus the Messiah says and does describes the nature of the kingdom he is sent to establish on earth.

As we read the Gospel story we will see that the people of Israel had wrong expectations for what God's kingdom would look like and how it would be established. These wrong expectations created conflict between Jesus the Messiah and many of the religious leaders of the Jews.

Both before and after the time of Jesus, revolutionary leaders arose claiming to be the Messiah who would free the people of Israel from their Roman oppressors. From Gabriel's announcement to Mary we learn that Jesus did not set himself up to be the Messiah as he grew older; God had chosen him to be the Messiah from birth.

MARY VISITS ELIZABETH AND
PRAISES GOD (1:39–56)

When Gabriel tells Mary that she will be the mother of the Messiah, he also informs her that her relative Elizabeth will have a child in her old age (v. 36). So Mary seemingly throws her belongings together and hurriedly makes the three-day trip from her village in Nazareth to visit Elizabeth outside of Jerusalem. Her visit to Elizabeth shows not only her desire to obey God but also her joy and enthusiasm in the mighty acts of God that they are experiencing.

Jesus the Messiah and John now have a first, symbolic meeting while still in their mother's wombs.[7] John's role as a prophet will be to point people to Jesus the Messiah. We also remember Gabriel saying that God's Spirit would fill John even before his birth (v. 15). So when Mary enters the home of her cousin with the good news that she too is pregnant, God's Spirit causes the baby John to leap in Elizabeth's womb to greet the coming Messiah.

Mary responds to the favor God shows her by praising him with a song. Nearly every word of her song is a quotation from the Scriptures, which Mary has known from childhood. She praises God for the privilege she will have as God's young, humble servant to give birth to the Messiah-King. She then prophesies that God will extend his mercy to all who fear him and lift up all who are humble (vv. 50–55). But while God will exalt the humble, he will "[scatter] those who are proud in their inmost thoughts" and "[bring] down rulers from their thrones" (vv. 51–52).

The scholar Tom Wright asks a good question about Mary's song of praise. "What has the news of her son got to do with God's strong power overthrowing the power structures of the world, demolishing the mighty and exalting the humble?"[8] How can the son of a peasant woman from a small village in Galilee topple the rulers of Israel and the Roman Empire?

If God can do the impossible in causing a very old woman and a virgin to conceive, he can also rescue the poor and the humble from their oppression under proud, powerful rulers. How God will use his humble Messiah to dethrone powerful rulers constitutes the mystery of the Gospel story.

---

7. Bock, *Luke*, 64.
8. Wright, *Luke for Everyone*, 15.

THE BIRTH OF JOHN AND THE
PROPHECY OF ZECHARIAH (1:57–80)

Three months after Elizabeth receives a visit from Mary, she gives birth to John. After John is born, God opens the mouth of his father, Zechariah. Now he no longer doubts God's word, but praises God for fulfilling the promises he made to the prophets to rescue his people from their enemies.

The account of John's birth is much shorter than that of Jesus'. This is appropriate because John as a prophet is less significant than Jesus, who is God's Messiah, Prophet, and unique Servant. John's role is to preach the word of God so that the people of Israel will change their hearts and be ready to welcome Jesus as the Messiah.

The story begins with the phrase "When it was time." This and similar phrases suggest that everything happens according to God's plan and that God keeps his promises. By frequently referring to "the times" of the ruthless dictators Herod and Caesar Augustus, the Gospel implies that God is at work to bring down the kingdoms of proud, unjust rulers and to establish his kingdom of righteousness and peace through his Messiah.

Mary responded to God's favor toward her by composing a song of praise. Now Zechariah too praises God with a song of prophecy. It is interesting to note that while Zechariah served as a priest before God his entire life, now that God's Spirit is a work in him, he functions as a prophet! As he holds his newborn boy in his arms he thinks of John's destiny in human history. Zechariah says, "And you, my child, will be called a prophet of the Most High; for you will go on before the Lord to prepare the way for him" (v. 76). Zechariah praises God for the role his son, John, will have in preparing the people to receive Jesus as the Messiah (vv. 76–79). But he begins his praise to God by describing in detail what God will accomplish through the Messiah Jesus.

The Messiah will be God's instrument to bring salvation (or deliverance) to his oppressed people (v. 69). The word "salvation" is used three times in Zechariah's prophecy (vv. 69,71,77) and has a broad range of meanings. It can mean deliverance to those who are under political and social oppression, but it can also refer to the deliverance of being forgiven one's sins and the resulting freedom from the fear of death.

Zechariah makes astounding statements about the baby boy who grows in Mary's womb! God will raise him up as "a horn of Salvation" (v. 69).

The image of a horn suggests the strong horns of a buffalo or bull. So the Messiah will be God's strong, powerful Warrior who will wage war to deliver the people of God from their enemies.

The people of Israel believed the Messiah would wage war against the Romans and drive them out of their land. They believed the Messiah would then reign over Israel from Jerusalem as God's appointed King forever. But we know the story did not turn out that way. The Jewish people on the whole rejected Jesus as their Messiah, and God punished them by allowing the Romans to drive them from the land of Israel. So did the Messiah Jesus fail in his mission? Or did the people of Israel misunderstand the mission of the Messiah? As you read the Gospel story, take note of how Jesus defines the enemies of God and how he teaches that they are defeated.

THE BIRTH OF JESUS AND THE PRAISE OF ANGELS (2:1–20)

After John is born, his father Zechariah praises God, but when Jesus the promised Messiah is born, all of heaven breaks loose in praise.

Jesus' birth takes place when the Roman emperor, Caesar Augustus, decrees that a census be taken of the entire empire. By means of a census Caesar can control and tax the people under his rule.

Since Joseph is a descendant of King David, he and Mary must make a ninety-mile trek from Nazareth to Bethlehem, a small village just south of Jerusalem where David was born. There they will be registered.

Perhaps the town is flooded with families because of the census, or perhaps there was not much space for visitors to begin with. Either way, Joseph and Mary are forced to stay on the side of a small house, where animals are normally kept and fed. In rural Palestinian homes at the time, a family could sleep on an elevated platform a few steps away from the animals' feeding trough.[9]

While Caesar Augustus lives in luxury in Rome and gives orders, controlling his empire and increasing his might and luxurious living, the one who will overthrow his reign is born in a room for keeping animals.

---

9.   I. Howard Marshall, *The Gospel of Luke*, The New International Greek Testament Commentary: A Commentary on the Greek Text (Grand Rapids, MI: Eerdmans, 1978), 107.

We remember that Mary prophesied that her son, the Messiah, would bring down rulers from their thrones (1:52). The one who will lift up the humble is given a humble birth.

Except for the lowly surroundings of Jesus' birth, the story so far reads like any other birth account. But what seems to be a normal occurrence on earth becomes a cause for celebration in heaven. While shepherds are watching over their sheep in fields outside of Bethlehem, an angel suddenly appears to them. The angel announces, "I bring you good news of great joy that will be for all the people. Today in the town of David a Savior has been born to you; he is Christ the Lord" (2:10–11). The day that the oppressed people of Israel longed for has come. This very day the promised Messiah has been born!

All of heaven erupts in praise. "Suddenly a great company of the heavenly hosts appeared with the angel, praising God and saying,

> 'Glory to God in the highest
> and on earth peace to men on whom his favor rests.'"
> (2:13–14)

The angels announce that this boy, Jesus, will be not only the Messiah but also Savior and Lord. To use the titles Savior and Lord for the boy Jesus is revolutionary. The birth of Caesar Augustus was also proclaimed throughout the Empire as "good news," Gospel. In addition, Caesar was given the title Savior because he boasted "that he had brought justice and peace to the whole world." And he proclaimed himself King and Lord.[10] Those who are familiar with these titles used for Caesar Augustus and now used for Jesus, God's Messiah, will see two kingdoms ready for conflict. How will the political and religious rulers respond to Jesus the Messiah when he announces that God's kingdom has arrived with his coming? How will a boy born in such humble circumstances overthrow the arrogant, oppressive rulers of this world?

The answer lies in the fact that it is the Mighty God who sends his beloved Messiah to bring peace on earth. The glory of God himself has appeared to the shepherds, and twice we read that God is given glory for the birth of the boy Jesus (2:14, 20). It is God who will ensure that

---

10. Wright, *Luke for Everyone*, 23.

the arrogant, power-hungry Caesars of this world fall by the work of his obedient Servant, the Messiah.

Mary, now at rest after giving birth to Jesus, ponders the words Gabriel spoke to her when she first discovered she would conceive. How can her son, lying helplessly in a feeding trough, deliver the poor and oppressed from such a powerful ruler as Caesar? How can he bring peace to earth when Caesar has such great military might?

A FOCUS ON THE ROMANS AT THE TIME OF JESUS

When Jesus lived, the vast Roman Empire stretched from present-day Spain in the west to the land of Palestine and beyond in the east. While the Romans are only occasionally mentioned in the Gospel stories, their presence is often felt by the mention of soldiers who occupy the land in order to enforce Roman rule.

Caesar Augustus, emperor at the time of Jesus' birth (2:10), dreamed of a world empire. But the world would not simply lie at his feet and welcome him as lord over their lands. So to achieve his goal of a worldwide empire, Augustus built a vast military machine to conquer new territories, suppress any dissent, and collect taxes to pay for his army. It is estimated that the emperor kept up to 100,000 soldiers ready to fight at all times.

Because Palestine was considered a hot spot for trouble, six legions—each legion consisting of three to six thousand foot soldiers and one to two hundred cavalrymen—were stationed nearby, four camping in Syria and two in Egypt. As an additional measure, Rome appointed a military governor called a prefect over Jerusalem. (Pontius Pilate was the Roman prefect in Jerusalem when Jesus visited it the last week of his life.)

It was not the good of the people but loyalty to Rome that drove local rulers like Herod and Pontius Pilate, both of whom eventually crossed paths with the Messiah Jesus. Thus the people of Israel resented both the political leaders and the Jewish elite in Jerusalem, who cooperated with the former in order to maintain their power, prestige, and wealth. In the decades before Jesus' public ministry, all-out revolt exploded from time to time in the region around Jerusalem, with self-appointed leaders gathering an army and proclaiming themselves to be Israel's promised Deliverer, the Messiah.

As mentioned earlier, on one occasion the Roman ruler in Syria led his legions down to Jerusalem to crush a revolt. To make a decisive statement, he crucified around two thousand Jewish insurgents. The insurgents involved had attacked not only the Romans but also the mansions of the Jewish aristocracy near the temple in Jerusalem. This revealed their contempt for their own leaders, who cooperated with the Romans in order to maintain their comfortable urban lifestyle while the common people, whom they were supposed to care for, suffered poverty and injustice.

This is the political climate in Palestine when Jesus appears and proclaims the arrival of God's kingdom. Will he be another revolutionary zealot who raises an army of insurgents to fight against the Romans? How will the people understand his preaching, that God is now establishing his kingdom through him?

Since Jesus avoids the larger cities of Sepphoris and Tiberias in Galilee and does not directly denounce the Romans in his teaching, preach political subversion by acts of violence, or raise an army, he is able to avoid direct conflict with the Roman authorities. It is not until he publically claims to be the Messiah during his final visit to Jerusalem that the leaders of Israel will be able to bring him before Pilate and pressure Pilate to take his claim seriously.[11]

THE INFANT JESUS AT THE TEMPLE IN JERUSALEM (2:21–40)

When Jesus is forty days old, his young parents take him to the temple in Jerusalem (al-Quds) to be dedicated to God's service. We are told five times in the story that Joseph and Mary obey what is "written in the Law

---

11. See R. B. Edwards, "Rome," in *Dictionary of Jesus and the Gospels*, 710–15; W. J. Heard, "Revolutionary Movements," in ibid., 688–98; Ben Witherington III, *New Testament History: A Narrative Account* (Grand Rapids, MI: Baker Academic, 2001), 49–61, 72–89.

The Births of John and Jesus   15

of the Lord" (vv. 22,23,24,26,39). The boy Jesus is to grow up in a God-fearing home that knows and obeys the holy books.

Just as in the first two stories of the Gospel it was Zechariah and Mary who responded to the angel, once again Luke records a man and a woman responding to the news that God has sent the Messiah. Simeon and Anna are two very aged residents of Jerusalem, both devoted worshippers of God. Simeon is only alive because God told him he was going to see the Messiah before he died. Anna, widowed in her twenties, is now possibly over one hundred years old.[12] In my opinion, Anna has to be one of the godliest persons who has ever lived; from the time her husband died she has "never left the temple but worshipped night and day, fasting and praying" (v. 37).

Imagine this elderly man and woman approaching the poor couple from Galilee in the grand temple in Jerusalem. Simeon and Anna have waited many years for God to send his Messiah to deliver Israel from their enemies. God has heard their prayers and brings them into contact with Joseph and Mary. As in the previous stories, the news of the Messiah leads to God being praised and prophetic utterances about the future of the child.

Simeon's prophecy partially confirms the previous prophecies about Jesus—he is the one God has sent to deliver his people. However, Simeon also adds new information about the mission of the Messiah. First, Jesus will be the source of salvation and light for the whole world—not just for the nation of Israel. He will be "a light of revelation to the Gentiles" (v. 32).

Second, life will not be easy for Jesus or his mother. Jesus the Messiah is destined for a life of conflict. Simeon says that he will "cause the falling and rising of many in Israel, and be a sign that will be spoken against" (v. 34). One would think that since Jesus is the Messiah and the Jews are longing for God to send a Deliverer, they will all respond with praise to God, just like Simeon and Anna. Simeon tells us that they won't. Many will oppose the Messiah and the message God gives him. The reason, in part, is because the Messiah's message will reveal the evil that is in people's hearts (v. 35). Will the people of Israel be humble? Do they want to love God from a pure heart, or are they deceiving themselves and merely

---

12. Bock, *Luke*, 94.

performing religious rituals? We will see the answers to these questions in the Gospel.

Finally, we learn that Jesus' life of conflict, rejection, and obedience to God will cause a sword to pierce the heart of his mother, Mary. Her once joyful song of praise at the news that she is the mother of the Messiah (1:46–55) will change, and sorrow will sweep over her.

We are beginning to see that the story of the Messiah's coming will be filled with tensions, riddles, and conflict. As readers of the Gospel we are invited, like Mary, to treasure up in our hearts all that has been said of Jesus and to reflect on the meaning of these words (2:19). We are encouraged to be open to God working in our hearts in ways we could never anticipate.

THE BOY JESUS TEACHES AT THE TEMPLE (2:41–52)

Since the Passover is an important Jewish celebration, Jesus has most likely traveled to Jerusalem each year to celebrate it with his parents. But this year is different. Jesus is now twelve years old, the symbolic age of manhood, and will enter adulthood with the responsibility of obeying God's word.[13] Jesus' obedience to God expresses itself in an unusual way in Jerusalem.

This story seems to depict Jesus as insensitive and even somewhat callous toward his parents, but this is not the case. Let me tell the story as I understand it after reading and reflecting on the writings of a number of scholars.

It took three days to travel by foot from Nazareth to Jerusalem for the Passover celebration. The festivities, during which the people of Israel remember how God rescued them from slavery and oppression in Egypt, have now concluded. Joseph and Mary, along with Jesus and the other children they now have, are travelling back to Nazareth after the Passover with their extended family and friends. There are two caravans for the pilgrims—one for women and one for men. Since Jesus is now a young man on the threshold between childhood and adulthood, he could travel

13. Ibid., 99.

with either caravan, so the confusion of not knowing where he is in such a large group of pilgrims is understandable.

After celebrating the Passover, Jesus stays behind in Jerusalem. It is true that he could have told his parents he wanted to stay longer, but Joseph and Mary also could have checked to see that Jesus was with the crowd of pilgrims when they left.

On the night of the first day of the return journey, Jesus does not come to sleep with his family. Joseph and Mary search for him among their family and friends and discover that he isn't in the caravan. So they travel back to Jerusalem and spend another day looking for him among the crowds.

They finally find their twelve-year-old son in the temple courts, sitting among the scholars and discussing the Scriptures! Jesus is listening to the teachers of the Scriptures and asking them questions. He is asked questions in return and is giving answers that astonish all those who are listening. Imagine—a twelve-year-old boy from a small village in Galilee interacting with the seasoned religious scholars of Jerusalem!

Joseph and Mary are also astonished at their son's understanding of the Scriptures. Yet they have just spent three days searching for him, and as his parents, they have been very worried. Mary expresses her great anxiety over not knowing where Jesus was. She asks him, "Son, why have you treated us like this? Your father and I have been anxiously searching for you" (v. 48).

Notice how Jesus responds to his mother. He says, "Why were you searching for me? Didn't you know I had to be in my Father's house?" (v. 49). In effect, Jesus is saying to Joseph and Mary, "You both know that God has chosen me to fulfill the Scriptures as his Messiah. So why didn't you look for me first in the temple courts, where I would discuss the purpose of God revealed in our Scriptures? You are my parents and I will continue to obey you (v. 51), but please understand that my first loyalty must be to God, who loves me like a father."

Notice the play on words between Mary's reference to "your father"—Joseph—and Jesus' response with "my Father." Loyalties will change as Jesus grows older and begins his mission as the Messiah. "Two loyalties hang in the balance. Already, as a child, Jesus indicates which must control his life, in spite of his mother's pain."[14]

This is the first incident that fulfills Simeon's prophecy of a sword piercing Mary's soul (2:35). Her son, Jesus, must live in obedience to God as his Servant and Messiah even when that will cause Mary pain. Jesus will love and respect his parents, but not at the cost of loyalty to God in fulfilling his mission as the chosen Messiah.

This story is sandwiched between two summaries that state how Jesus grew in wisdom and in favor with God (vv. 40,52). At the center of the story itself we read of how the religious scholars of Jerusalem are astonished at the wisdom and understanding Jesus has of the Scriptures. By now Jesus is highly familiar with the many prophecies of the Scriptures that describe the coming of the Messiah and God's kingdom. Jesus stays in Jerusalem interacting with the religious scholars so as to search the Scriptures and thereby better understand his mission from God. This story shows how the boy Jesus grew in his understanding of God's will for him and how that understanding created tensions even among his family.

---

14. Robert C. Tannehill, *Luke*, Abington New Testament Commentaries (Nashville, TN: Abingdon Press, 1996), 77.

PART TWO

PREPARATION FOR THE MISSION OF JESUS

In the first part of the Gospel we have read how the Mighty God is active in a powerful new way to bring his reign of peace to earth. John the Baptist is a key figure in fulfilling God's plan, but Jesus is the central agent in the story.

God sent angels to foretell their births, and by his Spirit godly people prophesied the ministries of John and the Prophet Jesus. We read of how the boys grew and became strong (1:80; 2:40). As we begin the next part of the Gospel, we read that both boys are now mature young men ready for their mission. We will first read of John and how he fulfills his mission of preparing the people of Israel to receive the Messiah, whom he will identify as Jesus. But John only begins his ministry when "the word of God came" to him (3:2). Again we are reminded that God is the primary actor carrying forward his plan on earth.[15] John does not act on his own initiative.

After John prepares the way for Jesus, Jesus is baptized, and as he is praying God's Holy Spirit comes upon him, enabling him to carry out his mission. God speaks from heaven, identifying Jesus as his beloved Messiah. After this short passage Jesus will begin to carry out his mission, and John the Baptist, whose only role is to prepare the way for him, will disappear from the story—except for one later account where he doubts whether Jesus truly is the Messiah.

JOHN THE BAPTIZER PREPARES THE WAY FOR JESUS (3:1–20)

John is now thirty years old, and we read of how he fulfills the prophecies made about him to bring back the people of Israel to the Lord so that they are ready to receive the Messiah (1:16–17). We meet John in the

---

15. Green, *Gospel of Luke*, 160.

desert. He does not take after his father, Zechariah, who was a priest and ministered in the temple in Jerusalem. John is a prophet, not a priest. And prophets can best hear God's word spoken to them when they are in the solitude of the desert. John does not begin to preach on his own initiative but because "the word of God came to him" (3:2).

The story begins with a list of rulers, starting from the current emperor in Rome, Tiberius Caesar, to the Jewish leaders in Jerusalem, Annas and Caiaphas. This list provides us with the historical context for the ministries of John and Jesus. But it also reminds us of the worldly powers the Messiah will challenge with his message of God's kingdom.

The word God gives John to preach is "a baptism of repentance for the forgiveness of sins" (v. 3). Baptism is a ritual cleansing with water. "Forgiveness of sins" implies that a person has built up a debt before God by not obeying his just and righteous commands, but that God in his great mercy will cancel the debt of one's sins if someone turns to him in humble repentance. But sin is not only a debt with a penalty; it is also a power that holds one imprisoned. Sins "are like a debt that cannot be repaid, robbing people of happiness and independence. The debt can grow huge so that people fall into debt bondage. Despair or hardened denial or responsibility could be the result, unless there is opportunity for a new start, free from this bondage."[16]John (and after him, the Prophet Jesus) proclaims the good news of a fresh start, a new beginning with freedom from fear and bondage through God's announcement that our sins are forgiven.

But there is a catch—and it is this catch that gets John thrown in prison and later beheaded. To experience this new beginning, a person must make a decisive change in their heart and actions. The Bible calls this repenting. A person must turn from a self-centered life to a life ruled by the way of God's kingdom. The baptism of John symbolizes this radical change of heart. Rather than receiving a ritual washing near the temple in Jerusalem, people come to John to be plunged below the waters of the river Jordan. The plunging into the water symbolizes the complete washing away of all sin and shame. The rising out of the water symbolizes a fresh new start.

Many people who come to the Jordan River to be baptized by John want the forgiveness of their sins without a change of heart. John sees through their hypocrisy and shouts at them, "You brood of vipers! Who

16. Tannehill, *Luke*, 79.

warned you to flee from the coming wrath? Produce fruit in keeping with repentance. And do not begin to say to yourselves, 'We have Abraham (Ibrahim) as our father.' For I tell you that out of these stones God can raise up children for Abraham. The ax is already at the root of the trees, and every tree that does not produce good fruit will be cut down and thrown into the fire" (vv. 7–9). John preaches that neither having the right religion nor being of a certain ethnicity—being a descendent of Abraham means both—guarantees that a person will escape God's judgment. God requires a change of heart, a heart that produces the good fruit of generosity and honesty in relating to others.

The crowd asks John, "What should we do then?" (v. 10). John responds by giving three examples, all related to one's possessions (3:10–14): A man with two coats and much food should give to those who have none. A businessman should not cheat in his affairs. And a soldier should not threaten people so that they give him money. In short, John says that God wants us to turn from our selfish, dishonest ways to become a people who are just, generous, and honest toward others. These qualities are the mark of a heart turned toward God in humility and obedience. And this is the word of God that has come to the prophet John to preach to the people of Israel.

John does not preach like the other prophets; his ministry is unique in that he preaches to prepare the people of Israel to receive the Messiah Jesus. His story begins and ends with an emphasis on one much greater than himself—the Messiah (vv. 4,16).

When some of the people believe John might possibly be the Messiah, he has integrity—as a true prophet of God should—and answers that he is not. The true Messiah is much more powerful than he. John only baptizes with water, but the Messiah will baptize "with the Holy Spirit and fire" (v. 16). The Messiah, as God's representative, will judge ("baptize with fire") those who reject the way of God's kingdom and will pour out God's Spirit in a new way on those who turn to God in humble repentance. As we continue to read the Gospel we will want to look for how and when Jesus as Messiah judges and gives God's Spirit to the people of God.

The story ends with John being put in prison by Herod, one of the rulers named at the beginning of the account (v. 1). This signals the beginning of the conflict between worldly rulers, with their selfish desires for a kingdom, and the kingdom of God, which is characterized by justice and mercy for the poor and marginalized. The Prophet John has faithfully fulfilled his role to prepare the people for the coming of the Messiah. He now fades out of the Gospel story as Jesus makes his public appearance.

THE BAPTISM AND GENEALOGY
OF JESUS (3:21–38)

The ruthless Herod refuses to accept the message God has given to the Prophet John. In striking contrast to Herod, Jesus accepts the baptism of John (vv. 21–22). Jesus is not baptized for the forgiveness of his sins; we never read of the Messiah Jesus sinning or asking God for forgiveness. Instead, he is baptized to demonstrate that he is fully united with the people he has come to deliver. He is also showing that he agrees with the message God has given John: that the people need to turn to God in repentance to prepare for the coming of God's kingdom.

The Gospel says, "When all the people were being baptized, Jesus was baptized too. And as he was praying, heaven was opened and the Holy Spirit descended on him in bodily form like a dove. And a voice came from heaven: 'You are my Son, whom I love; with you I am well pleased'" (vv. 21–22). The stress is more on what happens at the baptism of Jesus than on the baptism itself.[17] First, God gives Jesus his Spirit. The Holy Spirit is God's way of being present with Jesus to lead him and give him power to do his will. God gives his Spirit to the Messiah Jesus to enable him to fulfill what God has planned. Jesus is not to act on his own but in dependence on God's Spirit.

Second, while Jesus is praying, God speaks to him from heaven to assure him that he is his chosen Messiah. God says, "You are my Son, whom I love; with you I am well pleased" (v. 22). The text implies that God is *not* pleased with rulers like Herod or Tiberius Caesar. God is only pleased with his beloved Messiah, who will submit to him and establish his just, righteous, and merciful kingdom on earth.

We read earlier that the boy Jesus grew in wisdom and in favor with God (2:40,52). And it appears that when Jesus was twelve years old, he already understood that he had a special relationship with God as the Messiah (2:49). But as readers of the Gospel we may wonder if John and

---

17. Green, *Gospel of Luke*, 185.

Jesus will be faithful to fulfill the prophecies given them as infants. We have just read that John was faithful to his calling. He continued to preach the words of God even though it caused him to be imprisoned by Herod (3:1–20).

We now read that Jesus is thirty years old (3:23) and God's favor continues to rest on him. Jesus has continued to mature and live in obedience to God and is ready to carry out his mission. He needs the strength, guidance, and presence of God to carry out the task for which he has been chosen—and God provides it by coming to dwell in and with Jesus in the form of his Spirit. Jesus does not act independently of God, nor is he able to do the works of God without God's Spirit filling him and leading him. In one of the prophecies about the Messiah written centuries before, God said of the Messiah, "Here is my servant, whom I uphold, my chosen one in whom I delight; I will put my Spirit on him, and he will bring justice to the nations" (Isaiah 42:1).

It is clear that Jesus is God's Servant. But how are we to understand God calling Jesus his Son? As I wrote earlier, many Christians misunderstand the background of this term, and the misunderstanding has led to much confusion.

It is worth repeating that the meaning of the title Son of God as it is used for the Messiah comes from the older Scriptures, where God promised King David that one of David's descendants would be the Messiah, and that God himself would be like a father to him (2 Samuel 7:7–16; Psalm 2:6–7). God would have a unique love and a unique calling for the Messiah as he served him in carrying out God's mission.

We have already discussed how, in the Ancient Near East, it was common to speak of the relationship between a lofty ruler and the king who ruled under him in terms of father and son.[18] Thus Jesus the Messiah, chosen by God to rule over Israel as God's representative and viceroy, can be addressed as Lord, Son of God, or God's Servant.

Not long into his own ministry, Jesus hears that Herod has imprisoned the Prophet John for preaching the words of God. He knows his life will also include conflict and suffering. Remembering God's words of love and affirmation—"You are my Son, whom I love; with you I am well pleased"—strengthens him in his trials—one of which comes from

---

18. Barker, *NIV Study Bible*, 1016, note on Ps. 2:7.

God's chief enemy, Satan (al-Shaitan), soon after Jesus' baptism. We will soon read of how Jesus is led by God's Spirit into the desert, where he is tempted by the devil (Iblis) (4:1–13), and how Jesus then begins his mission in Galilee (4:14). But before that the Gospel includes a genealogy of Jesus (3:23–38).

Ancient cultures (and many still today) preserved long genealogies to identify and give status to those who belonged to a particular kinship group. The main intent of the genealogy of Jesus is to show that Jesus is a descendent of David, Abraham (Ibrahim), and Adam. As a descendant of King David, Jesus can rightly claim to be the Messiah promised to come from David's family line. As a descendent of Abraham, Jesus is qualified to be the one through whom God will bless all the nations of the world (Genesis 12:1–3).

But Jesus' family line goes all the way back to Adam, the first human being! In addition, Adam is called the son of God (3:38)! Again, this phrase contains no hint of physical relations; in this case it refers to Adam functioning as God's representative on earth to rule over his creation. So Jesus' connection to Adam, the first man, is especially significant. Not only is Jesus an Israelite and a descendant of King David, but as a son of Adam he is a human being standing in "solidarity with all humanity."[19] Messiah Jesus will act not only for Israel but for all humanity.

Jesus must succeed where his ancestors, though they were great men, failed. Satan tempted Adam so that he failed to obey God in representing God as his "son" to rule over creation. Likewise Abraham's descendants, the people of Israel, failed to carry out God's will on earth to bring justice and righteousness to the nations. Instead they worshipped the idols of the nations around them and practiced injustice. David, although he made many mistakes, was one of the few kings of Israel who genuinely loved and obeyed God, so God promised that one of his descendants would rule over God's kingdom. We see in the Gospel that God has kept his word: the long-awaited descendant is now ready to publically proclaim the arrival of God's kingdom on earth.

At this point in the story we might have serious doubts about how it will all work out. After all, Adam and Abraham's descendants gave in to temptation and failed to represent God's rule on earth. Will Jesus

---

19. Green, *Gospel of Luke*, 189.

remain loyal to God when he encounters temptation? In the next story Jesus meets the full force of Satan's assault against him. The devil is bent on preventing him from carrying out God's will on earth.

JESUS IS TEMPTED BY THE DEVIL (4:1–13)

To review, Jesus is now thirty years old and soon to begin his public mission. He has received God's empowering Spirit and heard the confirmation of his unique calling as the Messiah, God's Dearly Loved One. As the Messiah, Jesus will topple evil, oppressive rulers to establish justice and righteousness for those who are oppressed. Up until now we have been led to think that the emperor in Rome rules the world (2:1; 3:1), but with the temptation of Jesus we learn that there is an unseen evil force working through the rulers of the world—the devil.

How much the devil, God's chief opponent, understands about God's mission for the Messiah is not clear. But he clearly sees Jesus as a threat to his hold over human beings. Before Jesus even starts his public ministry, the devil seeks to derail him. Satan knows that God will be working by his Spirit in powerful ways through his Servant Jesus. The temptation of Jesus draws back the curtains that have kept these unseen realities hidden. We learn that the sending of the Messiah is really the beginning of God's assault on the devil and on his evil influence over human beings.

Twice the devil reminds Jesus that he is the chosen Messiah, the Son of God (4:3,9). The devil does not question Jesus' identity, but he seeks to get Jesus to act independently of God by using his power and position as the Messiah for his own benefit. If the devil is successful, he can maintain his evil, oppressive power over all humanity.

As we read the temptation story, we wonder if Jesus will succumb to the enticements of the devil and abandon the mission God has for him. Jesus knows God's mission will cause much personal suffering for him and his family. He will live in constant conflict with the political and religious rulers, who want to maintain their own power. Can his love, loyalty, and obedience to God remain strong when he is alone in the desert and has not eaten for forty days?

By the end of his fast, Jesus is near starvation. Seeking to exploit his weakened state, the devil tempts him to use his power as the Messiah to turn a stone into bread. The devil in essence says, "Since you are the

Messiah, you should not go hungry. You, as God's Special One, have a right to be comfortable and full" (v. 3).

However, Jesus will not please himself by performing a miracle apart from the will of God. He feeds on his close relationship with God and will only break his fast in God's timing and way. For forty days Jesus has been sustained by the words of God. Just as God's presence and words strengthened him at his baptism, he will continue to find joy, strength, and satisfaction in them. So Jesus refuses to use his power and position for cheap substitutes, however reasonable they may seem.

In the second temptation the devil gives Jesus, in an instant, a vision of all the nations of the world. The devil lies by promising something he cannot deliver: he offers Jesus a shortcut, an easy way to authority and splendor. He claims that Jesus can have all the kingdoms of the world, with all their power and wealth. There's only one catch. Jesus must submit to and serve him rather than God. Again, Satan's strategy is to make Jesus work independently of God.

Yet Jesus remains loyal. He knows God has chosen him to rule over his kingdom, but God's rule must come in God's time and way. Jesus answers this second temptation with the most basic command of the Scriptures: there is one God, and he alone is to be worshipped (Deuteronomy 6:4–5,12–14). Jesus will not be part of any rule that rivals God's authority. He will worship and serve God only.

The final temptation involves another instant vision put before Jesus. He sees himself at the highest point of the temple in Jerusalem (a 150 meter fall to the ground) and is challenged to jump and trust God's angels to rescue him. Since Jesus is God's Dearly Loved One, surely God will be present to save him.

In essence Jesus replies by saying that his special relationship with God is not the forum for public stunts to manipulate God into providing a miracle. Jesus will be in continual need of God's power and protection in the difficult years before him. But he will not put God to the test by asking for spectacular displays of power.

The devil knows God has sent his Messiah to take away the evil influence the devil has over human beings. His goal in tempting Jesus is to create a separation between Jesus and the One True God who sent him. If the devil can get Jesus to stray from the path God has set for him, then the devil's evil and cruel influence over mankind will remain intact.

But as this story ends we see that the Messiah has successfully resisted every temptation.

How does Jesus succeed in resisting the devil's temptations? No human being up to this time has ever succeeded. How does the Messiah Jesus overcome?

As we reread the story, we see that Jesus is immersed in God's holy word. In each temptation he quotes the words that God spoke through the Prophet Moses. The truth of these words counters the lies of the devil. The reason Jesus has immersed himself in God's holy word is because he loves God with all his heart and mind and soul, and he will only worship and serve the One True God.

Jesus' success in resisting the devil's temptations stands in contrast to Adam and the nation of Israel. They failed. At the end of chapter 3 the Gospel mentions Adam, the first human being God called to rule over his creation. We already know the story of how the devil tempted Adam and how he failed to obey God as his representative on earth.

After Adam, the people of Israel became God's chosen "son" to bring justice and righteousness to a world enslaved to evil and misery. God delivered the people of Israel from slavery in Egypt, showing them that he was the One True God. They were to worship and obey him alone. He gave the people of Israel his just and righteous laws to learn, obey, and share with the idolatrous nations around them. Yet they failed in their calling just as Adam failed. Shortly after God delivered them from their slavery in Egypt they turned to worshiping idols. They tested God. Right from the beginning of their calling they failed to represent God and his good and righteous ways to the world; and they continued to fail.

Jesus is tempted in similar ways as the people of Israel.[20] It appears that God wants to do through Jesus the Messiah what he always wanted to do through Israel. And he does! Jesus the Messiah succeeds where Israel failed.

Jesus' loyalty to God is tested during these intense trials, yet he remains faithful. He is now ready to engage in the mission for which God has sent him; but the spiritual war is not over. The devil has lost this battle, but he will return at "an opportune time" to tempt Jesus from the path God has laid out for him (4:13). We are meant to assume that the devil will be at

20. Ibid., 192.

work through the powers that oppose Jesus—the rulers of Israel and the Roman Empire. Will the devil succeed in turning Jesus from the path God has planned for him? We must read on to see.

A FOCUS ON THE SPIRIT OF GOD

When we begin reading the Gospel story we read of God's Spirit ("the Spirit," "the Spirit of God," or "the Holy Spirit") at work in a fresh and powerful way. God's Spirit is the means by which God works on earth through people; it is the way God is present with his power to work out his good purposes on earth. The prophets were able to speak the word of God with authority because God's Spirit was at work in them. God also filled some prophets with extraordinary power by his Spirit to perform miracles.

Since the prophets spoke the word of God by God's Spirit, and since he also gave his Spirit to the righteous King David so that he would rule with wisdom, righteousness, and justice, it is not surprising that David's descendant, the Messiah, is promised God's Spirit for his mission (Isaiah 42:1–2; 61:1–2). The Messiah Jesus is appointed to proclaim the good news of God's kingdom and reign over it.

Messiah Jesus, when he was among us, did not speak or act on his own authority. He did not live in our midst walking as if he were "a foot above the earth." His wisdom and teaching came through his close relationship with God and extensive times of prayer. He spoke the words of God with authority and did miracles by the power of God's Spirit, given to him at his baptism (Luke 3:22; 5:17). Jesus was strong to resist the temptations of Satan because he was "full of the Holy Spirit" (4:10); he emerged from his battle with Satan "in the power of the Spirit" (4:14). As God's Messiah, the Prophet Jesus experienced a constancy and a fullness of God's Spirit like no other prophet.[21]

---

21. M. M. B. Turner, "Holy Spirit," in *Dictionary of Jesus and the Gospels*, 341–51.

PART THREE

JESUS ENACTS THE KINGDOM OF GOD IN GALILEE (4:14–9:50)

In the first chapters of the Gospel we read of how God is now at work in a powerful new way in the world through the Messiah Jesus. Only a small group of people knows that Jesus is God's Messiah, but they are filled with joy and anticipation. They believe God has sent him to rescue them from their oppression under the Romans and to grant them peace in their land. But is this why God has sent his Messiah? As Jesus now begins his mission in Galilee, it is important to note that his teaching and actions do not always match the people's expectations.

It is also important to note how God continues to work out his purposes on earth. We have read of how God sends angels, fills people with his Spirit, and causes the miraculous birth of Jesus by his Spirit. Then God's Spirit descends upon Jesus at his baptism. From then on Jesus, God's Messiah becomes the focus of how God fulfills his purposes on earth.

As I wrote earlier, Jesus accomplishes God's will on earth by the power of God's Spirit. He never acts independently of God. "Throughout his ministry Jesus is God's agent, serves his aim, acts on his behalf, and works by his power."[22] The Gospel story is all about God and his will to remake the world. He accomplishes this through his obedient Servant Jesus. Since Jesus is completely dependent on God as he speaks and acts, he frequently takes time to be alone in prayer with God to renew his strength and receive guidance.

As the Messiah Jesus teaches and heals the sick, people are amazed at the power and authority God has given him. Many believe he is a prophet sent by God to help them. As readers of the Gospel we know that Jesus is also God's Messiah—but it is important to remember that the people in the story do not yet know this. So as the Gospel story unfolds, a major question becomes, "Who is Jesus?" Near the end of Jesus' ministry in

---

22. Green, *The Gospel of Luke*, 198.

Galilee, Herod, the ruthless ruler of that region, asks, "Who, then, is this I hear such things about?" (9:9). And Jesus' twelve closest disciples finally understand that he is more than a great prophet; he is the Messiah God promised to send to establish his kingdom (9:18–20).

Several other important themes reoccur. It is helpful, for instance, to observe how people respond to the teaching and healing work of Jesus. Note especially how a strict group of religious leaders called the Pharisees begins to oppose him. Why don't they believe God has sent Jesus? Another important theme is the way God expresses his love and mercy to women alongside men through his Messiah. Why does the Gospel emphasize the role of women as recipients of God's mercy?

In addition, we want to always try to understand what Jesus means by the kingdom of God and how his teaching and actions differ from the views and expectations of both the Pharisees and the people. Since Jesus teaches that God has sent him to establish his kingdom, it is important for us to take note of how he expresses and teaches the *meaning* of God's kingdom.

By way of summary, here are some questions to reflect on:
- Who do people say Jesus is?
- Why does Jesus say God sent him? What is God's purpose for sending the Messiah?
- How does Jesus describe the kingdom of God?
- What would the kingdom of God look like if people embraced it?
- How does Jesus help us better understand what God is like? If God sent his Messiah Jesus to accomplish his purposes, understanding those purposes can help us better understand the will and character of God.
- Finally, how do different people respond to Jesus? Why do they respond the way they do?

Enjoy following the drama of how people respond to the mighty words and works of the Messiah. Use your imagination and place yourself in the story. How would you respond to what Jesus said and did? Would you want to follow him?

JESUS BEGINS HIS MISSION
IN GALILEE (4:14–44)

Jesus Declares His Mission in
His Hometown (4:14–30)

The devil attempted to derail Jesus from his mission as Messiah with temptations, but the devil failed. Jesus was firm; he would worship and obey only God, no one else. In this next section we read in more detail about the mission God has given Jesus as the Messiah. It is this mission that the devil seeks to prevent Jesus from completing—the mission of freeing those who are in bondage to evil.

Jesus leaves his time of temptation "in the power of God's Spirit" (v. 14). He begins his public ministry in Galilee as strong as ever through the special empowerment given him at his baptism. The people are delighted when he teaches in their synagogues.

Jesus then decides to visit his hometown, Nazareth, and also teach in their synagogue. We don't know how long Jesus has been away from Nazareth, but everyone there knows him. Since it is a small town, he also remembers them by name—relatives, childhood friends and their parents, and those who frequented the shop where he worked with his stepfather, Joseph. By now the news of Jesus' miracles in Capernaum has spread to Nazareth. Jesus' teaching in Nazareth gives us a picture of what he has been teaching in other synagogues (v. 15). As we read, what does the story teach us about why God sent Jesus as his Servant, the Messiah? Let us look at the details of the story.

When Jesus visits Nazareth he attends the synagogue service on the Sabbath. This is his habit. In the service the people pray and read the Scriptures. On this occasion Jesus is asked to read the Scriptures from the scroll of the Prophet Isaiah (Al-Nabi Sha'ya"). He knows the contents of this scroll very well, so he chooses a text that summarizes the mission God has given him. He reads,

> The Spirit of the Lord is on me because he anointed me
>   to preach good news to the poor.
> He has sent me to proclaim freedom for the prisoners
> And recovery of sight for the blind,

To release the oppressed,

To proclaim the year of the Lord's favor. (Isaiah 60:1–2)

Jesus then sits down with all eyes fastened on him and says, "Today this Scripture is fulfilled in your hearing." What a dramatic moment! Jesus is openly claiming to be the Messiah who will fulfill the promises God gave through the prophets to establish his kingdom. But unlike the previous prophets who had been anointed with oil and spoke about God's kingdom coming, Jesus is anointed with God's very Spirit and announces God's kingdom has come!

This is the manifesto, or mission statement, given to Jesus by God. It explains what he will do as the Messiah and why God has sent him. When we look at this declaration, we see specific tasks for which God gave Jesus his Spirit.

First, Jesus will proclaim good news to the poor. All the prophets spoke of God's special compassion for the poor and his judgment on those who oppress them. So as God's promised Messiah, it is not surprising that Jesus will go primarily to those who are oppressed.

Second, Jesus will proclaim freedom for prisoners. Since Jesus does not demand that the Romans release all those in prison, it is best to understand this purpose symbolically as referring to those in bondage to sin and its consequences. We read how Herod piled up his sins and added to them the imprisonment of the righteous Prophet John. Yet everyone has created for themselves a debt of sin before God. The Messiah will proclaim a way for the debt to be canceled, for how we can be saved from the shame of our sins, and for all of our guilt to be removed.

Jesus will also restore sight to the blind. While we read in the Gospel of Jesus literally making the blind to see, these miracles also portray the spiritual light he will give to those blinded by spiritual darkness. Zechariah prophesied that the Messiah would be as "the rising sun, come to us from heaven to shine on those living in darkness and in the shadow of death" (1:78–79), and Simeon prophesied that Jesus would be "a light for revelation to the Gentiles" (2:32). When people encounter the Messiah, light will come, dispelling the darkness in their hearts and minds.

Finally, we read that the mission of Jesus is to release the oppressed. Again, there appears to be both an outward and a spiritual dimension to the mission of Jesus. In the visible realm, the poor will be relieved from their oppression as compassionate, just rulers replace greedy ones. But the Gospel also describes how the devil works through evil spirits (demons) to oppress people, keeping them in misery. Thus in the invisible realm, the Messiah is anointed with God's Spirit to release those oppressed by evil spirits.

These purposes of Jesus' mission as Messiah are summed up in the phrase "the year of the Lord's favor." In the ancient Scriptures, God established an ordinance called the Year of Jubilee in which, every fifty years, those who were forced to sell their property had it given back and those who had been forced into slavery were released. The Year of Jubilee signified a new start, a new hope, a fresh beginning. Jesus claims that God has sent him to give a new beginning for humanity, a new hope in life for all who are willing to receive it from him.

In essence Jesus is saying to his family and friends, "The time you have all been longing for has come. God has sent me and anointed me with his Spirit to fulfill the promises spoken by the prophets. I am the promised Messiah."

This is big news for a small village in Galilee. Initially the response from Jesus' hometown is cautiously positive. Then something goes wrong. What happens to make the people in Jesus' hometown drive him out of the village and seek to kill him by throwing him off a cliff? We can better understand the town's sudden, violent reaction in light of Nazareth's demographic and the meaning of Jesus' quote from Isaiah.

It appears that Jesus has startled everyone by stopping his reading from Isaiah with the phrase "to proclaim the year of the Lord's favor." The very next line speaks of "the day of vengeance of our God." Jesus must know that the Messiah is expected to avenge the people of Israel by destroying their Roman oppressors, and he surely knows the following verses in Isaiah, which speak of non-Jews serving the Jewish people by working as shepherds and laborers in their fields.

The scholar Kenneth Bailey points out that Nazareth was an all-Jewish settlement in Galilee. Many Gentiles had settled in the region, establishing new towns and villages for themselves, but the fearless and inflexible Galilean planned to gradually conquer Galilee and bring Jewish settlers up from Judea to inhabit the area.[23] Their hope was to make

---

23. Kenneth E. Bailey, *Jesus through Middle Eastern Eyes: Cultural Studies in the Gospels* (Downers Grove, IL: IVP Academic, 2008), 152.

Galilee all Jewish and make the Gentiles their servants. They felt that the Messiah's mission would be to lead them in their efforts to restore the governance of Palestine to the people of Israel.

In light of this hope, Jesus' omission of the next phrase in Isaiah—"the day of the Lord's vengeance"—is a contradiction of his people's expectations. But he goes further. Jesus reminds them of two stories from their own prophets Elijah and Elisha. In both stories there were many poor, needy people in Israel—widows and lepers. Yet God sent his prophets to help a poor Gentile widow (from modern Lebanon) and heal a Gentile enemy soldier (from today's Syria).

In presenting these stories Jesus is telling his townspeople that God, through his Messiah, is going to extend mercy to the Roman soldiers who occupy their land and to the Gentiles living around them. The time of God' judgment will come, but it is not now. Instead, God is offering mercy, compassion, and grace to all.

To the people listening, Jesus' whole message seems backward—it is a scandal. This is why Jesus anticipates that they will use the proverb "Physician, heal yourself" against him (4:23). In their eyes, there is clearly something wrong with him.

The people of Nazareth are furious with Jesus. They want to kill him because he is not proclaiming God's judgment on those they hate or satisfying their expectations about the kingdom God will set up for Israel. This is why they drive Jesus out of town and attempt to push him off a cliff to his death.

However, in some miraculous way God protects his Messiah from death. Jesus then leaves Nazareth and continues with the mission God has given him. Even though his own hometown has rejected him, he carries on in obedience to God. His mother, Mary, is no doubt crushed by this event. Most likely she remembers the words of Simeon spoken to her at the temple when Jesus was an infant: "Your child will cause a sword to pierce your soul" (2:35).

As we read the Gospel story the question we want to keep asking ourselves is, "Why did God send Jesus as his Messiah?"

Up until this incident in Nazareth we have been limited to the prophecies of Zechariah, Mary, Simeon, and others. These prophecies seem to show us that the Messiah will come as a mighty military king like King David to defeat Israel's enemies and establish Israel as a nation at peace in their land. Yet with this speech Jesus himself speaks out publically about what it means for him to be the Messiah! Jesus understands the prophecies about the Messiah differently than his fellow Jews do. Rather than a political deliverance for the people of Israel, Jesus speaks about a spiritual deliverance. There is a spiritual bondage, blindness, and oppression greater than that of the evil Romans (4:18–19).

Yet there is something even more startling in Jesus' illustrations of the prophets Elijah and Elisha (vv. 25–27). Jesus is saying that God will not only show mercy to the Gentiles but withhold mercy from the people of Israel if they reject what he seeks to accomplish through his chosen Messiah.

Simeon made a similar point at the temple when Jesus was an infant. He said, "This child is destined to cause the falling and rising of many in Israel, and to be a sign that will be spoken against" (2:34). Sadly, and surprisingly, Jesus' own hometown has decided to speak against him!

Jesus Demonstrates His Mission in Capernaum (4:31–44)

Jesus' hometown of Nazareth has rejected him and his mission as the Messiah. They have even tried to kill him for his message of mercy to those who aren't Jews. But Jesus moves on in obedience to God. Consumed by God's love and strengthened with his presence, Jesus travels with resolve down to Capernaum on the northern shore of the Sea of Galilee (or Tiberias). Capernaum, not Nazareth, will become the home base for his mission.

What Jesus announced he would do in Nazareth—release the poor from evil and oppression—he now does in Capernaum. We are reading what it looks like in practice for Jesus to be the Messiah. Four brief scenes from one day in Capernaum illustrate why God has sent Jesus as his Messiah.

The rest of chapter 4 (vv. 31–44) describes the authority God has given Jesus both to teach his Word and to rescue people from many kinds of sicknesses and evil spirits.

The crowd is amazed at the authority by which Jesus speaks. The tradition at that time was that the person who spoke would mention the famous religious scholars who agreed with him in order to support his point.[24] Yet when Jesus speaks, we see him speak the message of God directly without mentioning anyone.

---

24. Bock, *Luke*, 147.

The crowds are also amazed at Jesus' authority to command evil spirits to come out of people. What is amazing is that they do not yet understand who Jesus is—but the evil spirits do! They say, "What do you want with us, Jesus of Nazareth? Have you come to destroy us? I know who you are—the Holy One of God" (v. 34).

The devil knew who Jesus was in the wilderness, and the evil spirits know that God has sent his Messiah to destroy them and deliver all who have lived under their fear and oppression (v. 34). Jesus said in Nazareth that his mission was to proclaim freedom for the prisoners and to release the oppressed (4:18). Now we are able to see exactly what he meant. We are learning to see that the real enemy the Messiah came to destroy is not human beings, human rulers, or any earthly kingdom. The ones Jesus came to destroy are the spiritual forces of evil. The kingdom of God is a powerful work of God's Spirit through his Messiah, invading the kingdom of Satan to set people free from spiritual oppression, fear, and misery. The devil, of course, knows this is the mission God has given his beloved Messiah. This is the reason the devil sought to tempt Jesus and keep him from fulfilling his mission.

Twice Jesus commands the evil spirits not to reveal that he is the Messiah (vv. 34–35,41). This is puzzling. Why would Jesus not want people to know who he is? If God wants people to receive him as his Messiah, why would Jesus forbid the demons not to shout it out for all to hear? This is a question we need to keep asking ourselves as we continue reading the Gospel story.

This chapter ends with Jesus again declaring why God has sent him. He says, "I must preach the good news of the kingdom of God to other towns also, because that is why I was sent" (4:43). This is the first of many times Jesus will state that God has sent him to proclaim the arrival of his kingdom on earth. As you read the Gospel, try to understand what Jesus means by the kingdom of God. The Jewish leaders will challenge Jesus over this—over what God's kingdom is and how it is supposed to come. But Jesus will be bold and uncompromising in his obedience to following God's way. But just as it happened with all the previous prophets, the Prophet Jesus' unswerving commitment to proclaim and practice the word of God will cause him to suffer.

A Focus on Galilee at the Time of Jesus

Jesus spent most of his life and ministry in the region called Galilee. Galilee was about forty kilometers in diameter from east to west, with most towns and villages easily reached by walking in less than a day or two. The region was roughly equivalent to the area today north of the West Bank in Palestine to the southern border of Lebanon and Syria. The Jordan River and the Sea of Galilee made up the borders on the east, with the western border ending around ten kilometers short of the Mediterranean Sea.

The majority of the two to three hundred thousand people who lived in Galilee were poor farmers who lived in one of the 204 villages of Galilee that had populations ranging from three hundred to five hundred. The majority of these poor farmers were Jews who sought to live according to God's commandments revealed in the Torah. While pious, the Galileans were at the same time known to be fearless and inflexible, making Galilee a center for Jewish revolt against the Roman occupation. The rebel Judas, a Galilean, is an example of a violent revolutionary who fought passionately against the occupation of Palestine by the idolatrous Romans, seeking to drive them from the land and reestablish it as the place where the One True God of Israel was worshipped and his law alone obeyed.

Judas the Galilean believed he was the messianic king who would deliver Israel from its oppression under Rome. Since many others like Judas had taken up the sword to fight against Rome at the time of Jesus, both the Roman and the Jewish authorities in Jerusalem would have taken seriously Jesus' claim to be the Messiah, the promised King of Israel—even though he preached and practiced a kingdom in which love conquered one's enemies. Yet he preached his message in a volatile, hostile environment where politics and obedience to God were deeply intertwined.

The many stories (parables) Jesus tells to teach about the kingdom of God are based upon the imagery of farming in Galilee: there are farmers planting seeds and harvesting crops, wealthy landowners hiring laborers, and other familiar themes. In his teaching Jesus warns the wealthy landowners who buy up small family farms and oppress the poor that they need to abandon their love for money and possessions, and instead love God and show his compassion and justice for the poor.

Though Nazareth was only a village, Jesus did not grow up in the backwoods. There were fifty other villages in the surrounding area, major international roads that passed near Nazareth, and the nearby capital Sepphoris, a city of about fifteen thousand, a mere six kilometers away. The other major city in Galilee, Tiberias, was comparable in size and distance.

The Gospel does not record Jesus proclaiming his message in Sepphoris or Tiberias. He may have avoided these major cities in order to avoid confrontation with Herod and other political leaders while he was training his disciples and spreading the good news of the kingdom of God throughout the villages of Galilee.

Because of their part in a revolt against Rome at about the time of Jesus' birth, Sepphoris was burnt to the ground and its inhabitants enslaved. But the governor of Galilee, Herod Antipas, later rebuilt Sepphoris as his capital, making it the ornament of Galilee.[25] There he built a luxurious palace for himself, incorporated pagan symbols of the Greek and Roman gods into the public buildings, and sent out Roman soldiers to Nazareth and other villages to collect excessive taxes for his ambitious building projects.

From his home in nearby Nazareth, Jesus would have seen the city being built on "a hill that rises steeply 350 feet (115m) above the surrounding plain."[26] Jesus would have been a teenager during the reconstruction of Sepphoris by Herod, and it is very likely that his father, Joseph, who was not a farmer but a builder, traveled there to work. There is a good chance that Jesus and his brothers, who would have been trained by their father, joined him to help rebuild Sepphoris. (How much construction could they do in their small farming village of Nazareth?) But since Sepphoris was predominantly Gentile, Joseph and his sons would have been

---

25. Horsley, *Galilee*, 165.
26. Ibid., 163.

uneasy working among people who worshipped the Roman gods and ignored God's commandments in the Torah.

While there is no foolproof evidence that Jesus worked as a young man in Sepphoris, we can be certain that due to its proximity to Nazareth, its place as a center for revolutionary sentiments, its violent suppression by the Romans, and its disregard for the One True God and his commandments, Sepphoris would have often been the center of discussion in Jesus' home and village. As Jesus immersed himself in the vision of God's kingdom portrayed by the prophets, he would have contrasted it with the vision of life on display in Sepphoris. Herod's greedy pursuit of wealth and power and his unjust treatment of the poor would come to exemplify the kind of leadership and way of life Jesus often preached against.[27]

JESUS CALLS HIS FIRST DISCIPLES AND CREATES CONTROVERSY (5:1–6:11)

Jesus Calls His First Disciples
and Heals a Leper (5:1–16)

Up until now Jesus has proclaimed God's word alone. Now he begins to select his first followers, ordinary fishermen, whom he will prepare to help him spread the good news of God's kingdom (vv. 1–11). This story takes place in the town of Capernaum by the Sea of Galilee, a stone's throw from the synagogue and the house where Jesus heals Simon's mother-in-law.

As a prophet, Jesus continues to teach the crowds the word of God (v. 1). But then he turns to speak to Simon, the fisherman whose boat Jesus was using while teaching the crowd that stood on the shore. Jesus reveals to Simon knowledge of the depths of the sea that could only come from God. A sense of awe, even terror, immediately overwhelms Simon. How can this "son of a carpenter" from the hillside of Nazareth know the waters so intimately? Simon realizes that God's presence and power are with the Prophet Jesus in a very special way. He falls at Jesus' knees and says, "Go away from me, Lord; I am a sinful man!" (v. 8).

---

27. R. Riesner, "Galilee," in *Dictionary of Jesus and the Gospels*, 252–53; Witherington III, *New Testament History*, 111–17.

While Simon (also called Peter) and his fishing partners do not yet understand that Jesus is the Messiah, they see that Jesus is uniquely holy and sent by God. The story concludes with Jesus telling Simon and his fellow fishermen that from now on they will no longer catch fish here in the sea. They will follow Jesus and rescue people from the sea of evil in the world.

After these things, Jesus travels to a town nearby where he heals a man from leprosy (vv. 12–16). Leprosy was a hideous contagious disease that kept a leper socially isolated to prevent the disease from spreading to others. According to Jewish law, a person became unclean by touching a leper. Will Jesus touch the leper?

In a dramatic display of love and compassion, Jesus not only heals the leper but also touches him. Jesus, the holy one, the clean one from God (4:34; 5:8), touches the unclean leper. But instead of Jesus becoming unclean from the leper, the leper is cleansed by contact with Jesus. Most likely the poor leper had not been touched in years—no greeting of embrace from his friends; no embrace from his wife; no children climbing up in his lap.

But with the touch of compassion and the authoritative command "Be clean," Jesus heals the leper of his disease and restores him to his family and community. The man can now live and work among them. The Messiah Jesus has been sent not only to rescue people from the effects of sin but also to restore them to the life God has created them for. Jesus' work of rescuing and restoring the sick, the poor, and the ostracized illustrates the nature of God's kingdom.

Jesus Claims the Authority to Forgive Sins (5:17–26)

The news of a prophet in Galilee who teaches and heals with a unique authority from God has now spread all the way to Jerusalem. As a result, many of the strict religious leaders of the Jewish people—Pharisees and teachers of the law—come from all over the land to hear Jesus teach. Since they are religious leaders, they sit near Jesus in front of the large crowd that has forced its way into the house where he is teaching. On this particular occasion "the power of the Lord was present for him to heal the sick" (v. 17). Jesus does not heal all the time, but only when the power of God's Spirit is present with him to heal.

When some men learn that the power of God is present with Jesus to heal, they bring to Jesus a friend who is paralyzed to have him healed. But instead of healing the man, Jesus announces that the man's sins are forgiven! While he eventually heals the man, the emphasis of the story comes here in the middle when the Prophet Jesus makes the astonishing claim that God has given him the authority on earth to forgive sins. We have previously read how Jesus heals the sick, drives out demons, and teaches with a unique authority from God. Now we learn that God has also given his Messiah the authority to forgive sins on earth! The tense of the Greek verb used when Jesus says, "Friend, your sins are forgiven" (v. 20), implies that the man's sins are forgiven by God in heaven, but that God authorized Jesus to pronounce the forgiveness of sins on his behalf. [28]

But the Pharisees protest at this claim. They believe that the forgiveness of sins can only take place through the offering of sacrifices at the temple in Jerusalem. It is the priests in Jerusalem who speak for God and declare a person's sins forgiven—and only after a lamb has been sacrificed. But now Jesus, a Galilean villager claiming to be a prophet from God, asserts the unique authority to forgive sins! By announcing the man's sins forgiven, Jesus undermines the authority of the Jewish leaders who oversee the cleansing of sins at the temple in Jerusalem.

Jesus defends his right to declare the man's sins forgiven by claiming to be the Son of Man. He says, "The Son of Man has authority on earth to forgive sins" (v. 24). This is the first time Jesus refers to himself as the Son of Man, a title he will often use rather than Messiah. The Prophet Daniel used the title Son of Man centuries before. Daniel wrote that he saw in a vision "one who is like a son of man, coming with the clouds of heaven. He approached the Ancient of Days and was led into his presence" (Daniel 7:13). Daniel goes on to write that God gives the Son of Man a kingdom over which to rule (7:14).

From this we learn that the Son of Man is a human being with heavenly origins who is led by angels into the presence of God to rule over an eternal kingdom. The Son of Man has a unique relationship with God. One scholar describes the identity of the Son of Man in this way:

---

28. Green, *Gospel of Luke*, 240.

"The Son of Man image in Daniel describes a human figure who bears authority from God and who rides the clouds as God does."[29]

So Jesus now claims to be the very Son of Man spoken of by the Prophet Daniel! And he says that as the Son of Man, God has given him unique authority on earth to forgive sins! God, of course, is the Supreme Ruler of the universe and can do whatever he pleases. We learn here that God has been pleased to give the Messiah Jesus the authority to forgive sins. But as far as the Jewish authorities are concerned, Jesus is a renegade prophet from Galilee acting on his own. He speaks and acts without the authority of the legal scholars or the prescribed rituals for cleansing from sin at the temple in Jerusalem. This incident is the first of many conflicts Jesus will have with the Jewish leaders. Meanwhile the people praise God for what he does through his Servant Jesus. We read, "Everyone was amazed and gave praise to God. They were filled with awe and said, 'We have seen remarkable things today'" (v. 26).

This story gives us much to reflect on. Why does Jesus call himself the Son of Man instead of the Messiah? How is it possible for God to give him the authority to forgive sins on earth? And how will the Jewish leaders continue to respond to the mission God has given Messiah Jesus?

The Pharisees Challenge Jesus about Feasting and Fasting (5:27–39)

Jesus now leaves the house where he pronounced the paralytic's sins forgiven. As he goes along, he sees a tax collector named Levi at work. Jesus invites Levi to follow him, just as he had invited Peter and his fishing partners. What will be their reaction to this? The Jews despised tax collectors, because although they were fellow Jews, they collaborated with Roman officials in squeezing as much money as possible from the already poor and struggling rural population. "They were extortionists. And, more than that: they were working with the Romans, or for Herod, and their necessary contact with Gentiles put them under political suspicion (collaborating with the enemy) and ritual exclusion (they might well be unclean)."[30]

---

29. Bock, *Luke*, 158.
30. Wright, *Luke for Everyone*, 63.

In the previous story Jesus claimed the authority to forgive sinners. Now we read that he actively seeks out sinners like Levi to extend God's mercy and forgiveness to them! Jesus socializes and dines with the very kind of people the Pharisees despise and avoid contact with. Meals throughout the Mediterranean world "symbolized shared lives—intimacy, kinship, unity."[31] Jesus becomes the friend of sinners and extends the offer of God's mercy and forgiveness to them.

But the Pharisees again protest. They complain that a true prophet from God would not socialize with tax collectors and sinners as Jesus does. Jesus answers the Pharisees by saying, "It is not the healthy who need a doctor, but the sick. I have not come to call the righteous but sinners to repentance" (vv. 31–32). Jesus states that his mission is like that of a doctor: God has sent his Messiah to seek out people who are spiritually sick and weary from their shame so that they may be cleansed.

The Pharisees also complain that Jesus' followers do not fast the correct way (v. 33). Jesus and his followers do fast, but not like most of the other Jews at the time, for whom fasting "was a sign of waiting, of bewailing the present time when God's kingdom still had not arrived."[32] Jesus, of course, proclaims that the time of waiting and wailing is over; God's kingdom has arrived! God defeats evil and delivers the oppressed through his Servant Jesus. Now is the time to celebrate, not to wail!

Jesus gives two illustrations about the kingdom of God: it is like a new piece of cloth and new wine. His point is that just as a new piece of cloth cannot be attached to an old garment, and new wine cannot be poured into old wine skins without ruining them, so the fresh, life-giving, forgiving mercy God extends to sinners through his Messiah Jesus cannot be mixed with the self-assured, rigid, rule-regulated religion of the Pharisees. The leaders of Israel have developed a system of religious practices and beliefs that so distort the intention of God in the Scriptures that the message Jesus proclaims cannot be joined to it.

---

31. Green, *Gospel of Luke*, 246.
32. Wright, *Luke for Everyone*, 64.

A FOCUS ON THE SCRIBES (TEACHERS OF THE LAW) AND THE PHARISEES

Because most people could not write at the time of Jesus, scribes, or teachers of the Torah, had the important task of writing up business and marriage contracts, along with other important documents. But their most important task was to carefully copy the message of God revealed to the prophets and recorded in the Scriptures. Even though the scribes had memorized the Scriptures, they would still place a copy of the Scriptures before them when copying in order to accurately reproduce them for others.

In addition to being copyists, the scribes were scholars who interpreted and taught the Scriptures to the people. The leading scribes belonged to the ruling council (Sanhedrin) in Jerusalem and taught the Scriptures in the temple. But there were also scribes scattered throughout the villages of Palestine. It was these scholars from the towns and villages of Galilee who often teamed up with the Pharisees to challenge the teaching and practices of Jesus. Scribes, who had their own disciples, were no doubt worried that their followers could be attracted to the message of Jesus.

A scribe expected the young disciples under him to be more committed to him than even to their parents. The disciples often addressed their teacher as "my lord" or "my master" and were expected to memorize and teach others what they had been taught. Since Jesus' disciples committed themselves to him as their teacher, and since they believed that he was a special prophet sent by God (and in time that he was the chosen Messiah), they were careful to memorize and teach others the message God had given him.

The scribes and Pharisees added many detailed traditions to the Torah to ensure that the people properly obeyed it. Together they promoted and defended their interpretations. But these many laws had become a heavy burden for the common people, who were already burdened by sickness, poverty, and cruel oppression from the Romans.

At times Jesus deliberately, provocatively, and publically criticized and broke the laws the scribes and the Pharisees had added to the Scriptures. He did this not only because the regulations had become such a burden to the people but also because following them had become such a source of pride for the scribes and the Pharisees. Their preoccupation with following the minutiae of their laws resulted in their neglect of the weightier, more important parts of God's will—his love, compassion, and justice for all people, especially the poor.[33]

JESUS CONFRONTS THE PHARISEES (6:1–11)

If you have been following the story carefully you may have noticed the tension that is growing between Jesus and the Pharisees. Complaints about Jesus now mount to fury and talk of getting rid of him. In 6:1–11 we first read a story that takes place out in a grain field, followed by one that takes place in a synagogue. What connects the two is that they both take place on a Sabbath, and Pharisees are present, criticizing Jesus' actions.

It may seem strange to us that the Pharisees cause such a commotion about Jesus' disciples taking grain from the fields to eat on a Sabbath, and then also complain about Jesus healing a man on the Sabbath. But the Jewish people, especially the Pharisees, have come to build their identity on precise ways of keeping the Sabbath, avoiding certain foods (and people!), circumcision, and other external practices. The Pharisees have even added thirty-nine of their own man-made laws to the Scriptures for what a person can and cannot do on the Sabbath.

As I noted above, these laws have become a burden to the people. So many things to do and not do. This emphasis on living by external laws easily leads to spiritual pride and shifts the focus away from justice and compassion for the sick and poor. Jesus' disregard for the Pharisees' man-made laws undermines their authority over the people and threatens to unravel the religious way of life they have established. The Pharisees believe God's kingdom will come once the people of Israel faithfully follow their strict way of life, but Jesus believes that the Pharisees' emphasis

---

33. Ibid., 312–16; Witherington III, *New Testament History*, 45–48; S. Westerholm, "Pharisees," in *Dictionary of Jesus and the Gospels*, 609–14; G. H. Twelftree, "Scribes," in ibid., 732–35; J. R. Porter, *Jesus Christ: The Jesus of History, the Christ of Faith* (New York: Barnes & Noble Books, 2004), 30, 162.

on keeping their many external laws takes the focus off of the central command of God to help hurting people.

Jesus says to the Pharisees, "The Son of Man is Lord of the Sabbath" (v. 5). He means that he, as the Son of Man, has the authority to correctly interpret the Scriptures and teach how the Sabbath is kept. What is at stake is not just how the Sabbath is kept but, more importantly, who has the authority to correctly interpret the will of God as revealed in the Scriptures. The Prophet Jesus boldly claims that it is he.

Jesus, the Servant of God, always obeys God's word. But he will not follow the traditions the Pharisees have added to it—especially when those traditions keep him from doing what is most important: doing good and saving lives. When Jesus heals a man whose right hand—his working hand—is shriveled, the Pharisees accuse him of working on the Sabbath, which is forbidden. But Jesus believes that it is more important to heal the man so that he can work again, and thus live, than to keep the man-made laws of the Pharisees. So he challenges them: "I ask you, which is lawful on the Sabbath: to do good or to do evil, to save life or to destroy it?" (v.9). Jesus implies that the Pharisees are on the side of evil, destroying life by allowing their many laws to keep them from doing good to people who are hurting.

The Pharisees are now filled with rage and begin making plans to get rid of Jesus. He doesn't fit their view of how to live for God. He must be stopped since he is a false prophet who misleads the people.

A FOCUS ON JESUS THE LORD

Even though Jesus is primarily revealed to be God's Messiah, Servant, and Prophet in the Gospel, at times he is also addressed as Lord. This can cause confusion, because God is also referred to as the Lord. Understanding the wide variety of ways the title "lord" was used by both Gentile and Jewish people at the time of Jesus can help us better appreciate what they would have meant when they addressed him as Lord.

While the title "lord" could be used simply as a polite form of address, more often it was used to address any male figure of authority. Slaves addressed their masters as "lord." The head of a family, a wealthy landowner, or a ruler of any kind would be addressed as "lord."[34] In the eastern part of the Roman Empire, people prayed to their gods as "lord." Thus the Emperor August could easily demand that he be addressed as "lord" in a divine sense, like a god, even though he was a human being.

The Jewish people, like others in the empire, commonly addressed their masters and superiors as "lord." Yet they refused to refer to the emperor this way because of the unique devotion he sought with the title. They would only ascribe this kind of honor to the One True God. Still, while the people of Israel addressed God as Lord, there is evidence that "God could give a unique place and role to a particular heavenly figure or agent . . . who could speak and act for God with divine authority and power."[35] Thus, this heavenly agent of God who would act with God's authority could also be addressed as Lord in an exalted way.

It is in this sense that Jesus is at times addressed as Lord (along with the more common sense of the term). His closest disciples come to believe that he has been given a unique power and authority as the Messiah to bring about the coming of God's kingdom to earth. Jesus is Lord because God has chosen to give him a kingdom to rule over as his King. (And God, of course, can do what he pleases to do.) God gives Jesus the power to teach his word with divine legitimacy, to heal the sick, and to free those oppressed by the devil (e.g., 4:31–44). God also gives him, as his Messiah, the authority to forgive sins (5:24), to correctly interpret the Scriptures, to clarify their most central commands, and to show us what it looks like to live by them (e.g., 6:5; 10:25ff.). Thus Jesus is to be obeyed as the unique Lord, the one God has chosen to reveal and fulfill his purposes on earth (e.g., 17:5,10) [36]

---

34. Porter, Jesus Christ, 163.

35. B. Witherington III, "Lord," in Dictionary of Jesus and the Gospels, 486.

36. Ibid., 484–92; Porter, Jesus Christ, 163.

JESUS TEACHES HIS DISCIPLES TO LOVE THEIR ENEMIES (6:12–49)

Jesus Chooses the Twelve Apostles and Blesses all his Disciples (6:12–26)

In spite of growing opposition from the Pharisees, larger crowds seek out Jesus to be healed and to listen to him teach. In light of the increasing conflict with the leaders of Israel, Jesus seeks the guidance of God. We read, "Jesus went out to a mountainside to pray, and spent the night praying to God" (v. 12). As he prays, God reveals to him who his closest disciples should be. At the time, a disciple was a person who diligently learned from his teacher (or rabbi), observed how his teacher practiced his teachings, and sought to pattern his life after him.

Jesus chooses his disciples to also be apostles (Saiyiduna). An apostle was a person sent by one with authority with a special commission. Thus, as apostles the twelve closest disciples would become Jesus' authorized representatives. They are always with Jesus and so would become reliable witnesses and specially commissioned representatives of his life and teachings. There appears to be symbolic significance to Jesus choosing twelve apostles in the fact that the nation of Israel consisted of twelve tribes. We already sense that the leaders of the Jewish people may reject Jesus as the Messiah. Will the twelve apostles become the new leaders of God's people, who embrace the message of the Messiah Jesus?

After coming down from the mountain with his disciples, Jesus is met by a crowd of other disciples and a great number of people from as far south as Jerusalem and as far north as the Gentile cities of Tyre and Sidon. The Gospel says that God's "power was coming from him and healing them all" (v. 19). After Jesus heals the poor who have come to him, he encourages them by teaching them the word of God. The rich have socially and economically marginalized them, and now the Pharisees ridicule and castigate those who follow Jesus as the Messiah (v. 22), so the Prophet Jesus strengthens and encourages them with words of assurance. Looking at them, he says,

> Blessed are you who are poor,
> for yours is the kingdom of God.
> Blessed are you who hunger now,

for you will be satisfied.
Blessed are you who weep now,
    for you will laugh.
Blessed are you when men hate you,
    when they exclude you and insult you
And reject your name as evil,
    because of the Son of Man.
Rejoice in that day and leap for joy, because great is your
reward in heaven. For that is how their fathers treated
the prophets. (vv. 20–23)

The disciples will continue to be oppressed by the rich and ridiculed and rejected by their religious leaders, friends, and even family, but Jesus assures them that they have made the right decision by believing and practicing his message about the kingdom of God. They already belong to God's kingdom now, and they will inherit it when it comes in its fullness in the future. They are the ones who belong to God, not the religious leaders who exclude them. They are the ones who are truly rich. They are the ones who are fortunate, who are blessed. Those who mistreat them are to be pitied and prayed for, because they are blind to the realities of the kingdom of God manifest in his Messiah Jesus.

From this we learn that Jesus creates a reversal of how we look at people in the world. He turns the world upside down. Those we often envy are to be pitied, and those we pity are to be envied. While the rich are well-off in this life and the poor suffer, their roles will be reversed in the future manifestation of the kingdom of God.

But the poor, those that society ostracizes, are not automatically part of God's kingdom. They must turn to God and receive the mercy he offers through his Messiah. And they must learn to extend that same mercy to others—even their enemies—if they are to be part of God's kingdom. And while it is more difficult for the rich to humble themselves before God, some do and become shining examples of life in the kingdom of God. (See 19:10 for the example of the wealthy tax collector Zacchaeus, who embraced the Messiah Jesus and his message and gave half of all his possessions to the poor).

A FOCUS ON A DISCIPLE

At the time of Jesus, "disciple" referred to a student who committed himself wholeheartedly to learning and practicing the teachings of a leader in order to promote his ideology. There were disciples of philosophers, of religious leaders, and even of political revolutionaries. Jesus' disciples were devoted to both learning his message and observing how he practiced it. With Jesus as their teacher (or rabbi), the disciples were called to immerse themselves in his teaching and participate in extending the movement he launched—the kingdom of God. We will read that both men and women followed Jesus as his disciples.

As we are reading the Gospel, it is interesting to note the various reasons people become disciples of God's Servant Jesus. Often they are drawn to him because they witness God's power in his teaching and miracles. But more often it is his compassion for the poor and love for "sinners" that leads people to follow Jesus. Yet because he teaches that following him might result in hardship and even rejection by family and friends, many who first begin to follow him do not continue to do so. While Jesus shows and provides the way to life, love, and peace with God, he also alerts potential disciples of the high cost of following him and inheriting God's kingdom.

Jesus selects twelve from the larger crowd of disciples to be apostles. As his closest companions, the twelve are privileged to witness all that their Master Jesus says and does. In this way they become trustworthy, reliable witnesses of his life and teachings and effective leaders in spreading the message of the kingdom of God (6:12–16). The Messiah selects and carefully trains the twelve in order to ensure the continued expansion of the kingdom of God. The mission of God is not to depend on the fluctuating commitments of the crowds who follow him.

Among these twelve disciples are men who led a fishing business, a despised tax collector, a zealous revolutionary, and a man who will betray Jesus. They are young men from the towns and villages of Galilee, impulsive at times, and they show the roughness and vigor of the Galileans. But Jesus sees potential in them, and slowly, very slowly, they learn his ways.

At times when we read the Gospel it can be difficult to understand whom "disciple" refers to. The context then becomes our best guide for understanding. Often the reference is to the twelve disciples who are with Jesus at all times. At other times the reference is to the twelve and everyone else who is following him. We also often read of a large crowd around these core disciples who are amazed by the miracles and teaching of Jesus. Not all from this crowd are true disciples. Perhaps they have considered following Jesus but have not yet made the commitment. Jesus repeatedly warns wavering disciples of the necessity of practicing what he teaches in order to inherit God's kingdom.

By way of summary, disciples of Jesus are people who entrust their whole lives to God and commit themselves to learning and practicing the ways of God's kingdom as taught and embodied by his Servant Jesus. A disciple is an apprentice to the Messiah, committing to join Jesus in remaking the world according to God's good and perfect will for all people.

Disciples follow the example of their Master Jesus by selflessly pouring out their lives (however imperfectly) for the good of others—even their enemies. Disciples are called to emulate the love, compassion, justice, and righteousness of their Master. This causes them to also seek out the poor, the abused, the marginalized, and those burdened with sin, extending to them the freedom and forgiveness of God. [37]

Jesus Teaches the Disciples to Love as God Loves (6:27–49)

In the midst of performing many miracles, Jesus now teaches at length on the necessity of loving our enemies. His disciples, like most people, tend to only show acts of kindness to people like themselves and limit the way they live out their "religion" to a prescribed set of practices and beliefs. Jesus teaches that God's central command for us is to actively and generously do good to others, even our enemies. The love Jesus describes is constantly on the lookout for ways to give for the good of others, and this is the way Jesus expects his disciples to live. Love acts creatively,

---

37. M. J. Wilkins, "Disciples," in *Dictionary of Jesus and the Gospels*, 176–82.

spontaneously, throughout the day, and the collective expressions of love by the disciples are to be the way God remakes the world.

Jesus' disciples gather around him on a mountain plain outside of Capernaum. As he teaches them, many from the large crowd also listen (7:1). He has just warned his disciples that they may be hated, excluded, insulted, and rejected for following him (6:22). Now Jesus teaches his disciples how they are to respond to those who mistreat them. He says, "But I tell you who hear me: Love your enemies, do good to those who hate you, bless those who curse you, pray for those who mistreat you" (vv. 27–28).

Who would the enemies of the disciples be? They could be the cruel, oppressive Roman soldiers stationed in their towns; the Pharisees who criticize and exile them from the community for following Jesus; or the greedy landowners, who oppress their servants as they work hard in the fields. What does it mean to love people who have hurt you? It doesn't mean we will necessarily like them. But it does mean we are to intentionally do good to them, bless them, and pray for them. We can choose to act in kindness towards those we do not like, even towards our enemies. God can even use acts of love to turn an enemy into a friend! God sent his Messiah to show us the way of love so that the cycles of hate and vengeance could be broken—in our families, in our communities, and among the nations.

Jesus gives three examples of what it could look like to bless and do good to our enemies (vv. 29–30). He says, "If someone takes your cloak, do not stop him from taking your tunic." Jesus is not giving new laws for three specific situations; rather, he uses forceful, imaginative language to create in us a spirit that will learn to love in any and every possible context.

Jesus knows our inclination as human beings to limit our acts of kindness to those who are like us or to those from whom we want something in return. He knows that in reality we often act out of selfish motives—secretly we want something in return for our acts of kindness. Jesus teaches that it is no grand expression of love to give and lend to our family and friends with the expectation that they in turn will help us out. Everyone does that. So Jesus teaches,

> If you love those who love you, what credit is that to
> you? Even "sinners" love those who love them. And if
> you do good to those who are good to you, what credit

is that to you? Even "sinners" do that. And if you lend to those from whom you expect repayment, what credit is that to you? Even "sinners" lend to "sinners," expecting to be repaid in full. But love your enemies, do good to them, and lend to them without expecting to get anything back. Then your reward will be great, and you will be sons of the Most High, because he is kind to the ungrateful and wicked. Be merciful, just as your Father is merciful. (vv. 32–36)

God's kind of love, the kind of love the Messiah has and expresses, is shown when we do good to others without expecting anything in return. But more than that, when we practice God's kind of love we will not limit our acts of kindness to those who are like us or to those we like. Jesus challenges us to love even our enemies—those who hate us, curse us, and mistreat us! God's way is the only way we can break down the walls between us and put an end to our hatred and hostility. God's way is the way to peace among us.

Jesus bases the command to love our enemies on the nature of God. God "is kind to the ungrateful and wicked." Therefore, his people are to be kind to the ungrateful and wicked. They are to be merciful, just as God is merciful (vv. 35–36). Most people, most religions, would say that God is merciful. But then they define God's mercy in a way that supports the way they want the world to be. The people from Jesus' hometown, Nazareth, believed that God is merciful, but then they sought to kill him because he taught that God wanted to bless their enemies!

How does Jesus describe the mercy of God? He teaches that God's mercy lies at the very core of his being and determines how he relates to mankind. He teaches that God is so filled with mercy that he shows love and compassion to all people—even to those who don't believe in him or live for him. He shows mercy to the Romans, who worship idols, and to greedy tax collectors, who abuse and betray the poor. God has sent his Messiah Jesus to socialize with sinners and offer them forgiveness. Jesus reveals what God is like when he seeks out sinners and extends to them his love.

Jesus' disciples must learn to love as God loves. It is not natural to love someone who has hurt you, ridiculed you, or excluded you.

It requires humility and deep inner strength. We show our inner weakness when we simply respond to our enemies in anger, but we are strong when we choose against our anger and act in the way of love and join God in creating peace.

God has given Jesus his Spirit and unleashed a new power on earth. God's power enables his people to love his way. A love that gives without an agenda lies at the heart of God's kingdom. Because God is love, he wills for all his creation to be penetrated with love.

The Messiah then teaches his disciples, "Do not judge, and you will not be judged. Do not condemn, and you will not be condemned. Forgive, and you will be forgiven" (v. 37). Jesus may be warning his disciples to not be like the Pharisees, who walk around like moral police, pointing out the faults of others. They judge, condemn, and withhold forgiveness from sinners rather than reach out to everyone in humility and love. Jesus implies that proud judging is deeply at odds with God's way of love.

The Pharisees carefully examine the behavior of others, but they are blind to their own pride, self-righteousness, and lack of compassion. Because they do not know or understand the depths of God's mercy, they cannot teach it to others. The Pharisees travel far to make disciples like themselves. But they are like a blind man leading another blind man; both will fall into a pit (vv. 39–40). Jesus says, "Why do you look at the speck of sawdust in your brother's eye and pay no attention to the plank in your own eye?" (v.41). Jesus compares the pride of being right—of having the right religion, of having righteous behavior—to a big board in our eye that keeps us from seeing straight. Such things keep us from knowing the love of God.

Thus far Jesus has stressed the importance of loving, of doing good to our enemies. Now he compares a good man to a tree with healthy roots that bears good fruit (vv. 43–45). What does this comparison mean? What is a good man, and what are the good things he brings out of the good stored up in his heart? The context suggests that a good person is the person who has learned to live selflessly for the good of others—even his enemies. God has sent his Messiah to show us the way to love and to make us into good people, people who give of themselves to others.

We know a tree is healthy because of the quality of the fruit we see on it. So we will know if a person truly loves and obeys God as his Messiah teaches by the selfless acts of love we see in their life. They will love even those who have mistreated them. They will love without expecting acts of kindness in return. They will not limit their love to those who are like them or to those they like. They will learn to love as God loves.

Just as a healthy tree naturally produces good fruit, so acts of kindness towards others becomes the natural overflow of such people's lives. As a tree matures with time, so also the disciples can mature so that selfless, uncalculating love for others characterizes their lives. They store up goodness in their hearts through prayer and constant reading of the Gospel to learn how Jesus embodied God's love as his Messiah.

Jesus concludes his extended teaching on love by warning that it is not sufficient to listen to his words and believe them (vv. 46–49). To be his disciple, a person must put Jesus' teaching into practice. A person may acknowledge Jesus as God's Messiah and Lord; they may even know and believe all he has taught; but to avoid God's judgment (here likened to the collapse of a building), they must put into practice the way of love. To love is to believe. To love is to build one's life on the solid foundation that will endure God's righteous judgment.

God has sent the Messiah to both show us how to live and teach us how to live. He does not teach new rituals to practice, nor does he teach an elaborate set of beliefs. God has sent his Servant Jesus to create in us hearts of selfless love, to make us good on the inside so that we can extend love to a hurting, hostile world.

I have a theory that many people act religiously—or if they are not religious, they promote a certain political or social ideology—instead of doing the hard work of humbling themselves and having their hearts changed. It is hard, unnatural work to learn to live for the good of others, to learn to love our enemies. But this is the way of God's kingdom and establishing his peace on earth.

REVIEW: Where are we in the story?

God has given his Messiah the mission of bringing his kingdom to earth. God has given Jesus his Spirit to guide and empower him for this mission. The mission involves invading the dark forces of evil to release those in fear and in bondage. When Jesus releases those in bondage, he also restores them to a new life in God's kingdom. As participants in God's kingdom, they have peace with God. They no longer live in fear and shame. In addition, they have the power to begin loving all people as God loves them.

In chapter 6 we have learned more about what led God to send his Messiah. The motive that moved God to act in sending his Servant Messiah is his generous, uncalculating mercy for mankind. We will now read of how Jesus continues to reveal and extend the mercy of God to those who are outsiders to the religion of the Jewish people.

JESUS DEMONSTRATES HE IS THE MESSIAH, BUT JOHN DOUBTS HIM (7:1–50)

The Extraordinary Faith of a Roman Military Officer (7:1–10)

After Jesus teaches God's will for us to build our lives on love— love even for our enemies—he enters the village of Capernaum, where he demonstrates God's wide-reaching kindness through an act of mercy toward a Roman military officer (7:1–10). If Jesus were a Pharisee, he would have two things against this man upon meeting him. First, he is a Gentile and therefore "unclean" to socialize with. Second, he is a prominent officer in the very military that oppresses the Jewish population. And yet Jesus is willing to answer his request. The most extraordinary part of this story is that the Roman soldier believes Jesus can heal his dying servant without Jesus actually coming to see and touch him. He believes Jesus has the authority to just "say the word" right where he is, and his servant will be healed (vv. 7–8).

Apparently Jesus does speak a word of healing, for when the officer returns home, he finds his servant healed! While the story emphasizes the extent of the authority God has given the Messiah Jesus to heal, great emphasis is placed on the officer's faith. Jesus turns to the largely Jewish crowd and says, "I tell you, I have not found such great faith even in Israel" (v. 9). Jesus commends the Gentile soldier for believing in the power of God at work in him. Jesus may be contrasting his faith with the unbelief of the Pharisees, who want to get rid of Jesus simply for healing a man on the Sabbath (6:6–11).

Jesus Raises a Widow's Only Son to Life (7:11–17)

Shortly after this Jesus leaves Capernaum, followed by his disciples and a large crowd. As they approach the small village of Nain, they are met by another large crowd—a crowd mourning the death of a widow's only son. Since her husband has already died, this second tragedy will make her poor, destitute. Being without means, she will be forced out to the margins of society, deprived of financial support and social status.[38]

This story has clear contrasts with the healing of the Roman officer's servant in the first part of the chapter. The officer is a man, a Gentile, and a person of great wealth and authority. The widow is a female, a Jew, and a poor, destitute woman. But the most dramatic contrast in the stories is in what influences Jesus to restore life in each case. The officer's faith is described in considerable detail, while the widow doesn't even say a word! Perhaps she is so overcome with wailing that in her flow of tears she doesn't even see Jesus. The important point of the story is that Jesus sees her. And he speaks to her! From a heart filled with compassion, he simply says to the widow, "Don't cry."

Jesus then steps forward to stop those carrying the coffin and raises the young man to life—right in the middle of the funeral procession! And with another beautiful act of compassion, he gives the boy back to his mother. Her wailing turns to joy.

Jesus said that he would turn weeping into laughing, that the poor would be part of God's kingdom (6:20–21). This simple story reveals the depths of the compassionate love of God as he expresses it through his Messiah. God did not give his Messiah power and authority to dazzle the crowds, but to reveal his love and lift up those who are beaten down.

The crowds who see the boy raised from the dead respond with praise to God. They say, "A great prophet has appeared among us. God has come to help his people" (7:16). As readers of the Gospel, we know that Jesus is more than a great prophet. He is God's Messiah sent on a unique mission to establish God's kingdom. Yet most of the people do not yet understand this.

A FOCUS ON THE PROPHET JESUS

The Gospel records that both Jesus' disciples and many of the people who heard him teach and witnessed his miracles believed that he was a great prophet sent by God, similar to but greater than

---

38. Green, *Gospel of Luke*, 291.

the previous prophets. While prophets at times predicted what God would do in the future, their primary role was to speak God's words of comfort and warning. The messages prophets received from God came to them in different ways—in dreams, visions, visitations from angels, or moments of being caught up in close communion with God. We often read in the Gospel story that the Prophet Jesus went alone to the mountains to spend entire nights in prayer. During these times of close communion with God, he also received strength, guidance for his mission as the Messiah, and the words of God that he was to speak to the people.

A prophet's message was distinguished from that of a religious teacher or a spiritual advisor in that the prophet believed God himself was speaking to him and through him. Thus, the prophets of God believed that they spoke God's words with God's authority, not their own words with their own authority. People were often amazed at the Prophet Jesus' teaching because he did not quote other religious authorities to support his message, a common practice with other religious teachers. He spoke directly to the people with God's authority, knowing that what he said was the message he had received from God. The Prophet Jesus experienced the fate of many others prophets of Israel: he too was ridiculed and rejected because he spoke the words of God to a people who did not want to receive them.

While the Gospel story primarily emphasizes Jesus' identity and mission as the Messiah, Jesus was also considered an exceptional prophet, greater than any previous prophet. Yet, like previous prophets, he warned people of God's judgment if they did not love and obey him from their hearts. Like previous prophets, he also offered words of comfort and blessing to all those who suffered in their poverty but turned in humility to God for help. And like the previous prophets, but even more so, the Prophet Jesus had visions, heard the voice of God, knew what was in people's hearts, predicted the future, and performed great miracles by God's mighty power.

But the Prophet Jesus distinguished himself; he set himself apart from all the previous prophets by proclaiming the arrival of God's kingdom to earth through himself as the chosen Messiah. While the prophets of old had foretold the arrival of God's kingdom on earth with the coming of God's Messiah, the Prophet Jesus claimed that *he* was the long-awaited Messiah. And he taught that he fulfilled the prophecies of all the previous prophets by establishing God's kingdom on earth.

As God's obedient Messiah, Jesus stands alone, far above all other prophets. By his obedience he begins the process of rescuing and restoring the world according to God's good purposes. It is the Prophet Jesus' attempt to link the coming of God's kingdom to himself and his claim to uniquely know the heart and will of God (in contrast to the leaders of Israel) that causes the leaders of Israel to label him a false prophet.

In conclusion and by way of illustration, we should note that the people who hear Jesus teach and who witness his miracles believe he is a great prophet sent by God. On the occasion when Jesus raises the only son of a poor widow from the dead, the people are filled with awe and praise God, saying, "A great prophet has appeared among us. God has come to help his people" (7:16). And much later, after the leaders of Israel in Jerusalem have rejected the Prophet Jesus, two of his closest disciples express their grief by saying, "He was a prophet, powerful in word and deed before God and all the people" (24:19). Jesus believes himself to be a prophet of God. When his message is rejected in his hometown of Nazareth, he says to the people of his village, "No prophet is accepted in his hometown" (4:24). And on another occasion Jesus claims that he is a greater prophet than the Prophet Jonah, who preached God's word to the great city of Nineveh, leading all the people of Nineveh to turn to the true and living God in repentance (11:32).[39]

The Prophet John Doubts Jesus (7:18–35)

We have not read about the Prophet John since we learned that Herod put him in prison (3:120). John believed that Jesus was the Messiah and preached to prepare the people to receive him. But now he doubts whether Jesus really is the Messiah (7:18–23). So he sends two men to ask Jesus, "Are you the one who was to come, or should we expect someone else?" (7:18). John apparently reasoned, "If Jesus is the Messiah, why am I still

---

39. G. F. Hawthorne, "Prophets, Prophecy," in ibid., 636–43

suffering in prison? Why hasn't Jesus raised an army to defeat Herod? Why does he praise the faith of a Roman soldier and heal his servant? And why does Jesus forbid people from telling others that he is the Messiah?"

Jesus responds to John's doubts by sending John's two disciples back to him to tell him what they see Jesus doing. "The blind receive sight, the lame walk, those who have leprosy are cured, the deaf hear, the dead are raised, and the good news is preached to the poor" (7:22). John knows that the Scriptures say these are the very things the prophets predicted of the Messiah.

At the same time, Jesus knows that John (and many of the Jewish people) expect the Messiah to also bring about a political deliverance for Israel and to judge their Roman oppressors. For this reason, Jesus is patient with John and others. He knows that their preconceived notions of how God's kingdom comes will require change. That is why he says, "Blessed is the man who does not fall away on account of me" (7:23). That is, blessed is the person who continues to follow Jesus even when he doesn't fit their expectations for the Messiah.

After John's disciples leave, Jesus commends John to the people (7:24–28). Instead of criticizing John for doubting, Jesus honors him for his bold resolve in preparing the people for the coming of God's kingdom.

The people respond by affirming that they believe in the way of God as taught by the Prophet Jesus (7:29–30). By accepting John's baptism, they prepared their hearts to receive the Messiah and live according to the message he would teach. In contrast, "the Pharisees and experts in the law rejected God's purpose for themselves, because they had not been baptized by John" (7:30). God wants the leaders of Israel to also humble themselves, be healed of their pride, and experience God's peace and forgiveness. But most of the religious leaders have missed out on the life-changing purposes God has for sending his Messiah.

Jesus Forgives a Sinful Woman (7:36–50)

We have just read that when the people hear Jesus' teaching, they acknowledged that it is God's way, but that the Pharisees reject it (7:30). They criticize Jesus for "eating and drinking with sinners" and claiming that God has given him authority on earth to forgive sins. The story of "the sinful woman" vividly illustrates the growing contrast between the people who believe God is at work through Jesus, and the Pharisees, who do not believe he is a prophet from God.

The scene is a large banquet hosted by a prominent Pharisee (later in the story we learn his name is Simon). The Pharisee invites Jesus to join him and his friends for a meal so that they can learn more about Jesus' message. Perhaps some of these Pharisees are open to Jesus being a prophet sent by God.

According to custom, guests recline on the floor to eat. Their heads faced the center of the room towards the food, with their feet extended out toward the walls. It was customary in this culture to leave one's doors open during the day, and at a banquet such as this, beggars and curious passersby could enter the house to stand by the walls and listen in on the conversation. The hungry could receive leftover food.

One of the guests who enters positions herself by the wall behind the feet of Jesus. This "sinful woman" is not a sophisticated prostitute from a large Roman city; she is a simple woman from a small village in Galilee who sells her body for sex to the Gentiles who pass through town. She is a poor, ostracized, beaten down, lonely woman; her only friends are a few other prostitutes in the village. She may have been forced into prostitution as her only option for survival, or sold into it by her parents because of their poverty.[40] She is a vivid example of the poor, marginalized, shame-filled people God has sent Jesus to rescue and offer forgiveness to.

In contrast to "the sinful woman", the Pharisee believes he is righteous and worthy of God's coming kingdom because he separates himself from sinners like her. He does not know that in reality he is sick. Deep in his heart he is sick with religious pride. Above all he lacks love—the little love he has he limits to people like himself (see 6:32–34). He is blind to the extravagant love of God expressed through the Messiah. He cannot see the kingdom of God at work in the Messiah, a kingdom that seeks to rescue and restore the poor.

The woman stands by the wall, by the feet of Jesus, and begins to weep. Wetting his feet with her tears, she then breaks all social norms by letting her hair down in public to wipe the feet of Jesus. Then she astonishes the Pharisee and all his guests by profusely kissing the feet of Jesus.

---

40. Green, *Gospel of Luke*, 309.

How does Simon the Pharisee respond to Jesus allowing himself to be touched by the prostitute who has come into his house? He concludes that Jesus could not be a true prophet sent by God.

Knowing the Pharisee's thoughts, Jesus tells him a short story to teach him that the woman is demonstrating an extravagant (if a bit socially awkward) love for God because he generously forgave her many sins. In a dramatic turn of events, Jesus turns to the woman—still kissing his feet!—and asks Simon to look at her. Three times in quick succession, Jesus points out how Simon has treated him rudely by not even showing him common courtesies as a guest: not having Jesus' dusty feet washed, not giving the customary Eastern greeting of a kiss, and not providing olive oil for his hair, which is dry from walking in the intense Middle Eastern sun. Meanwhile the woman lavishly welcomes him as a guest, and this is not even her house!

Notice that Jesus does not respond rudely to Simon. He wants Simon to experience the love and mercy of God, and he wants to help Simon look at the woman with different eyes—God's eyes. Instead of seeing her as a sinful woman, he is to see a woman who has been changed within, forgiven, and is deeply grateful to God for the love she has encountered in Jesus. Simon too has sins in his heart, but they are different kinds. Simon's sins are the deeper, more deceitful sins of spiritual pride, a hard heart, and a love that limits itself to those who are like him, to those who share his beliefs. Perhaps Simon will reflect on Jesus' words, humble himself, and later embrace the message of God's kingdom. I would like to think that he does and that this is why his name is recorded in the Gospel story.

In conclusion, more than any other story thus far, the story of the sinful woman and Simon the Pharisee describes how God sends his Messiah Jesus to socialize with sinners and offer them the new life God desires for them. The story also illustrates how sinners are to express love and gratitude to the Messiah for being the vehicle of God's love and for extending his forgiveness. Finally, the story paints a clear contrast between how the Pharisees understand God's purposes and how Jesus understands them. Jesus represents God's love and demonstrates God's desire to receive and forgive sinners. In contrast, Simon the Pharisee views Jesus' contact with sinners as wrong, proving that Jesus is a false prophet.

JESUS PROCLAIMS AND DEMONSTRATES
THE POWER OF GOD'S KINGDOM (8:1–56)

How People Respond to the
Message of Jesus (8:1–21)

After Jesus speaks words of love, forgiveness, and peace to the formerly "sinful woman" in Simon the Pharisee's house, he continues to travel from town to town "proclaiming the good news of the kingdom of God" (8:1). The Prophet Jesus has previously declared why God sent him as the Messiah with this message. He said, "I must preach the good news of the kingdom of God to other towns also, because that is why I was sent" (4:43). The present summary (8:1–3) reminds us that Jesus has been loyal to God in fulfilling his mission as the Messiah. The summary also reminds us that the Messiah's miracles of healing and deliverance from evil spirits are expressions of the kingdom of God he proclaims. Jesus both teaches and embodies the way of God's kingdom in all that he does.

We then read that "some women who had been cured of evil spirits and diseases" accompany Jesus and the twelve disciples "to support them out of their own means" (vv. 2–3). It may seem unusual for women to travel with Jesus and his disciples due to the separation of the sexes in first-century Jewish society. However, it was common at this time for godly women to assist traveling rabbis with their financial needs. In addition, it is good to recall that there are large crowds present wherever Jesus and his disciples travel.

But who are these women? A few of them may be wealthy, but most of them are like the poor prostitute of the previous story. They are widows, former prostitutes, and women Jesus has healed and delivered from evil spirits. To one degree or another they have all been ostracized by their communities and left to cope alone as best they can. Jesus allows these women to follow him, not only so he and his disciples will receive provisions for their travels, but also to provide the women with a new community where they can feel safe, accepted, and forgiven.

In addition, Jesus trains these women as disciples, as workers in the kingdom of God. These female disciples play an important part in Jesus' mission to heal others who are sick and weary of life. Imagine the discussions they have with other women in a village as they enter it with Jesus, having had their lives transformed by him. Their transformed lives would add credibility to the words Jesus speaks about the good news of God's kingdom. (Toward the end of the Gospel we will read of the important role these women have when Jesus fulfills his mission in Jerusalem.)

In one of the towns, Jesus tells a parable to a large crowd and proclaims the good news of the kingdom of God (vv. 4–15). Apparently Jesus has proclaimed the word of God long enough for his closest disciples to ask him why many who have listened no longer follow him. So Jesus tells a story to illustrate why people respond as they do to his message about the kingdom of God. In the parable, the farmer who sows seed in his field represents Jesus. As the Prophet-Messiah he has been faithful in sowing "the word of God" (vv. 11,12,13,14). The word of God he proclaims ("sows") is the good news of the arrival of God's kingdom on earth (vv. 1,10). It is the good news that God rescues and restores the lives of people like "the sinful woman" and the widow of the previous stories.

The parable teaches us not to doubt that Jesus is God's Prophet-Messiah or that he speaks the word of God. It teaches us that while many people do not receive his message, or if they do, do not persevere in practicing it, the reason is the condition of their hearts. The pursuit of wealth, delight in sinful pleasures, anxious worries, and pressure from family and friends for following Jesus can choke out the life they once received when they embraced his message.

The story serves at least two purposes. First, it encourages Jesus' disciples to continue to follow him even when many in the crowds are leaving him. The story is a challenge to his followers to continue to listen carefully to God's word and put it into practice. They are to be like the seed that fell on good soil. They are challenged to be like "those with a noble and good heart, who hear the word, retain it, and by persevering produce a crop" (v. 15). Second, the story invites us as readers of the Gospel to reflect on how we have received the message of Jesus. Will we be among those who keep reading the teachings of the Prophet Jesus and building them into our lives so that our lives make a difference? Or will we allow worries, the pursuit of wealth, and sinful pleasures to choke the life out of our souls?

After teaching how people respond to the word of God, Jesus then teaches that God's light, his all-knowing sight, will eventually reveal what is hidden in our hearts (vv. 16–18). We can hide what is in our hearts from others; it is easy to do this by appearing to be religious, like the Pharisees. But we cannot hide from God. God, who sees and knows all, will judge us for how we receive and put into practice the message he has given his Messiah.

Suddenly Jesus' mother and brothers show up in the crowd (vv. 19–21). They seem to doubt if Jesus is truly a prophet from God, or at least how he is carrying out his mission. While Jesus respects his biological family, he insists that God's spiritual family takes precedence over them. He says, "My mothers and brothers are those who hear God's word and put it into practice." Earlier, at the age of twelve, Jesus told his parents that he must give priority to obeying God over pleasing them (2:49). He remains loyal in his obedience to God.

Through his Messiah, God is building a spiritual family that is not made up of the Pharisees and other religious leaders but of those who receive the words of Jesus and put them into practice. Participating in the kingdom of God involves not only believing that Jesus is God's Servant-Messiah but also putting into practice the message he teaches and demonstrates in his life: generous, sacrificial living for others—even for your enemies and those of different ethnicities. It is a bit shocking to read about a woman like "the town prostitute" (7:36–50) becoming part of God's spiritual family while those in Jesus' biological family—at least at this time—are outside it!

Jesus Quiets Raging Storms (8:22–39)

Jesus is now traveling across the Sea of Galilee with his twelve disciples in a small fishing boat when suddenly a raging storm overtakes them (8:22–25). When the disciples panic in fear, Jesus rebukes them for their lack of faith. Jesus has earlier demonstrated his command of the sea (5:1–11). Since that time Jesus has continued to demonstrate his authority from God in remarkable ways. He rightly feels that by now his twelve closest disciples should show greater calm and trust in his control over the "storms" they encounter. The more they come to understand of who Jesus is and the authority God has given him, the more they will trust in his power and his care.

Jesus again shows his disciples that he has full authority over the forces of nature. Even the winds and the waters—like the evil spirits—must obey his commands. What does this tell us about who Jesus is?

The twelve disciples whom Jesus chose to be closest to him still do not understand who he is! "Who is this?" they ask. "He commands even the winds and the water, and they obey him" (v. 25). As readers of the Gospel we are also challenged to ask, "Who is this?" Do we believe that Jesus is God's Messiah and has the authority to calm the raging waters of our lives?

As soon as Jesus and the disciples pull their boat to shore, they encounter another violent storm—this time from the forces of evil inhabiting a Gentile man (vv. 26–39). As Jesus commanded the storm at sea to be calm, so he will now overcome the raging forces in a demon-possessed man and bring peace and calm to his life.

We have already read often of Jesus' authority over evil spirits. This story of deliverance from oppressive demonic forces is unique in two ways. First, it occurs in a largely Gentile region. Jesus purposely travels to a non-Jewish region east of Galilee to show that God desires to rescue and restore all people, no matter what their nationality.

Second, the condition of the demon-possessed man is described in pitiful detail. We read, "For a long time this man had not worn clothes or lived in a house, but had lived in the tombs." The demons in him had often "seized him, and though he was chained hand and foot and kept under guard, he had broken his chains and had been driven by the demons into solitary places" (vv. 27,29).

The demon says his name is "Legion," a military word used for some 5,600 Roman soldiers.[41] This detail, along with the sheer strength of the demon(s), seems to suggest that Jesus is engaged in a battle of cosmic proportions. The description of the demon-possessed man's terrible state also reveals the devil's purpose for all human beings: the man lives chained up like a beast. He is scarcely human, living where the dead are buried. No one can help him.

This story vividly shows how Jesus, God's Warrior over evil, easily fulfills God's desire to rescue and restore the pitiful man. Three times the many demons in the man beg Jesus not to send them to the Abyss, where they will be bound and tortured. They know they are helpless against God's Mighty Warrior, Jesus the Messiah, and plead for his mercy.

The devil's evil hold over the man is broken. We read that the man is now able to sit "at Jesus' feet, dressed and in his right mind" (v. 35). He calmly takes the posture of a disciple, eager to hear the words of God

---

41. Ibid., 330.

spoken by the Prophet Jesus. And he receives the honor of being the first person sent by Jesus to go out and proclaim the good news of what God is doing through Jesus. (v.39).

Surprisingly, the people from the nearby town respond not in joy but in fear over the tremendous power and authority at work in Jesus. They can't explain such a power, and they are afraid that if Jesus continues his work it will upset the economy and life of their town. Sadly, they ask Jesus, the one who loves and liberates, to leave.

But Jesus does not retaliate or rebuke them. He gets in the boat with his disciples and returns to the other side of the lake. Except for the deliverance of the demon-possessed man, it appears that the word of God has not fallen on good soil (vv. 4–15). Yet Jesus will not push the good news of the coming of God's kingdom on people who resist it. He continues to proclaim and embody the good news of God's work to restore the world. People must decide for themselves how they will respond to what God offers the world through his beloved Messiah.

A Lowly Woman Models Faith for a Religious Ruler (8:40–56)

As Jesus and the twelve disciples return to Capernaum and pull their boat up to shore, a large crowd welcomes them (8:40–56). The ruler of the synagogue, a man named Jairus, is among the crowd and pleads with Jesus to come to his house to heal his twelve-year-old daughter, who is dying. But as they walk through Capernaum, with the crowds almost crushing Jesus, a woman who has hemorrhaged for twelve long years sneaks up behind him. She reaches out to touch Jesus so that she can be healed of her bleeding. When she manages to touch the Messiah's garment she is instantaneously healed.

In spite of Jairus' urgent need for Jesus to come to his house and heal his dying daughter, Jesus stops to find out who touched him. He felt the power of God in him go out to heal someone. As readers, we wonder why the Prophet Jesus would stop to inquire from the crowd when Jairus' need is so urgent. It seems that Jesus stops out of compassion and to complete the woman's faith.

The lowly woman has been physically healed, but Jesus knows she has been isolated from her community because of her "unclean condition" of constant bleeding. In Jewish culture she would have lived in a perpetual state of ritual uncleanness for twelve long years and anyone who touched her, or anything she had touched, would be considered unclean (Leviticus 15:25-30). So in the presence of all the people Jesus says, "Daughter, your faith has healed you. Go in peace" (v. 48). By being affirmed as clean in front of everyone, she is immediately restored to a new life in the community. In addition, Jesus addresses her as "daughter." In this way he assures her that she is now part of the new spiritual family God is creating. She experiences the fullness of peace the Messiah was sent to give (2:14).

But it is important to see that Jesus also stops to talk with the woman so that Jairus' faith can be strengthened by hers—because while he and the woman are talking, someone runs to inform Jairus that his daughter has just died. The Prophet Jesus knows he can change the situation even if the girl has died before they get to the house. In essence Jesus says to Jairus, "Don't be afraid. Believe that God's power and compassion are present in me and that your daughter will be healed, just like this woman was healed. Let her example of faith challenge you to believe that I can raise your daughter from the dead."

Thus we read that a woman again becomes the hero in a Gospel story. The lowly woman's faith shines especially bright in contrast to the mockery of the crowd outside Jairus' house, who laugh in disbelief at Jesus.

In addition, we are again reminded that Jesus is the Holy One of God (4:34). In Jewish culture not only the hemorrhaging woman, but also the dead corpse of Jairus' daughter would be considered "unclean." To touch either of them would make a person ritually unclean. But Jesus, the Holy One sent by God, touches both of them, making them whole. Is Jesus as the Messiah in some way taking the uncleanness, the shame of mankind upon himself?

THE IDENTITY OF JESUS AND THE MEANING OF DISCIPLESHIP (9:1–50)

The Mission of Jesus Expands (9:1–9)

While the twelve disciples still struggle to understand the full identity of Jesus (8:25), they understand more than the crowds, since they have always been with Jesus to see him heal the sick and hear him proclaim the good news of God's kingdom. So Jesus determines that they are now ready to be sent out on their own to heal the sick and proclaim the good news that God's kingdom has arrived. We read, "When Jesus had called the Twelve together, he gave them power and authority to drive out all demons and cure diseases, and he sent them out to preach the kingdom of God and to heal the sick" (9:1–2).

God gave his Spirit to his beloved Messiah at his baptism so that Jesus would have power and authority to carry out the mission of establishing God's kingdom. (3:21–22). Significantly, Jesus now calls his twelve disciples together and gives them the power and authority of God before sending them out to assist him in establishing God's rule on earth. While Jesus gives the authority to heal and drive out demons, it is important to note that he conveys the power and authority for the kingdom he himself has received from God. Jesus does not work independently of God but always in unity with God's will.

The twelve disciples set out on their mission. Just as the Messiah Jesus learned to trust in God for his provision, so now he trains the twelve to learn to trust in God for their mission. He tells them, "Take nothing for the journey—no staff, no bag, no bread, no money, no extra tunic" (9:3).

But danger looms. Suddenly a dark cloud is cast over the mission of Jesus and the work of the twelve disciples.[42] Herod, the governor of Galilee, the ruthless ruler who beheaded John the Baptist for his preaching, now hears "about all that was going on" (v. 7). He is perplexed and alarmed. He has heard that a Jewish prophet preaches the coming of God's kingdom. He has learned that the prophet and now some of his followers heal the sick. The crowds flock to them.

Herod is both curious and worried. If someone proclaims the arrival of God's kingdom, perhaps they believe they will be the king. Herod thinks, *Who is this who challenges my ambition to become king over Israel?* He asks, "Who, then, is this I hear such things about?" (v. 9).

We again see that the coming of the Messiah causes a clash with those in authority. We remember once more that when Jesus' parents presented him as an infant to God at the temple, Simeon prophesied that the Messiah was "destined to cause the falling and rising of many in Israel, and to be a sign that will be spoken against, so that the thoughts of many hearts will be revealed" (2:34–35).

---

42. Ibid., 360.

The question of Jesus' identity now becomes more and more the focus of the Gospel story.

The Miraculous Feeding of Thousands (9:10–17)

The twelve disciples return from their mission and report to Jesus their success in healing the sick and proclaiming the kingdom of God (9:10). What they witnessed Jesus say and do they have now said and done. They have experienced God's power to heal for themselves. They were enabled to do miracles similar to those prophesied of the Messiah (7:18–23). This experience no doubt put aside any lingering doubts that Jesus is the promised Messiah who will deliver Israel from their enemies.

After this the twelve disciples are allowed to participate with Jesus in miraculously multiplying five loaves of bread and two fish to feed thousands of people. This will help confirm their belief that Jesus is the Messiah of God, for the people of Israel believe that the Messiah will provide a great banquet with an abundance of food when he appears. While an abundance of bread and fish in a remote area of Galilee may not seem like a great banquet, bountiful food for so many people would trigger associations of what was said of the Messiah.

Peter's Confession and Jesus' Prediction (9:18–27)

In this section we read of some good news, but also of some that is strange and shocking and disturbing. First, let us look at the good news. The question of Jesus' identity has slowly become the focus of the Gospel. Since this is so, Jesus now asks his twelve closest disciples, "Who do the crowds say I am?" (9:18). They answer with what King Herod has heard the crowds are saying: Jesus may be John the Baptist raised from the dead. He may be the Prophet Elijah. Or he may be another ancient prophet who has come back to life.

Jesus, in response, asks the twelve directly. "But what about you? Who do you say that I am?"

Peter, speaking for all twelve disciples, answers, "The Christ of God,"—that is, the Messiah sent by God (v. 20). ("Christ" is from the Greek translation of the word "Messiah.") So the good news is that Jesus' twelve closest disciples now understand that he is not only a prophet but also the Messiah, even though Herod and the crowds believe Jesus is only the former.

The strange part of the news is that Jesus warns his disciples not to tell anyone he is the Messiah! The twelve disciples have finally come to believe who he is; yet Jesus strictly warns them, as he warned the evil spirits earlier (4:34–35,41), not to tell anyone. Then Jesus immediately refers to himself as the Son of Man instead of the Messiah (9:22)!

Why does Jesus want to keep this a secret? Is it connected to the shocking news he is about to share with them? Almost in the same breath Jesus tells them that he, as the Son of Man, "must suffer many things and be rejected by the elders, chief priests and teachers of the law, and must be killed and on the third day be raised to life" (v. 22).

After traveling from village to village healing the sick, raising the dead and announcing the arrival of God's kingdom, Jesus now tells his disciples that he will be rejected and killed. This is a surprise. It is a shock. God's chosen Messiah—rejected and killed?

While the news of the Messiah's death comes as a blow to the disciples, as readers of the Gospel we have been partially prepared. Jewish leaders as far away as Jerusalem have begun to oppose Jesus' mission, and Simeon prophesied early in the story that Jesus would be "a sign that will be spoken against" (2:34). In addition, a reading of the Scriptures that came before shows us that the people of Israel have a long history of killing the prophets God sends to speak to them.

But questions still naturally rise in our minds. Why would God plan for his beloved Messiah to suffer and be killed? What possible purpose could God have in his beloved Messiah's death? How will the kingdom of God be established on earth if the Messiah dies? Could there be a connection between the Messiah's mission to rescue and restore the poor and those oppressed by sin, and his death and resurrection? As readers we have a lot to think about.

A detail of the Greek language, the language the Gospel was originally written in, is important at this point. The word translated "must" is used by Jesus twice in verse 22 and literally means "it is necessary." This word is used repeatedly in the Gospel to stress the necessity of the Messiah's death to fulfill God's will (13:33; 17:25; 22:37; 24:7,26,44).

This is the first of many times that the Prophet Jesus tells his twelve closest disciples about God's plan for him as the Messiah to suffer and die. His mission as Messiah is defined by pouring out his life for the good of others. The devil tried to entice Jesus to pursue his own power and glory, but he rejected these temptations (4:1–13). Instead he has obeyed God in serving, healing, and giving his life in humility for the good of others—especially the poor, the weak, and the marginalized. This continual outpouring of his life will culminate in the ultimate act of obedience to God, when he allows himself to be arrested and killed in Jerusalem.

In response to the question, Who is Jesus?, Jesus essentially answers, "I am the one who suffers and serves and gives his life." This is the way of the cross, the path that God has called him to walk. The way of the cross defines the Messiah's life on earth; it reveals his identity and shows us how God establishes peace.

Immediately after Jesus startles his disciples with the revelation that he must suffer and die, he begins to teach them that they too must be ready to suffer and die (9:23–27)! He says to them, "If anyone would come after me, he must deny himself and take up his cross daily and follow me. For whoever wants to save his life will lose it, but whoever loses his life for me will save it. What good is it for a man to gain the whole world, and yet lose or forfeit his very self?" (vv. 23–25).

When a person saw someone carrying a cross in the time of Jesus, they would think what we think when we see a man in a movie standing before a firing squad, or with a rope around his neck: his life is over. He is as good as dead.

The twelve disciples now believe that Jesus is the Messiah—and yet they don't. For at this point they still do not truly understand what it means for him to be the Messiah, and they are far from patterning their lives according to his way of the cross—the way that involves humbly pouring out their lives for others, even their enemies. The Prophet Jesus must teach the twelve that a disciple is not someone who simply believes he is the Messiah but someone who patterns his or her life according to the Messiah's.

So the path for Jesus' life must also be the path for their lives—if they are to be his disciples. To follow him means to follow him in selfless service and suffering, even if that leads to death. They too must resist the temptations the devil tempted Jesus with- to pursue power and glory. They too must die to every selfish ambition and submit to God's will for them.

Paradoxically, by losing their life they will save it, or find true life. Submission to the way of the suffering, serving Messiah is the path to peace.

We all want to hold on to our life, live the way we want to live; but it is only by submitting to God and losing it that we find true life.

This call to identify with Jesus by taking up their cross daily in order to follow him must have also startled the disciples. As the twelve closest companions of the Messiah, they expected to receive positions of power and prominence in the kingdom they believed he would establish in Jerusalem. As we continue to read the Gospel story we will see how Jesus, through words and actions, repeatedly seeks to capture the hearts and minds of his disciples so that they too will embrace the way of the cross. His path is to become their path, his story their story, his obedience their obedience.

A FOCUS ON JESUS THE MESSIAH

The title Messiah occurs 531 times in the entire New Testament. It is the most common way to identify Jesus and the best way to understand God's purpose for sending him. Because the New Testament was written in Greek, the Greek word for Messiah, *Christos* (rendered "Christ" in English), has influenced many Christians and popular culture to speak of Jesus Christ rather than Jesus the Messiah. Unfortunately, when "Christ" is used, it is often wrongly understood as a second name or surname for Jesus. Because of this misunderstanding, the rich background for the title Messiah in the Prophets is often overlooked.

The background for this title is a Hebrew word that means to anoint a person with oil for a special task to which God has called them. A prophet, priest, or king could be chosen and anointed for God's service. However, in time the prophets began to speak of one special person, a descendant of King David, who would be God's Anointed, a King who would deliver Israel from her enemies and reign over God's kingdom on earth.

By a decisive military victory the Messiah was expected to establish God's justice and righteousness in the land of Palestine and extend it to the entire world. The Messiah was supposed to cleanse the temple in Jerusalem so that the One True God would be worshiped in righteousness. He would secure the land of Palestine for Israel so that they could live there in peace. In other words, the people of Israel believed that God would send the Messiah primarily for them, and once he had liberated them from their enemies, the nations would come to Jerusalem to serve them and learn the ways of God.

It is Jesus' refusal to fulfill this expectation for the Messiah that is central to the confusion, conflict, and drama that we read in the Gospel story. The Prophet Jesus knows that a correct understanding of the Scriptures reveals a different mission for him. Because he knows that the people of Israel have wrong expectations for what the Messiah will do, and because the Roman authorities are quick to kill anyone who claims to be the Messiah, king of Israel, Jesus is careful to not identify himself publicly as the Messiah. It is not until he approaches Jerusalem at the end of his life that he begins to publicly confirm suggestions that he is the chosen Messiah (18:38–39; 19:38–40).

Until that time, he commands those who know he is the Messiah—Satan, evil spirits, and then in time even his twelve closest disciples—to be quiet, to reveal it to no one! He needs time to slowly show and teach the nature of his mission as Messiah. He needs time to show the people who the real enemies of Israel and of all mankind are. He needs time to show and teach how they will be defeated in order to live in freedom, without fear. So in the meantime, instead of calling himself the Messiah, Jesus most often refers to himself as the Son of Man, a more neutral, less familiar title that he can gradually fill with the Scriptures' meaning in order to clarify the nature of his mission. Other titles are used alongside this one to cast additional light on the meaning of "Messiah."

One prominent New Testament scholar summarizes Jesus' essential identity in the Gospel as "the Messiah-Servant-Prophet."[43] Messiah-Servant-Prophet is a good way to begin to understand who Jesus is. The titles Servant and Prophet especially enable us to understand the mission of Jesus as the Messiah. As God's Servant, Jesus humbly obeys God even to the point of suffering and death. As God's Prophet, he uniquely knows the will of God and speaks

---

43. Bock, "Luke, Gospel of," in *Dictionary of Jesus and the Gospels*, 504.

the word of God with fearless authority, even though it will lead to terrible opposition.

But other titles are also used alongside "Servant" and "Prophet" to fill out the meaning of Jesus' chosen task as the Messiah. For example, as the Son of David, Jesus is a descendant of King David, who was given a kingdom by God to rule over. As the Son of Man, Jesus fully identifies with us as human beings and is escorted by angels into the presence of God to receive a kingdom. And as the Son of God, a synonym for "Messiah," Jesus is the descendant of King David whom God promised to love and care for in a unique way (2 Samuel 7:12–16). This title too includes the promise of a kingdom to rule over.[44]

Three Disciples See Jesus in His Glory (9:28–36)

How would you feel if you were Peter or one of the other disciples who has left everything to follow Jesus, and suddenly you heard him say that he will suffer and die and that you too must be ready to die? Like John the Baptist, whom Herod recently beheaded, you too might begin to doubt if Jesus really is the Messiah and if you want to continue following him. We will see, however, that the disciples do not really register the full implications of his statement; they do not believe Jesus will literally die. So they express no doubts and continue to follow him. But when the time comes and the Messiah Jesus is put to death, they are meant to remember his promise that God will raise him from the dead, and that he will return to earth "in his glory and the glory of the Father and of his holy angels" (9:26). His death will be his path to glory in the presence of God.

Eight days after the Messiah Jesus reveals the news of his coming death, he gives Peter and two other disciples a glimpse of his glory, a glory hidden to men on earth. It is the glory of Jesus as the Son of Man who is led by angels into the presence of God to receive a kingdom (Daniel 7:13–14). The disciples see "the appearance of his face changed, and his clothes became as bright as a flash of lightning" (v. 29). The purpose of Jesus revealing his heavenly glory to the disciples is to seal in their minds that he is God's chosen Messiah despite what the Jewish leaders say about

---

44. L. W. Hurtado, "Christ," in *Dictionary of Jesus and the Gospels*, 106–17; Bock, "Luke, Gospel of," in ibid., 503–4.

him. The vision of the Messiah in his glory will help them persevere when they begin to doubt and suffer because of their loyalty to him.

The whole scene is saturated with the language of glory. Not only is Jesus seen in his glory, but the prophets Moses and Elijah also appear with Jesus "in glorious splendor" (v. 31). And while God does not reveal his own glory to the three disciples, he speaks to them from a cloud that envelops them (v. 34)!

It is crucial to note what God says to Peter, James, and John. Do you remember what God spoke to Jesus when the Prophet John baptized him? He said, "You are my Son, whom I love; with you I am well pleased" (3:22). Now God says something very similar to the three disciples: "This is my Son, whom I have chosen; listen to him" (9:35). God assures the disciples that Jesus is his beloved Messiah whom he will make King— even if Jesus now begins to speak of his sufferings and death. They must continue to listen to him and obey him even when he teaches them to deny themselves and to be ready to die for the sake of God's kingdom (v. 23). Most important of all, they must listen to the Prophet Jesus when he stresses that it is God's plan for him to die.

But we learn something else crucial from this account. While Jesus prays on the mountain, Moses and Elijah, two great prophets who died hundreds of years ago, appear and talk to him. What a remarkable scene! What are they discussing with the Messiah Jesus? They speak with him "about his departure, which he was about to bring to fulfillment in Jerusalem" (v. 31). But what could they mean by Jesus' "departure"?

This same word is used in the Scriptures for when the people of Israel were liberated from their slavery in Egypt and departed by the great power of God. Since Jesus has recently taught that he will be killed and then raised to life again, it is logical to understand his death and resurrection as the "departure" they discuss. Since the people of Israel killed many of the prophets God sent to them, it should not surprise us that the Prophet Jesus will also be killed. Here we have another hint of God's purposes for his Messiah: his death will bring about a new deliverance of which his miracles are only a taste.

Why can't Jesus continue to send out more and more disciples to heal the sick, deliver people from demons, and proclaim the good news of God's kingdom? It appears that the Messiah's death and resurrection will bring about an even greater release. Can the Messiah Jesus' death and resurrection fulfill the scripture he quoted when he stated his mission in Nazareth—"to proclaim freedom for the prisoners, recovery of sight for the blind, and release for the oppressed"? (4:18). It is very important for us to try to understand the purpose God has for allowing his Messiah to be put to death by the leaders of Israel.

A FOCUS ON JESUS THE SON OF MAN

Even though Jesus knows that he is God's chosen Messiah, he does not publicly acknowledge it until he arrives at Jerusalem in the last week of his life. Instead, Jesus almost always refers to himself as the Son of Man. Why would Jesus prefer this title?

In the Aramaic and Hebrew languages, which Jesus speaks and reads, "son of man" simply means "mortal" or "human being."[45] Thus, by calling himself the Son of Man, Jesus expresses his full identification with us as human beings. He knows what it is like to be human and shows us how to be human, fully human and fully alive to God and his world. But Jesus has other reasons for speaking of himself as the Son of Man. The Prophet Daniel spoke of "one like a son of man" who was given a kingdom by God. In a vision Daniel recorded, he said he looked, and before him "was one like a son of man, coming with the clouds of heaven. He approached the Ancient of Days and was led into his presence. He was given authority, glory, and sovereign power" (Daniel 7:13–14).

Because the Son of Man in Daniel's vision is given a kingdom to rule over, just like the Messiah, some Jews believe the Son of Man spoken of in Daniel 7 refers to the Messiah. However, since non-Jewish people and even most Jews do not equate the Son of Man in Daniel 7 with the Messiah, Jesus is able to use this more obscure title to cryptically explain the nature of his mission.

At the time of Jesus, a person claiming to be the Messiah would quickly be put to death. "In the volatile political climate of Roman Palestine, anyone suspected of claiming to be the Messiah was unlikely to survive long, and so it proved with Jesus: the inscription affixed to his cross, which all four Gospels record, makes it clear that

---

45. Wright, *Luke for Everyone*, 317.

he was crucified as a dangerous messianic revolutionary."[46] Thus, by avoiding the public use of the title Messiah and instead using the more obscure title Son of Man, Jesus controls the timing of his death, giving him the time he needs to explain the nature of the kingdom of God to his disciples and prepare them to extend it after his departure.

Jesus speaks of himself as the Son of Man twenty-three times in this Gospel, using the title in three basic ways. First, he speaks of the authority God has given him as the Son of Man. For example, he says, "The Son of Man has authority on earth to forgive sins" (5:24); he also asserts that the Son of Man is Lord over the Sabbath—that is, he has the authority to teach how to practice the Sabbath (6:5,9). Even more, he embodies in his life and teaching the central purpose of the Sabbath: rest for the weary soul, peace with God.

Second, Jesus uses the title to teach his twelve closest disciples that as the Son of Man he must suffer, be rejected by the leaders of Israel, and be killed, but then after three days be raised from the dead by God (9:22,44; 18:31–33; 22:22; 24:7). Because the Jewish people believe it is impossible for God's Messiah to be put to death by their enemies, Jesus speaks of his own sufferings and death using the figure of the Son of Man. His disciples are probably more confused than they would be if he had said he would be put to death as the Messiah. It is only after God raises Jesus from the dead that they are able to understand that it was God's plan for him to die as the Messiah.

There is a third context in which Jesus speaks of himself as the Son of Man. In addition to the unique authority God has given him as the Son of Man—and his unique sufferings and death—Jesus often refers to himself by this title when speaking about the events after his sufferings and death, when God will exalt him to his right hand (a place of honor and authority) and later send him back to judge all mankind (12:8,40; 17:22–23,26,30; 21:27; 22:69–70).

It is interesting to note that after his resurrection Jesus consistently refers to himself as the Messiah instead of the Son of Man.

46. Porter, *Jesus Christ*, 165.

This is because the disciples now understand that it was God's will for him, as the Messiah, to die. Now that it is obvious that Jesus died as the Messiah, against all their expectations, there is no need to be secretive about his messianic identity. By way of summary, Jesus uses the title Son of Man to speak of the unique authority given him by God and of God's plan for him to suffer and die, but then of his exaltation to God's presence in heaven.

But there are two other, even more important reasons Jesus might speak of himself as the Son of Man. In Daniel's vision the Son of Man represents the righteous people of God in the presence of God. In the vision, the people of God suffer at the hands of an evil beast that represents the Roman Empire. But God delivers them and grants them possession of his kingdom (Daniel 7:21–22).

Thus, the Prophet Jesus may be using the title Son of Man to imply that he is "the son of man" in Daniel 7, who represents the people before God and suffers instead of them. He claims to fulfill in his person, as an individual, what was said collectively of "righteous Israel." As the Son of Man, representing the people before God, Jesus suffers death at the hands of the Romans but is delivered from death by God and given a kingdom. In addition, just as the saints of the Most High God are promised a kingdom to possess in Daniel's vision (Daniel 7:18,22,27), so Jesus promises his disciples that they will rule with him in his kingdom (Luke 22:28–30).

Finally, in Daniel's vision the Son of Man comes with the clouds of heaven to be escorted by heavenly servants into the very presence of God. Because the Son of Man seems to have a heavenly origin, is closely associated with God, and is "given authority, glory, and sovereign power" by God, many believe Jesus understood himself not only as fully human but also as having come from God's very presence in heaven to earth.[47]

---

47. Wright, *Luke for Everyone*, 317; Witherington III, *New Testament History*, 122–24; I. H. Marshall, "Son of Man," in *Dictionary of Jesus and the Gospels*, 775–81.

Jesus Teaches the Twelve Disciples
about True Greatness (9:37–50)

The next day when Jesus comes down from the mountain, we are reminded why he could not stay there as Peter requested. A man in the gathered crowd asks Jesus to heal his only child, who is being destroyed by an evil spirit. We see once again that Jesus must continue his mission to defeat the forces of evil. God will only glorify him after he fulfills his mission in Jerusalem.

The other nine disciples, who did not join Jesus on the mountain, are unable to deliver the boy from the demon. Previously, when Jesus sent out the twelve with the authority "to drive out all demons" (9:1), they succeeded. Why do they now fail to free this boy from an evil spirit? Jesus is clearly frustrated with their lack of faith to heal him.

While Jesus was praying on the mountain and discussing his coming death with Moses and Elijah, they may have discussed their greatness in the kingdom of God instead of praying. In any event, this story and the following three sayings of Jesus (9:44,48,50) show the spiritual dullness of the disciples. (This theme continues: even after God has raised Jesus up, they are not yet ready to continue his mission.)

The crowd marvels at the greatness of God's power expressed through the Prophet Jesus. But the mood shifts sharply as he turns to the twelve disciples and again tells them he will be rejected. "'Listen carefully to what I am about to tell you: The Son of Man is going to be delivered into the hands of men.' But they did not understand what this meant. It was hidden from them, so that they did not grasp it, and they were afraid to ask him about it" (vv. 44–45). As Jews, the disciples cannot conceive of the Messiah suffering and being killed. While Jesus speaks of a literal betrayal, death, and resurrection, the twelve disciples appear to believe that he is speaking in riddles as he does when teaching in parables.

Sadly, instead of discussing Jesus' statement about his sufferings, his twelve closest disciples now begin to argue about which of them will be greatest in the coming kingdom of God (vv. 46–48)! Their selfish ambitions prevent them from standing by Jesus as he approaches his final conflict. They continue to show little understanding of the nature of God's kingdom. For them the kingdom of God presents an opportunity for power, positions, and prominence. It is tragic to see in this moment how much their hearts are like those of the leaders of Israel.

In order to teach the disciples the nature of God's kingdom, Jesus has a small child—whom society would brush off as insignificant—stand beside him. He says to the disciples, "Whoever welcomes this little child in my name welcomes me; and whoever welcomes me welcomes the one who sent me. For he who is least among you all—he is the greatest" (v. 48). The disciples must begin to receive the small and insignificant if they want to become great before God. Instead of scheming and striving for positions of power and prominence, Jesus teaches them that true greatness before God consists in putting aside self-importance to humbly serve those societies casts aside.

The same elitist mentality and desire for power and prominence surfaces again when one of the twelve disciples seeks to prevent a man who is not one of them from casting out demons (49–50). Jesus again rebukes the disciples for their proud hearts. Their pride now expresses itself in seeking to control the work of God. While the man who drives out demons is not one of the chosen twelve, he is doing the work of God and should be left alone.

In summary, verses 37–50 show us that the twelve disciples still have much to learn about the nature of God's kingdom and true greatness. They still have much to learn about God! After all, it is God who reveals his nature and will through his Servant Jesus.

Jesus will now "resolutely set out for Jerusalem," where he will bravely face his sufferings and death (v. 51). On his journey he will patiently teach the twelve disciples the nature of God's kingdom so that they will be prepared to carry on his mission after he has been raised up to God. At this point they seem ill equipped. They seem so unlike the Messiah who gives his life in service for the good of others. As we continue to read the Gospel story, we will often wonder if they will ever be fit to carry on the work of the kingdom of God.

Review of the first part of the Gospel: LUKE 1:1–9:50

What have we learned so far in the Gospel story?

- We have learned that God has given Jesus his Messiah power and authority through his Spirit to establish his kingdom on earth.
- We have learned that the nature of God's kingdom is different than the nationalistic, political kingdom the Jewish people expect the Messiah to establish. This is why Jesus does not openly claim to be the Messiah at the present time.
- We have read of open conflict between Jesus and the religious leaders of Israel, and of their growing rejection of him.
- Most recently we have read that Jesus will suffer and die in Jerusalem, and that he now teaches his disciples that they too must be ready to suffer and die. But they cannot understand what Jesus means.
- In obedience to God, Jesus remains strong in his resolve to travel to Jerusalem in spite of threats and opposition from the Jewish leaders and the knowledge that he will suffer and die there.
- Finally, we have learned much about the nature of God's kingdom. Jesus teaches and embodies God's kingdom, his will to rescue all people from the devastating effects of sin and Satan so that they may be restored and live in peace with God and one another.

As we continue reading the Gospel we find ourselves curious about how the story will unfold:

- How can Jesus' message from God be called good news if he must suffer and die?
- How can Jesus' mission to rescue and restore the poor and the broken continue if he dies?
- What possible purpose could God have in allowing his beloved Messiah to suffer and die? How will God turn the apparent defeat of Jesus into victory?
- What will happen to the disciples when Jesus dies? What will they do when they see the leaders in Jerusalem reject Jesus by causing him to suffer and die? Will they run to save their lives?

As we have finished reading the first part of the Gospel, we may want to also ask where we find ourselves in the story. Are we open to Jesus being sent as God's Messiah to remake the world for justice and goodness? Hopefully we are, even if at this point we may be somewhat confused. Do we find ourselves being drawn into the goodness, love, power, and peace God reveals in Jesus his Messiah?

PART FOUR

JESUS' JOURNEY TO JERUSALEM (9:51–19:44)

This part of the Gospel story is often called the travel section because it records Jesus' journey to Jerusalem to fulfill God's plan. The section begins, "As the time approached for him to be taken up to heaven, Jesus resolutely set out for Jerusalem" (9:51), and ends with repeated references to his final movement to Jerusalem (e.g., 19:11,28,41). The actual route and locations for Jesus' journey are seldom mentioned and are of little concern. The emphasis lies rather on how and why Jesus is journeying to Jerusalem—he travels there to suffer and die as God's Suffering Servant who fulfills God's will.

The Prophet Jesus has only recently told his disciples he will suffer and die at the hands of Israel's leaders (9:22). Now, because his sufferings and death are imminent and so central to God's plan for him, he speaks of them on many occasions (e.g., 9:44; 12:49–50; 13:31–33; 17:25; 18:31–34). The people of Israel have a long history of killing the prophets God sends to proclaim his message. So we should not be surprised that the great Prophet Jesus will also suffer and be killed. Yet as readers of the Gospel we know (and the twelve disciples have recently confessed) that the Prophet Jesus is also God's chosen Messiah. So we are challenged to reflect on why God would allow his Prophet and Messiah Jesus to be put to death. How can God's kingdom be established, how can the Messiah rule over it, if he is killed?

Throughout this part of the Gospel we are often reminded that the Messiah's journey to Jerusalem, and the path it depicts, is to be the pattern for how his disciples walk through life. The path the Messiah walks is one of love and loyalty to God no matter the cost; it is the path of selflessly suffering for the good of others—even one's enemies; it is the path of humility and service, of caring for the poor and the ostracized, of sharing meals with "sinners" and offering them God's forgiveness, of breaking down hostilities and making peace between tribes and religions; it is the path of establishing justice and righteousness.

It is this way of life—the way of the Messiah, who models the way of God's kingdom—that his disciples are so slow to understand, accept, and emulate. Their pride and frequent pursuit of high positions, power, and honor stand in glaring and disappointing contrast to God's Servant Jesus, the teacher they are to pattern their lives after. In fact, as we read this section of the Gospel we are often amazed at their spiritual dullness and wonder if there is ever any hope for them to understand—and more importantly, practice—the way of the kingdom seen and taught by Jesus.

Because the disciples so highly value prestige, positions, and pursuing authority over others, Jesus must devote much time on the journey to Jerusalem to teach them the way of life in God's kingdom. Their values, behaviors, and goals for life will require a complete reconstruction if, after Jesus has been raised up to God, they are to live as he lived and be qualified to lead the kingdom movement he has launched.

(On this subject, it is interesting to note that the disciples of Jesus were first called people of the Way, or the Path, not Christians; see Acts 9:2; 19:9,23; 22:4; 24:14,22. The way referred to was the Way of Jesus the Messiah. Sadly, at some point in history the humble, selfless Way of the Messiah became too organized, too hierarchical, and an organized religion called Christianity emerged, with many of its leaders competing for power and positions, just as the Pharisees had. The Way of Jesus was never lost, but it became less and less visible in a church that valued political power and prominence.)

While in the previous section of the Gospel we often read of Jesus healing and rescuing those in despair, on the journey to Jerusalem we read more about his teaching. Everything he teaches is related to the nature of God's kingdom and how to participate in it. He teaches his disciples to practice mercy and justice and warns them of practicing the hypocrisy of the Pharisees, especially their pride and greed. He teaches that God's kingdom is offered to all peoples, not just to the people of Israel. He teaches, by word and deed, of God's extravagant love for sinners. By sharing meals in the homes of "sinners," Jesus maintains that he is like God by loving them and inviting them to turn to God so that they might receive his life, love, and peace.

But the more Jesus teaches and acts in ways that the leaders of Israel disapprove of, the more tensions escalate as he approaches Jerusalem. Earlier in the Gospel the godly Simeon prophesied concerning Jesus, "This child is destined to cause the falling and rising of many in Israel, and to be a sign that will be spoken against, so that the thoughts of many hearts will be revealed" (2:34). Jesus is increasingly spoken against as he journeys to Jerusalem, and there the hearts of Israel's leaders are revealed to us, the readers of the Gospel. The more the Messiah speaks and enacts the nature of God's kingdom, claiming that he and not the leaders of Israel knows and represents it, the clearer it becomes to them that his teaching undermines their authority over the people. Thus, at the end of this section, the setting is ripe for bitter conflict as Jesus approaches Jerusalem for the last time.

PROCLAIMING AND PRACTICING THE WORD OF GOD (9:51–10:42)

Jesus Begins His Journey to Jerusalem with Resolve (9:51–62)

When Jesus met with Moses and Elijah on the mountain, they discussed "his departure, which he was about to bring to fulfillment in Jerusalem" (9:31). In referring to the Messiah's death as a departure (or exodus), the Gospel suggests that the Messiah's death will bring about a new liberation for those who are spiritually enslaved and oppressed when he comes to Jerusalem. We now read, "As the time approached for him to be taken up to heaven, Jesus resolutely set out for Jerusalem" (9:51).

Jesus knows that God will take him up to heaven after he has suffered and died. Jesus will not be surprised when his sufferings and death come upon him; nor will he die as a weak, helpless victim. He is not confused or cowardly. He travels to Jerusalem with full resolve, in obedience to God's will. Yet at this point in the Gospel story we only have a few hints as to why God would plan to have his beloved Messiah suffer and die.

Somewhat surprisingly, the first village Jesus visits on his journey rejects him, a rejection that forebodes what awaits Jesus in Jerusalem. The village that turns the Messiah away is in the region of Samaria, located between Galilee and Jerusalem. The Samaritans and the Jewish people hate each other. At times their hatred erupts into violence. God has sent his Messiah to bring peace between hostile groups like these; Jesus arrives wanting to heal the sick and proclaim the good news in Samaria also.

This would help bring peace between at least his Jewish disciples and the Samaritans who receive him. But he is rejected.

However, Jesus does not respond to this rejection with threats and retaliation. He is prepared to travel on to the next village. In sharp contrast to Jesus, two of his closest disciples, James and John, "intoxicated with their own sense of power,"[48] respond by asking him, "Lord, do you want us to call fire down from heaven to destroy them?" (v.54).

This astounds me. What a startling request! Jesus has taught the disciples to love, pray for, and do good to all people—even their enemies (6:27–36). Now a few of them want to ask God to destroy an entire village with fire. This shows how far the disciples are from understanding the love of God revealed in his Messiah. It is a love that conquers one's enemies by doing good to them, even suffering for them. It can conquer one's enemies by turning them into friends. It is this love that Jesus abounds in but his disciples still lack. So Jesus rebukes the disciples and continues on to another village.

As Jesus continues his journey to Jerusalem, three potential workers for the kingdom of God approach him to become his disciples (vv. 57–62). The first eagerly says, "I will follow you wherever you go." But Jesus and his disciples have left their home base of Capernaum in Galilee, and as they travel they are not always received into a village for lodging. On such occasions they must travel on to another village or sleep out under the stars. So Jesus says to the potential disciple, "Foxes have holes and the birds have nests" (to return to rest in each night), but as the Son of Man he "has no place to lay his head" (v. 58). Is the would-be disciple ready for this? His initial enthusiasm wears thin at the thought of a cold night out in the open and little food for the morning.

It is important to point out that at this particular phase Jesus' mission is so urgent, so intense, that workers must be ready to put the work of God's kingdom above even the central command to honor their parents. To perform the funeral rites for a person in Jewish society at this time is a twelve-month long process. So when the second potential disciple asks to first bury his father, Jesus responds by saying there is no time for that now. The urgent need to proclaim the kingdom of God on the way to Jerusalem must take priority over even the most honorable duties.

---

48. Green, *Gospel of Luke*, 405.

The third potential worker also wants to fulfill the custom of honoring his family, returning to his village to say goodbye before he travels with Jesus. Jesus says again that the critical nature of his mission at this point takes precedence over even this honorable custom. He responds, "No one who puts his hand to the plow and looks back is fit for service in the kingdom of God" (v. 62).

The ancient prophets taught that honoring one's parents is God's will and is an important way to show love and obedience to God. But at this particular time, as Jesus makes his crucial and dangerous journey to Jerusalem, joining him must take precedence over even honoring one's family. While these commands appear to be colored by the critical context of Jesus' increasingly hard and perilous mission, the lesson is still clear: if any disciple at any time is forced to choose between family and following God's Messiah, he or she must choose loyalty to Jesus.

Jesus Sends Out Seventy-Two More Workers (10:1–24)

After three potential workers for the kingdom make excuses for not following Jesus on his mission to Jerusalem, Jesus successfully recruits others for the task (10:1–9). God's work continues even when some will not pay the price to do it. The Servant of God resolutely continues his mission from God.

Jesus earlier appointed twelve disciples to be with him and spread the good news of God's kingdom (9:1–2). He now appoints and sends out seventy-two more. More and more people seek to be healed and touched by the love and power of God, and Jesus cannot be everywhere at once. Besides, he is headed to Jerusalem, where he will die and be taken up to God, so he must train more workers to continue his mission.

When Jesus first chose the twelve apostles (9:1–6), he implied that they would be the new leaders of Israel, replacing those who will reject him in Jerusalem. While the number twelve represents Israel with its twelve tribes, the number seventy-two represents all the nations of the world. (According to the earlier Scriptures, this is how many there are; see Genesis 10.) By sending out seventy-two workers, Jesus suggests that the blessings of God's kingdom offered through him as the Messiah are for all the peoples of the world, not just the people of Israel.

After giving specific instructions to the seventy-two before sending them out (10:3–8), Jesus tells them what he earlier told the twelve disciples: they are to "heal the sick . . . and tell them, 'The kingdom of God is near you'" (v. 9). By now we have come to understand that the power and presence of God's kingdom reside in Jesus his Messiah. But how can the kingdom of God be near the people in these towns if it is the seventy-two and not Jesus who visits them?

At times Jesus speaks of the kingdom of God as coming in the future, at the end of time. But at other times he teaches that the kingdom of God is already present in him, seen in what he says and does. As God's beloved Messiah, Jesus has been given his Spirit to exercise the power and authority of his kingdom on earth. When Jesus heals, drives out demons, teaches, and forgives sins, he does so by the authority of God, which has been given to him. Remarkably, Jesus himself now confers that same healing power and authority on the seventy-two, just as he did previously with the twelve (9:1). Through his Spirit, God will also be present with these workers to rescue people from the oppression of sin.

Soon after Jesus pronounces God's judgment on the towns in Galilee who rejected his message (10:10–16), the seventy-two workers return filled with joy because of the success of their mission. They say, "Lord, even the demons submit to us in your name" (v. 17). Jesus responds to their success in delivering the oppressed from evil spirits by declaring, "I saw Satan fall like lightning from heaven" (v. 18).

Satan dwells in the heavens as God's archenemy and works through his evil minions (demons) on earth to destroy lives. God has sent his beloved Messiah to invade Satan's kingdom and rescue people from his oppressive power. This clash of kingdoms intensifies when Jesus sends out seventy-two more workers to undo the works of Satan.

Jesus then reminds the seventy-two disciples that their power over evil spirits does not come from magic or their own spiritual might. He says, "I have given you authority . . . to overcome all the power of the enemy" (v. 19). We are again reminded of the enemy God has sent his Messiah to defeat: it is not the Roman Empire, an enemy to be defeated with swords, but sin and Satan, who can only be overcome with the power of God's Spirit.

Jesus reminds the seventy-two that their greatest joy is to be found in belonging to God, and that they can be assured of entering God's kingdom when it is consummated at the end of time. He says to them, "Rejoice that your names are written in heaven" (v. 20). Then Jesus makes yet another remarkable statement. He says, "All things have been committed to me by my Father. No one knows who the Son is except the Father, and no one knows who the Father is except the Son and those to whom the Son chooses to reveal him" (v. 22). We learn several important truths from this statement. First, as we have previously seen, God has given Jesus a unique authority on earth to establish his kingdom—to heal, forgive, judge, bring justice, and speak the words of God. He speaks with the full authority of the Messiah when he says that *all things* have been committed to him. Second, Jesus says that only God knows his true identity. While the crowds (and even his disciples) struggle to know who Jesus is and understand his mission, Jesus has peace in knowing that God knows his full identity and loves him through and through—the same way the best of fathers loves his son.

Conversely, Jesus makes the bold claim that no one knows the true essence of God but him! He says, "No one knows who the Father is except the Son." Jesus knows and shows the true essence of God when love drives him to seek out sinners to offer them forgiveness; when compassion drives him to weep for those who are in despair because of their mistreatment and poverty; and when mercy drives him to bring peace to fractured humanity. Jesus claims to know the very heart of God, a claim that sets him apart from all the previous prophets.

And finally, because only Jesus the Messiah knows the essence of God, only he can reveal the depths of God's being. Only Jesus the Messiah truly understands the love of God, the compassion that causes God to draw people near and heal them, and the mercy of God that forgives and restores them in him. And it is this love, compassion, and mercy that Jesus reveals in his life and words.

Many prophets have spoken of the mercy of God. But only Jesus, God's beloved Messiah, knows the full depths of God's mercy and uniquely reveals his abounding desire to seek out and save sinners.

Jesus Teaches the Nature of Love (10:25–37)

An expert in Jewish law now tests Jesus with a question. He asks Jesus the crucial question, "What must I do to inherit eternal life?" (10:25). When Jesus asks the lawyer how he would answer his own question, the man responds, "'Love the Lord your God with all your heart and with all your soul and with all your strength and with all your mind'; and 'Love your neighbor as yourself'" (v. 27).

Jesus agrees that these are the two central commands of Scripture and that they summarize what God has revealed to all the prophets. So Jesus says, "Do this and you will live" (v. 28). That is to say, if the legal expert loved God with his whole being and treated others the way he would like to be treated, he would inherit eternal life. All of the words of the prophets (i.e., the will of God) can be summarized with these two commandments. God is worthy of our complete obedience and love. And because God is, above all, a merciful God who shows mercy even "to the ungrateful and wicked" (6:35), those who say they love him are to love as he loves.

The Jewish people at the time of Jesus tended to limit their expressions of love to other Jews. They believed God loved them and did not look with favor on Gentiles and Samaritans. The strict party of the Pharisees and the experts of Jewish law felt no obligation to love even the "unrighteous" Jewish person. Jesus, of course, is ripping this narrow worldview—this world with a narrow love—wide open. He demonstrates God's love for all people and teaches his disciples to do the same—even if they are slow to practice his way of love.

When the legal expert seeks to justify limiting his love to other "righteous" Jews, Jesus tells him a story. The hero of the story is a Samaritan. (Recall that a Samaritan village recently refused hospitality to Jesus. Now Jesus makes a Samarian the hero of a story, as the one who loves his enemy and shows God's kind of love!)

In the story, two Jewish leaders, a priest and a Levite, are traveling from Jerusalem. When they see the victim of a brutal crime lying at the side of the road, they keep on going. They pass by this man, a fellow Jew who has been robbed, beaten, and left for dead on the dangerous road leading down to Jericho.

A Samaritan comes along. He is most likely a merchant traveling back home from Jerusalem. He too sees the half-dead Jewish man lying at the side of the road. But instead of passing him by, "he took pity on him" (10:33). This phrase "comes in the middle of the story to emphasize its importance."[49] It shows that the Samaritan models what it looks like to love your neighbor, who may also be an enemy. The Samaritan stops—

49. Ibid., 431n125.

in spite of the danger of also being robbed and beaten—and extends tangible, costly love to the beaten Jewish man.

The implication is clear. It is the Samaritan who will inherit eternal life, for he has put into practice the two greatest commandments: to love God completely and to love his neighbor, who is anyone in need. The Jewish man whom Jesus is talking to, an expert in the Jewish law, must do as the Samaritan did if he wants to inherit eternal life.

To fully grasp the impact of the story it is helpful to recall that the Jewish people at the time felt repulsion and hatred toward the Samaritans. In fact, the Jews cursed Samaritans in their public prayers, asking that they would not share in eternal life! Sadly, the feelings were mutual. The hatred between Jews and Samaritans had gone on for hundreds of years. Both groups had their own temple for worship and their own version of the Scriptures. They regarded each other as infidels and enemies.

This story has greater impact on us if we imagine a modern Palestinian teenager stopping to help a Jewish settler who has taken his land and who has been robbed, beaten, and left for dead by some Jewish activists. While Orthodox Jewish leaders pass him by, the young Palestinian pays for a taxi to take him to a clinic where he will be treated for days. This too the Palestinian boy pays for.

After telling the story, Jesus asks the expert in Jewish law, "Which of these three do you think was a neighbor to the man who fell into the hands of robbers?" The man replies correctly: "The one who had mercy on him." Jesus then tells him, "Go and do likewise" (vv. 36–37).

As readers of the Gospel, we are meant to ask ourselves if we will "go and do likewise." Will we put limits on our love? Or will we begin to love other people regardless of their race and religion? Will we love God completely and learn to love as he loves?

Jesus Praises a Female Disciple (10:38-42)

As Jesus and his disciples continue on their way to Jerusalem, they are hosted for a meal at the home of two sisters, Mary and Martha (10:38–42). Martha, one of the sisters, frantically works in the kitchen to provide the perfect meal for Jesus and his disciples. Mary, the other sister, leaves the kitchen (the women's domain) to sit at the feet of Jesus as he teaches the word of God.

It was customary for disciples to sit at the feet of their teacher to be taught. It was here the disciple listened, asked questions, and learned the rabbi's teaching with the intent of putting it into practice and teaching it to others. [50]

The shocking point of this story is not that Mary does not help her sister in the kitchen—it is that she boldly enters the room full of men to hear Jesus teach about the kingdom of God. Jesus commends Mary for her hunger to learn the word of God.

JESUS TEACHES THE DISCIPLES A NEW WAY TO PRAY (11:1–13)

One day, after the Prophet Jesus finishes praying, one of his disciples approaches him to ask if he would teach them to pray, just as John taught his disciples to pray. Jesus' disciples have been praying, but they notice that Jesus prays in a new way in light of his special relationship to God and of the kingdom of God coming to earth through him. When the Messiah Jesus prays he speaks to God uniquely as his Father and prays for God's strength to enable him to establish his kingdom on earth.

Jesus does not focus on special techniques or times for prayer. He emphasizes that we can be intimate with God in prayer. He teaches his disciples that the nature of God is good and generous and that he loves them like the best of fathers loves his children; God eagerly desires to give them what they ask for. Jesus repeats the verbs "ask" and "give" many times in these few verses in order to encourage the disciples to freely and boldly ask God for help.

Jesus teaches his disciples that they can approach their Mighty Creator God as an affectionate, caring Father. He is not a distant, demanding, impersonal deity, but a loving God whom they can know and relate to as if he were the best of human fathers. Jesus begins and ends his instruction by addressing God as Father (vv. 2,13). Some Jews at the time of Jesus used the more formal "ab or abi" (father) to address God. But Jesus uses the more familiar term "Abba," which means something like "Father dearest."

---

50. Wright, *Luke for Everyone*, 131.

The term "Abba" implies both the intimacy and endearment we can have in our relationship with God.[51]

It is important to note that while the disciples can pray to God as "our Father," Jesus prays to God as "my Father." As the Messiah, Jesus has a unique and unusually intimate relationship with God. God has revealed his purposes on earth to the Messiah Jesus in ways he has revealed them to no one else. And God has chosen Jesus as his Messiah for the task of accomplishing those purposes—a task that no one else could fulfill.

Jesus then instructs the disciples to pray, "Father, hallowed be your name." They are to pray for God to be known, honored, and obeyed for who he is. As their love for God grows they will want others to acknowledge the beauty of who God is—especially the great mercy and compassion he reveals through his Messiah Jesus.

Next, Jesus teaches the disciples to pray for God's kingdom to come. God's kingdom is seen in the Messiah Jesus as he delivers people from the oppression of sin, shame, and Satan, offering them instead God's love, forgiveness, and peace. The kingdom of God advances wherever Jesus heals and teaches and people put his teaching into practice. The disciples must pray for more and more people to be delivered from their sin and despair. Implicit in the prayer is a challenge: as we pray for God's kingdom to grow, we are to envision how we can participate in selflessly giving of ourselves to help hurting people.

Jesus has taught us to begin our prayers with a focus on God—on his honor and his kingdom growing. Now he teaches about prayer within the community of disciples. For the majority of poor disciples and their families in Galilee, food is scarce. Many are forced to hire themselves out as day laborers on the farms of wealthy landlords. Because of this they need to pray for work and provisions for the day.

Jesus then teaches his disciples to pray to God to forgive their sins. While the Messiah has been given authority on earth to forgive sins, ultimately sin is against God, and he is the one we are to ask for forgiveness. At the same time, we must be ready to forgive those who have sinned against us! It is hypocritical for us to ask God to forgive us when we harbor bitterness and hatred in our hearts towards those who have hurt us. Jesus often points out the inconsistency of asking God for forgiveness

---

51. Witherington III, *New Testament History*, 125.

while withholding it from those who have wronged us. We must learn to show mercy just as God shows mercy.

Finally, Jesus encourages the disciples to pray that they will not be led into temptation (or better, "testing"). Since both Jesus and his disciples have faced times of testing (4:1–13; 6:22), it is difficult to understand what he means by this. Perhaps Jesus means that we should ask God to strengthen us so that we can endure times of testing and come out of them strong, in the power of God's Spirit, just as Jesus did when tested by the devil (4:14).

As Jesus continues to teach his disciples how to pray, he focuses on *what God is like* and how God eagerly wants to help us. First he tells a short story (11:5–10) to illustrate that God wants to help them much more than even their best friends do. It is helpful to recall yet again that Jesus extends God's love to "sinners" and outcasts on the fringe of society. Many have been made to feel unworthy of God's love because of the many demands placed on them by the Pharisees. They live with shame and fear. In this first story Jesus stresses that those who have sinned much in the past, and thus might feel unworthy to approach God in prayer, can feel confident that they may approach God boldly in prayer without shame.

The Greek word translated "boldness" (or "persistence" in some translations) in verse 8 can also be understood here to mean "shameless-ness." Imagine in this story a small village in Galilee with houses in close proximity to one another. A peasant farmer sleeps on a floor mat in his one-room house with his wife and children. The family sleeps together to keep warm and has been asleep for several hours. Then a good friend who lives nearby bangs on their door late at night—he is requesting food for a friend who is visiting unexpectedly.

In the society Jesus lives in it would be dishonorable to turn the friend away and not provide him with food. So the man who is woken from his sleep preserves his honor by getting up to give food to his friend, even though the friend acts shamelessly by waking up the man and his family and disturbing their neighbors.[52] What is Jesus' point? He seems to speak especially to those disciples who feel unworthy of God. He comforts and encourages them by saying that they are not to let their feelings of fear and shame keep them from approaching God in prayer. God is a good and merciful God and wants to receive and help us.

---

52. Tannehill, *Luke*, 189.

If the logic behind the first story is that God loves us much more than a friend would, the logic behind the second story (vv. 11–13) is that we can expect God to love and care for us much more than the best of earthly fathers. There is no evil in God. Goodness and mercy permeate his being. Jesus says to us, as humans who do evil, "If you then . . . know how to give good gifts to your children, how much more will your Father in heaven give the Holy Spirit to those who ask him!" (v. 13).

Jesus says God will "give the Holy Spirit to those who ask him"! He is suggesting that the Holy Spirit is the greatest gift God could give us and thus the greatest gift we could ask for. What could this mean?

The Spirit of God is the presence of God on earth. God gave his Spirit to his beloved Messiah Jesus in order to strengthen him and lead him in establishing his kingdom. In the same way, God wants to be present through his Spirit with the disciples to make them aware of his love for them and to strengthen them for service in his kingdom.

JESUS EXPOSES THE HYPOCRISY OF THE PHRAISEES (11:14–54)

Jesus Overpowers Satan's Kingdom by the Spirit (11:14–28)

Jesus has just taught his disciples to pray for God's kingdom to come. He has encouraged them to pray for God to give them his Spirit to extend God's kingdom. He now delivers a man from a demon by the power of God's Spirit and then teaches that his mission to deliver people from the forces of evil is an attack of God's kingdom on Satan's. Satan and the forces of evil are strong, but God's Messiah is by far the stronger and easily overpowers them.

The Jewish leaders who oppose Jesus cannot deny the power that is at work in him. But if they admit that Jesus' power comes from God, they will also need to admit that God has sent him and that his words are true. This they will not do. So they make the outlandish, blasphemous claim that Jesus has made an alliance with Satan and casts out demons by Satan's power! They say, "By Beelzebub, the prince of demons, he is driving out demons" (11:20).

Jesus responds to his accusers with a simple observation (vv. 17p–18). There is a fatal flaw in their logic. Everyone knows that princes in the same kingdom who war against each other for control will weaken the kingdom and lead to its ruin. The Messiah is launching a major attack against the forces of Satan. Why would Satan give the Messiah authority to destroy his rule over people? It doesn't make sense.

Jesus then responds with another simple observation based on logic (v. 19). The very leaders who accuse him of driving out demons by the power of Satan have followers who are driving out demons. Why aren't they placed under the same scrutiny for the source of their power? If Jesus is driving out demons by the power of Satan, then logically they would be doing the same.

In his final reply to his accusers, Jesus states the source of his power to overcome Satan's strong grip over human lives. He says, "But if I drive out demons by the finger of God [i.e., God's Spirit], then the kingdom of God has come upon you" (v. 20). The expression "finger of God" is used in the Scriptures as an image for God being present with his great power to deliver the people of Israel from their bondage in Egypt (Exodus 8:19). Jesus is saying that the same power of God's Spirit is now at work in him to bring about a new deliverance—a deliverance from the bondage of sin and Satan.

Thus, there is a clash of kingdoms—the kingdom of God and the kingdom of Satan—beneath the surface of what people see in the mission of Jesus. Satan works through evil spirits to keep people in misery and bondage and to prevent them from experiencing the love, peace, and freedom found in God's kingdom. Satan is strong in the world. But the good news of the kingdom of God is this: God's Messiah is stronger.

Jesus depicts Satan as a mighty soldier who is heavily armed to protect his property. He says, "When a strong man, fully armed, guards his own house, his possessions are safe. But when someone stronger attacks and overpowers him, he takes away the armor in which the man trusted and divides up the spoils" (vv. 21–22). While Satan's grip on human beings is strong, he is no match for God's powerful Messiah, who is equipped with truth, righteousness, and the authority of God's Spirit.

Satan seemed to know that Jesus, as the Messiah, would attack his rule over humanity. That is why he tempted Jesus by offering him all the kingdoms of the world if he would worship him instead of serving God. But Jesus would not be derailed from his loyalty to and love for God. He will worship the Lord his God and serve only him (4:5–8).

The Crowds Are Challenged to
Believe in Jesus (11:29–36)

The crowds continue to increase. The tension continues to mount. Jesus now responds to an earlier demand to show a spectacular sign from heaven (11:16).

Those who challenge Jesus to perform a spectacular sign belong to what he calls "a wicked generation." They are a wicked generation because even though Jesus does the signs predicted of the Messiah (7:20–25), they demand a more sensational one. They do not really want to believe. A more spectacular sign won't cause them to repent and live in light of God's kingdom. So the only additional sign they will receive is what Jesus calls "the sign of Jonah" (11:29).

Just as God rescued the Prophet Jonah (Yunus) from the belly of a great fish after three days, so God will rescue his Messiah Jesus by raising him from the dead after three days. Jesus has earlier predicted that this will happen after he is killed by the leaders in Jerusalem (9:21). This is the sign he refers to. His enemies will claim that Jesus' death proves he is not the Messiah, but his resurrection will prove them wrong.

Then Jesus warns the wicked generation of Jewish leaders who reject him (11:31–32.) He reminds them that two great non-Jewish nations, Arabia and Assyria, humbled themselves before God when they received the messages of King Solomon (Sulayman) and the Prophet Jonah. But now the leaders of Israel are rejecting Jesus the Messiah, who is greater than both Solomon and Jonah! At the judgment these non-Jewish nations who received God's word will rise and speak against the current leadership of Israel.

Jesus continues to warn the leaders of Israel in the crowd (vv. 33–36), who claim he works for Satan and demand a spectacular sign of him. God has sent his Servant Jesus as a light, to show his love for the world. How can the leaders of Israel not see the light of God revealed in his Messiah Jesus? Jesus says it is because their hearts are full of darkness.

The Hypocrisy of the Pharisees (11:37–54)

The Background to His Critique
After Jesus speaks words of warning to those who demand a sensational sign to prove he is from God, he accepts an invitation to a meal from a prominent Pharisee and his friends. It is likely that these Pharisees were part of the crowd that accused Jesus of driving out demons by the power

of the devil and challenged him for a sign. The setting of the meal is tense. Jesus is under close scrutiny.

The host immediately casts a critical look at Jesus when he does not follow the Pharisees' practice of washing before a meal in order to cleanse themselves of contact with "unclean sinners and Gentiles." The Pharisee knows that Jesus has been in contact with such people. He knows that Jesus even touches them when he heals them. The Pharisee reasons that if Jesus were a righteous prophet sent by God, he would know that he must wash away the impurity that clings to him as a result of his contact with sinners.

I suggest that Jesus deliberately avoids washing according to the traditions of the Pharisees in order to provoke them to think about what is most important to God. It is true that Jesus does not follow good social protocol as a guest. But he has a good reason for not doing so. He wants to shock his host and the other guests so that they will understand what is at stake by rejecting him and the message of the kingdom.

Jesus is harsh in his critique of the Pharisees and the scribes, but we should give him the benefit of the doubt and try to understand his reasons. While Jesus shares many of the same beliefs as the Pharisees—a belief in one God, the prophets, angels, and a resurrection at the end of the ages, followed by judgment—there is a fundamental difference between his understanding of God and God's purpose for the world, and theirs. And this fundamental difference—"the key to knowledge," as Jesus later puts it (11:52)—makes all the difference in the world.

Jesus proclaims that God's kingdom has come to earth through him. His words and actions show that God wants to come near all people— especially the poor and the oppressed—to deliver them. God wants to save them from the oppression of sin. He wants to deliver them from the economic, social, and religious powers that marginalize and oppress them. God wants to break down the walls that separate people and restore them to life in his kingdom, where justice, love, peace, goodness, and forgiveness prevail. God has sent Jesus his Messiah to proclaim, embody, and bring into existence his kingdom on earth.

The Pharisees, along with their colleagues, the experts in Jewish law, have a different understanding of God and how his eternal kingdom will come. They make new policies (laws) for outward purity and put pressure on people to abide by them. Then they have created additional laws for how to be cleansed when someone breaks the law. Thus, they divide people into the "clean" and the "unclean."

One scholar points out that the Pharisees are not simply conservative religious leaders, but that they apply their laws and traditions to all aspects of life: the social, the political, and the religious. They enforce their rigid system of rules on the people in order to accomplish their political aims. According to the Pharisees, God will not send his Messiah to establish his kingdom until the people are pure—by their definitions of purity![53] For them it is quite clear Jesus cannot be a prophet of God. His way of socializing with sinners proves this.

Jesus knows what is at stake. If the Pharisees can convince people like the poor widow, the ostracized leper, the sinful woman, and the raging demoniac that Jesus is a false prophet who does not speak the words of God, they will not come to him to be rescued and restored! So the clash between the kingdom of God and the kingdom of Satan that we read about earlier in this chapter continues as Jesus now shares a meal with the Pharisees. Jesus views these religious leaders as pawns in the hands of the devil; they look good on the outside as they observe their manmade traditions, but on the inside they are full of greed and evil. With this background we can better understand the seriousness of Jesus' sever critique of the Pharisees.

Jesus' Critique of the Pharisees and the Teachers of the Law

Jesus contrasts the Pharisees' focus on an outward cleansing with his emphasis on an inner cleansing of the heart that produces goodness towards others (11:39–41). He compares their practices to washing the outside of a bowl but leaving the inside dirty—how foolish! "Did not the one who made the outside make the inside also?" While the Pharisees may impress the crowds with their outward practices of religion, they are "full of greed and wickedness" on the inside.

They are foolish not to see that God created both their bodies and their hearts. God desires clean hearts above all. If the Pharisees would begin by building good and generous hearts (6:45), by giving liberally to the poor, and by loving their enemies (6:35), then they would begin to become truly pure before God.

---

53. Wright, *Luke for Everyone*, 145–46.

Jesus now pronounces the first of six woes—three to the Pharisees and then three to the teachers of the law. The word translated "woe" was commonly used by the prophets of God to pronounce his just judgment. Jesus uses familiar prophetic language, warning the religious leaders of Israel of God's judgment just as previous prophets warned their generations.

While the Pharisees meticulously separate one in every ten herbs from their gardens as an offering to God, they fail to focus on what really matters to him. Jesus says, "You neglect justice and the love of God." Many of the prophets predicted that the Messiah would establish justice among all the peoples of the earth (Isaiah 9:7; 11:4; 32:1,6; 42:1,3–4). Jesus not only helps those who are treated unjustly—he speaks against those who neglect justice and even practice injustice.

Then, in an interesting play on words, Jesus reveals what it is that the Pharisees love rather than God: they neglect *the love* of God for *the love* of their own importance. They express their self-love by seeking the prominent seats at public prayers, where all can see them. And they parade around in public to be seen and greeted by the people. But hidden beneath their displays of devotion to God is passion for prominence and applause.

Jesus then warns the Pharisees that they "are like unmarked graves, which men walk over without knowing it" (11:44). Death and decay lie below the grass and flowers on the surface above. He is saying that, as teachers, the Pharisees fail to be sources of life to the people. They cannot show the way of life because they do not have the life of God in them. So the people, deprived of life with God, listen to their teachings without perceiving the rot that lies beneath the surface.

This illustration shows the irony of the Pharisees' demand for purity from the people. While they give the impression of being pure by following their many traditions, their hearts are as impure as a corpse. And since walking over a grave makes a person unclean, they make the people impure along with themselves.[54]

Jesus now speaks three woes to the experts in the law who are present at the meal with the Pharisees (vv. 45–54). The experts in the law and the Pharisees hold similar views and often appear together in the Gospel in their opposition to Jesus. When one of the experts in the law tells Jesus that by saying these things he is also insulting them, Jesus does not

---

54. Green, *Gospel of Luke*, 473.

apologize or hold back on his critique. As I have already stressed, Jesus knows the stakes are too high for social pleasantries. He acts provocatively and speaks prophetically to shock the Pharisees and scribes, so that they will understand how they misrepresent the true nature of God and what he plans to accomplish on earth through his Servant Jesus.

Jesus' first pronouncement against the scribes is because they burden the people with laws God has not given, and then they make no effort to help the people follow these laws. As experts in the law, they are diligent to create new laws or traditions to ensure that people keep God's commands. They do not feel it is enough to teach the people to keep the Sabbath; they have to add thirty-nine of their laws to ensure that the Sabbath is not broken. These thirty-nine laws for keeping the Sabbath, along with hundreds of others they have created, become a burden loaded on the people.

We can sense the tension growing as Jesus makes an unfavorable comparison: he now links this group of Pharisees and legal experts with those who persecuted and killed the prophets of old! The people of Israel ridiculed and killed the prophets rather than change their ways and obey the word of God. Now it is happening all over again. Jesus is sent to Israel to speak the words of God, and the leaders of Israel ridicule him! Jesus knows that the increasing hostility in these leaders will ultimately contribute to him being killed.

When the scribes and Pharisees build and venerate the tombs of Israel's prophets, they live a lie with a false interpretation of history. They are not like those who accepted the previous prophets; rather, their rejection of Jesus links them with those who killed them. It is ironic that these legal experts, who meticulously study God's word, fail to see that the Messiah Jesus fulfills what they read.[55]

Jesus is sent by God to fulfill what the prophets predicted of the Messiah. He embodies, speaks, and reveals all that the prophets described and longed to see—right before the eyes of the Jewish leaders. By rejecting and ultimately killing him, the present generation of Jewish leaders show themselves to be the leaders of all who have killed God's prophets in the past. God's severe judgment will fall upon them, the accumulated judgment for every past act of murder and rejection.

---

55. Ibid., 474.

Finally, Jesus warns the experts in the law of the disaster that awaits them because they have taken away "the key to knowledge" (v. 52). By using this phrase, I understand him to be referring to the good news of the kingdom of God that he proclaims. Receiving that message is the key that leads to experiencing the love, peace, and forgiveness of God and empowers us to practice God's justice and mercy towards others.

The experts in the law have not received the message of Jesus and entered the kingdom of God. More seriously, by criticizing Jesus they hinder people who are on the way to entering the kingdom. Their guilt is great. They claim to be teachers of God's ways to the people, but they themselves are on the wrong path. As Jesus said earlier, they are like the blind leading the blind.

The account ends with Jesus leaving the home of the Pharisee. Jesus has clearly drawn the line, showing the sharp contrast between the way of God's kingdom, which he represents, and the ways of the Pharisees and teachers of the law. It is now clear to them that Jesus will not be one of them. He doesn't fit their system.

So they begin to fiercely oppose him, challenging him with questions to try to expose him as a false prophet before the people. The conflict between the leaders of Israel and Jesus continues to be a prominent theme on his journey to Jerusalem. Once he is in Jerusalem it will reach its climax.

JESUS CHALLENGES HIS DISCIPLES NOT TO FEAR (12:1–13:9)

Fear God, not Man (12:1–12)

The crowd that gathered to witness Jesus cast out a demon (11:14) has now swollen from the hundreds to the thousands. The crowd tramps on one another as they seek to get a closer look at Jesus and hear what he says. We have read that the Pharisees now fiercely oppose Jesus and seek to get rid of him as a false prophet of God. So Jesus now speaks directly to his disciples, who stand closest to him in the huge crowd, and warns them not to practice the hypocrisy of the Pharisees (12:1–3). He then challenges them not to fear those who threaten to kill them (vv. 4–7).

What is the hypocrisy of the Pharisees that the disciples are to guard themselves against? A hypocrite is a person who pretends to be something that he isn't. But hypocrisy begins with the failure to sincerely love God from the heart and leads to the failure to treat others the way you yourself would like to be treated (11:42). When a person does not sincerely love God and obey him from the heart, they tend to focus on outward acts and behaviors as a substitute in order to appear pious before others.

Jesus spoke of hypocrisy when he said, "You Pharisees clean the outside of the cup and dish, but inside you are full of greed and wickedness" (11:39). He spoke of hypocrisy when he said to them, "You give God a tenth of your mint, rue and all other kinds of garden herbs, but you neglect justice and love for God" (11:4). Now Jesus warns hypocrites that what they hide in their heart will not be hidden forever. He says, "There is nothing concealed that will not be disclosed, or hidden that will not be made known" (12:2). We can fool others by pretending to be something that we really aren't, but we cannot fool God. One day, who we really are will be "proclaimed from the roofs" for all to hear.

After warning his disciples not to practice the hypocrisy of the religious leaders, Jesus warns them not to fear them either. The verb "fear" is used five times in verses 4–7. Rather than fear their enemies, whose power is limited to killing the body, the disciples are to fear God, who determines their eternal destiny. Yet the disciples are not to live in a constant, dreadful fear of God. Jesus reminds them that God, whom he has taught that they can pray to as Father, cares deeply for them. God loves them; he knows everything that happens to them, and they are very valuable to him.

Jesus has spoken of how the disciples are to relate to God. Now he speaks of their relationship to him as their Teacher and Messiah. He makes another astonishing claim, saying, "I tell you, whoever acknowledges me before men, the Son of Man will also acknowledge him before the angels of God. But he who disowns me before men will be disowned before the angels of God" (12:8–9).

Jesus teaches that it is not enough to fear the One true God. To truly believe in God means to entrust one's life to his Chosen Messiah and commit oneself to practicing the message God has given him. To reject Jesus as God's Messiah means we cut ourselves off from the love, life, forgiveness, freedom, and peace God offers us through him. It means we cut ourselves off from God's kingdom offered through Jesus. To not acknowledge Jesus as the Messiah means we cut ourselves off from him and from the love and life of God for all eternity.

A FOCUS ON HYPOCRITE

The English word "hypocrite" refers to a person who pretends to be something they aren't. It is often used of religious people who claim to live one way but in reality live another way. At the time of Jesus, the Greek word we translate "hypocrite" was used for actors in a play. In real life the actors were not the persons they portrayed in the play.

Jesus often challenges his disciples to not practice the hypocrisy of the leaders of Israel, who go to great efforts to look righteous before others, but in reality do not love God from their hearts and do not show his love and mercy towards the poor and those they deem less righteous than themselves. Jesus often warns of this inconsistency between outward acts of piety and the true condition of the heart. While the leaders of Israel are keen to display their outward acts of religion before others—their frequent public prayers, their somber appearance when fasting, their gifts to the temple, and other outward displays of their religiosity—inside their hearts are full of pride, greed, and self-promotion.[56]

Trust in God to Provide (12:13–34)

As Jesus continues to teach, a man in the crowd yells out to him, saying, "Teacher, tell my brother to divide the inheritance with me" (12:13). Jesus, being a prophet, knows there is greed behind the man's request, and this leads him to teach the man and the crowd around him about greed and possessions (vv. 13–21). Jesus says, "Watch out! Be on your guard against all kinds of greed; a man's life does not consist in the abundance of his possessions" (v. 15). Jesus challenges the man to reflect on the true meaning of life. Most people are shortsighted and live only for this short life, pursuing pleasures and building up their possessions. But true life (and thus true joy and peace) consists in knowing God and living for his purposes.

To illustrate the foolishness of building one's life on pleasures and possessions, Jesus tells a short parable. A rich landowner sees the opportunity to get even richer when his land produces an unusually good crop. The good crop is the result of the sun and the rain that God has provided, but the man does not thank God or consult him to determine what to do

56. R. H. Smith, "Hypocrite," in *Dictionary of Jesus and the Gospels*, 351–53.

with his money. He consults only himself and thinks only of himself. The rich man thinks, "What shall I do? This is what I will do. I will store all my grain. . . . And I'll say to myself, 'You have plenty of good things laid up for many years. Take life easy; eat, drink and be merry'" (vv. 16–19).

"Eat, drink, and be merry" is a common saying—but the man forgets how this classic ancient formula for hedonistic living ends. It ends with "for tomorrow you will die!" The man leaves God and God's compassion for the poor out of his planning, and he forgets that his short life on earth will one day end. In his case, it ends that very night. The man considers himself a good businessman, but God calls him a fool! His possessions will not follow him to the grave, but acts of compassion would have. Yet the rich man has none to take with him. "He did not realize that the bellies of the poor were much safer storehouses than his barns."[57]

Jesus now turns directly to his disciples to teach them how to use possessions in the kingdom of God vv. 22–34). There is a clear contrast between the outlook of the rich fool and how the disciples are to relate to possessions. The rich fool consults only himself as plans how to use his money. In contrast, the disciples are to consult God, considering his compassion for the poor and his eternal kingdom when they consider how to use their possessions.

There is a progression of thought in the main verbs Jesus uses here to teach about possessions. He begins with "Do not worry" (v. 22), then asks us to "consider" (v. 27), and ends with the challenge to "seek" (v. 31). Following this progression can help us better appreciate Jesus' teaching in these verses. First of all, he challenges his disciples not to worry about the basic necessities of life, such as food and clothing (vv. 22,26,29). He wants to free them from anxious striving and worry.

But just telling people not to worry does not work too well. Jesus knows that. So he then challenges the disciples to consider (the second set of verbs) God's presence and care in his creation. By stopping to observe and reflect on God's care for birds and flowers, the disciples will realize that they can count on him to provide for them. They are of much more value to God than the flowers of the fields, which are here today and then thrown into the fire tomorrow.

---

57. Augustine, Sermon 36.9, quoted in Bailey, *Jesus through Middle Eastern Eyes*, 304.

It is not until the third set of verbs ("Do not seek," "But seek") at the end of Jesus' teaching that his intended outcome becomes clear. In verse 29 and following, Jesus teaches the disciples to give their energies to the pursuit of God's kingdom, not to the pursuit of possessions. He says, "And do not set your heart on what you will eat or drink; do not worry about it. For the pagan world runs after all such things, and your Father knows that you need them. But seek his kingdom, and these things will be given to you as well" (vv. 29–30). God cares for the disciples infinitely more than the very best of earthly fathers. And he knows their every concern and need. Knowing that God knows and cares is enough to put their minds at rest and allow them to experience his peace.

Knowing that God knows their needs and that he has been pleased to provide them with a place in his kingdom (v. 32) frees the disciples to give liberally of their possessions to the poor (vv. 33–34). Rather than storing up possessions for themselves like the rich fool (v. 21), they are liberated to sell what they own and give the money to those in need. In this way they build up an investment in heaven that God will keep track of and keep safe.

Giving to the needy is the safest, most secure investment we can make. Again, the bellies of the poor are far safer repositories than our bank accounts.

Be Ready for Jesus' Return (12:35–48)

This passage can be difficult for modern readers. We are not used to reading about masters and servants—much less masters who beat their servants and even have them cut to pieces! It is important to remember that Jesus is teaching here with parables (12:35–39,42–48), which are short stories, and these parables are based on the often violent times he lives in. Normally a parable has one main point to teach and can include hyperbole, a figure of speech using exaggeration, as in the case of these three parables. The details of a parable are not to be interpreted literally. All this can help us understand some of the harsh descriptions in the present parables.

While the details of these three parables can be difficult to understand, their message is simple and clear. The words "master" and "servant" along with the challenge "to be ready" are repeated many times. Jesus is the disciples' Master, whom they must faithfully serve by continuing his mission after God has raised Jesus to be with him in heaven. Those who continue to faithfully serve him will be greatly honored. But those who become complacent and begin to live for themselves will face a harsh judgment.

These parables allude to the time when God will send Jesus his Messiah back to judge all the peoples of the earth. Jesus tells his disciples that they "must be ready, because the Son of Man will come at an hour when you do not expect him" (v. 40). As readers of the Gospel we know that Jesus travels to Jerusalem to die, and we also know that God will raise him from the dead after only three days. Because Jesus will faithfully fulfill the mission God has given him on earth as his Servant, God will exalt him to a position of glory in heaven. Then, at a time in the future known only by God, he will send the Messiah Jesus back to judge the world. These are the times and events Jesus refers to in these parables.

Jesus anticipates that it could be a long time before God sends him back to judge the peoples of the earth. Because of the long delay before he returns, his disciples might be tempted give up and begin to live for their own selfish pleasures rather than for God. But Jesus makes an incredible promise for the disciple who is faithful in his service: Jesus says that "he will put him in charge of all his possessions" (v. 44). Because this promise is part of the imagery of the parable, we cannot be exactly certain what Jesus means. But clearly he promises great rewards for the faithful, obedient disciple when the kingdom of God is consummated at the end of history.

Jesus Causes Division (12:49–59)

As Jesus travels closer to Jerusalem, where he will complete his mission, he expresses deep distress, because he wants it to be completed. He speaks of a fire he will bring on earth, a baptism he feels compelled to complete, and a division (not peace) he will bring. What can Jesus mean by these unusual expressions? Because these three short, puzzling statements say much about why Jesus is sent as the Messiah, it is important to try to understand them.

First of all, what is the fire Jesus says he has come to bring on earth? The prophet John said that the Messiah Jesus would carry out the fire of judgment. He warned that the Messiah would separate good from evil— those who produce the good fruit of love and generosity in their hearts from those who remain greedy and uncompassionate (3:8–9,16–17).

By longing for the fire to be kindled, Jesus longs for the day when God will have him rid the world of evil so that the earth is filled with only his love, justice, and righteousness. He longs for the day when women are no longer raped or abused; when corrupt presidents, kings, and prime ministers are no longer in power to oppress the poor; when Satan no longer enslaves and misleads people; and when the peace of the kingdom reigns supreme. Don't we all long for that day? Jesus must come with fire in order to bring it about.

But before that day, Jesus says he must first undergo a baptism. The prophet John has already baptized Jesus (3:21–22), so what baptism must he now undergo that so distresses him? The word "baptism" at the time was used for immersing or plunging someone completely into a life-consuming fire or water.[58] It appears that the baptism Jesus speaks of is his coming sufferings as the Messiah in Jerusalem. He will be plunged into ridicule and torment that will culminate in the violent, ignoble death of crucifixion. Jesus has not yet said much about why he must die—his closest disciples still do not even understand that he *will* die! But Jesus knows both that his death is certain and that there is a reason for it. And he is distressed until his sufferings are completed.

There remains one final puzzling statement to understand. Why does Jesus say he came to bring division on earth? Hasn't God sent him to bring peace (2:14)? Hasn't Jesus pronounced peace on the sick and the sinner when he has healed, forgiven, and restored them to their communities? But Jesus knows that people only experience God's peace when they humble themselves, turn to God, and open their hearts to the love, power, and forgiveness he offers through his Messiah. Because most do not receive Jesus and his message of the kingdom, "the immediate reality is division."[59] The different responses to his message create a rift. The result of following him or refusing him runs so deep that it divides not just friends, neighbors, and communities, but sadly, even families.

Jesus then speaks to the crowd, calling them hypocrites (12:54–59), just as he earlier called the Pharisees hypocrites (v. 1). He says, "Hypocrites! You know how to interpret the appearance of the earth and the sky. How is it that you don't know how to interpret this present time?" (v. 56). It appears that the Pharisees have now persuaded many in the crowds to reject Jesus as a prophet sent by God. The Pharisees and others

---

58. Tannehill, *Luke*, 213.
59. Ibid., 214.

in the crowd can predict what the weather will be like, but even though they diligently study the Scriptures, which predict the coming of God's kingdom with the Messiah, they don't interpret the Scriptures correctly and thus can't see the presence of the kingdom of God revealed in Jesus before their very eyes.

Jesus finishes by telling the crowd a short parable to warn them that they are headed for disaster if they do not wake up, receive his message, and enter the kingdom of God. The people in the crowds need to think for themselves instead of blindly believing what their religious teachers say. After all, it is their lives that are at stake!

Bear Fruit for God (13:1–9)

As Jesus travels from Galilee to Jerusalem, a few in the crowd tell him of a bloody atrocity recently committed in Jerusalem by the ruthless Roman ruler Pilate (13:1–9). While pilgrims from Galilee had been sacrificing in the temple, the pagan ruler Pilate entered the Jewish holy site and killed the pilgrims. He then mixed their blood with the blood of the animals they were to sacrifice to God!

Why is this abominable act reported to Jesus? Probably because Jesus is also from Galilee, and as he journeys to Jerusalem he is announcing the arrival of a kingdom other than Rome's. This could be viewed as an act of sedition against Rome and, if it becomes known, could lead to his crucifixion. So perhaps those who tell Jesus about Pilate's slaughter of the pilgrims at the temple in Jerusalem want to warn him not to continue his journey to Jerusalem. However, it is also possible that they report the massacre to challenge Jesus. If he plans to deliver Israel from their Roman occupiers—as the people who follow him expect—what will he do when he arrives in Jerusalem? Where is his army? Is he brave enough to continue his journey after hearing what Pilate has done?

Jesus does not respond to the possible threat to his life. Instead, he uses the occasion to teach that all people need to turn to God in repentance. He rejects the common assumption that people suffer more because they have sinned more. He rejects the idea that there is a direct link between disasters and God's judgment. Jesus does not explain why people suffer. Instead, he stresses that all of us ("all" is repeated four times) will be judged if we do not turn to God in humility and change. In this way he challenges the false assumption of some people, like the Pharisees, who are confident that their religious acts earn them God's favor. In short, Jesus teaches that everyone needs to turn to God in repentance and bear fruit for him from the heart in order to be forgiven.

Jesus then tells a parable to emphasize that God is more concerned with how we live from within our hearts than with the details of what we believe or with our outward acts of religion. The point of the parable is that God looks for fruit in our lives—this is repeated three times. We are to repent (vv. 3–5) in order to live in a new way that causes our families and communities to flourish. The fruit Jesus envisions most likely refers to the way of God's kingdom that he has taught and exemplified. It is the way of loving God with our whole being and expressing that love by generosity to the poor, mercy to the sinner, and compassion for the sick. It is the way of selflessly giving of ourselves for the good of others, just as Jesus has done. This is the fruit God looks for. If we do not produce the fruit of good and generous love, we too will perish.

WHO WILL PARTICIPATE IN THE KINGDOM OF GOD? (13:10–17:10)

Jesus Heals a Crippled Woman on the Sabbath (13:10–21)

This story of Jesus delivering a poor, crippled woman from bondage reminds us again of why God has sent him. At the very beginning of his ministry Jesus said his mission was to preach good news to the poor, to proclaim freedom for prisoners bound by the effects of sin, to provide recovery of sight for the blind, and to release the oppressed (4:18). We have read often in the first part of the Gospel story of how Jesus has healed the sick. Now we read of it once again as a reminder of why he travels to Jerusalem.

The woman Jesus heals is "bent over and could not straighten up," a detail that symbolizes her social state as well as her physical condition.[60] For eighteen long years she has crept slowly along the village roads. Everyone knows her. Few have paid attention to her. And no one can help her. Bent over, with the crowd towering high above her as Jesus teaches,

---

60. Green, *Gospel of Luke*, 522.

no one can see her. But Jesus sees her! Then he speaks the compassionate word of release to her: "Woman, you are set free from your infirmity" (13:12). The woman immediately straightens up, praising God, with the crowd joining in her praise.

But not everyone in the crowd rejoices at the woman's restoration. The ruler of the synagogue is angry—just like the Pharisees—that the crowds come to Jesus to be healed on the Sabbath. He wants to control the crowds and put limits on when God's love is shown. But God's Servant Jesus will put no limits on the love of God. The love of God, shown in the healing of the crippled woman, dwells deeply in his Messiah. Jesus will not allow the deep, powerful love of God to be limited by the rules of men.

In reaction to the synagogue ruler's attempt to prevent the sick from being healed on the Sabbath, Jesus points out the hypocrisy of the religious rulers. They free their donkeys to go get water on the Sabbath, and that is considered work according to their beliefs. Their donkeys can survive one day without water. Yet this poor woman has been bound by her infirmity for eighteen long years! And she is not a donkey but a daughter of the great prophet Abraham. How hypocritical, how heartless, to complain about her being healed on the Sabbath!

After Jesus' rebuke to the synagogue ruler and the Pharisees, we read that all "the people were delight with all the wonderful things he was doing" (v. 17). But the religious rulers, humiliated, will still continue to oppose him. The crowds might wonder, will the growing opposition prevent Jesus from establishing God's kingdom on earth? Jesus immediately tells two short parables to teach that the kingdom of God will indeed succeed on earth.

At this point in time the kingdom of God may seem small and insignificant. Think about it: so far the kingdom of God is seen only in Jesus and his small band of disciples as they travel from village to village along the dusty roads of a remote province of the vast Roman Empire. At this point in time the kingdom of God is like a small mustard seed planted in a garden, or a bit of leaven mixed in with a large batch of flour.

But just as the small mustard seed contains within itself the potential to grow and become a large tree, and just as the small bit of leaven can work its way through an entire batch of dough, so the kingdom of God contains within itself the DNA to grow and one day permeate all of God's creation. Jesus knows that he is God's chosen Messiah. He knows that

God has chosen and empowered him to establish his kingdom on earth. So he pushes on, convinced that what may now seem small and insignificant will one day fill the earth.

Jesus Warns and Weeps for Unbelievers (13:22–35)

Because the kingdom of God has appeared with the coming of Jesus, he challenges the people to "make every effort" to enter it by embracing his message. It will be too late after they die. At the time of judgment, many of the people of Israel who heard Jesus teach in their villages will ask him for permission to enter God's eternal kingdom. They will say, "We ate and drank with you, and you taught in our streets." But because they did not acknowledge that God had sent him and did not build their lives on his teaching, he will say to them, "I don't know you or where you come from" (13:26–27).

Jesus expresses deep sorrow that most of the people who have heard him teach will not enter the kingdom of God when it comes in all its fullness at the end of time (v. 34). Still, he rejoices that God's kingdom will succeed and be full! He says that multitudes of non-Jewish people (Gentiles) "will come from east and west and north and south and take their places at the feast in the kingdom of God" (v. 29) Jesus depicts the kingdom of God at the end of time as a great feast, filled with the very people Israel considered to be their enemies and beyond the reach of God's mercy.

As Jesus finishes teaching, some from among the Pharisees advise him to leave Galilee because Herod wants to kill him. (Not all Pharisees are hostile towards Jesus.) Herod is the ruthless ruler of Galilee who beheaded the prophet John and who wanted to meet Jesus in order to find out who he claimed to be (v. 7–9). Herod wants to establish himself as king over the greater area of Galilee and will not allow anyone to challenge his authority.

Jesus responds to the news that Herod wants to kill him by sending the men who have warned him back to Herod: "Go tell that fox, 'I will keep on driving out demons and healing people today and tomorrow, and on the third day I will reach my goal'" (v. 32). As God's chosen Messiah, Jesus knows his life and destiny are in God's hands, not Herod's. Jesus will continue his journey to Jerusalem to fulfill God's plan for him. Jesus remains focused and full of resolve. He will resume his travels and arrive safely according to God's timing, in three days. Jerusalem is the appointed destiny for God's Prophet and Messiah, "for surely no prophet can die outside of Jerusalem" (v. 33).

Even though Jesus knows that the leaders of Israel will have him put to death, he wants them and all the people to receive him and be saved. Even though he sternly warns the people of Israel, he does it out of compassion, so that they will turn to God and be saved. Jerusalem has become a way of representing all of the people of Israel; thus Jesus laments, "O Jerusalem, Jerusalem, you who kill the prophets and stone those sent to you, how often I have longed to gather your children together, as a hen gathers her chicks under her wings, but you were not willing" (v. 34).

God longs to rescue his people Israel, but they are not willing to receive the one he has sent to rescue them. So God will withdraw his protection over them in the land of Palestine and leave them desolate. Around forty years after Jesus speaks these words, Roman soldiers will destroy Jerusalem along with its magnificent temple and drive the people of Israel from their land.

A Focus on Herod Antipas

Herod Antipas, one of the sons of King Herod the Great, was the governor of Galilee during the life and ministry of Jesus. He ruled over Galilee from 4 BC to AD 39, thus beginning his rule a few years before Jesus' birth and ending it a few years after Jesus' death. When he came to power, Herod was a friend of the emperor in Rome, but the emperor later deposed him because of his relentless scheming to be appointed king.

Since Jesus grew up just south of Sepphoris, the capital of Galilee, where Herod Antipas resided, Herod's politics and policies were most likely topics of discussion at home in Jesus' village of Nazareth. Later, when Jesus had begun his ministry, Herod became alarmed that Jesus and his twelve closest disciples were beginning to preach "another kingdom." As Jesus' popularity in Galilee grew, Herod tried to meet with Jesus, but Jesus avoided seeing him. And as he was on his journey to Jerusalem, he was told that Herod sought to kill him. Jesus responded by telling those who reported this to go back and tell Herod (whom he calls a

fox—i.e., a clever fool) that he would continue to heal the sick and travel to Jerusalem in obedience to God. His life was in God's hands, not Herod's.

Herod will be in Jerusalem when the leaders of Israel put the Prophet Jesus on trial for claiming to be the Messiah, the King. Then the Galilean governor's wish will finally be granted: he will meet with Jesus. Will Jesus confront "the ruthless fox" he had known from the time he grew up in Nazareth?

Jesus Challenges the Pharisees to Humble Themselves (14:1–24)

While there seem to be at least a few Pharisees sympathetic to Jesus' teaching, since some of them warned him about Herod, the majority of the Pharisees remain critical of Jesus. Now another Pharisee invites Jesus to eat at his house so that he and his associates can find fault with him. Jesus, however, knows their intentions and deliberately provokes them by healing a man in front of him who suffers from dropsy. It is a provocation because he does this on a Sabbath.

The disease of dropsy (now known as edema) causes a person to drink constantly so that their body retains too much fluid and thus swells. At the time of Jesus, the disease had become a metaphor for greed and hunger for power.[61] So there may be a symbolic hint in the healing of the man with dropsy—perhaps Jesus is challenging the power-hungry, greedy Pharisees to be healed of their love for money by embracing his message of the kingdom of God.

Like others in the Roman Empire, the Pharisees believe that the best way to build wealth is to get to know the right people. When Jesus notices how the guests of the rich Pharisee seek places of honor at the meal in order to enhance their status in the community, he challenges them to humble themselves (14:7–11).

Jesus earlier rebuked the Pharisees for their greed, for seeking positions of prominence at times of prayer, and for their neglect of justice and of love for God (11:39–43). They show this same lack of love today with the unfortunate man suffering from dropsy. They show yet again

---

61. Ibid., 547.

their greed and desire for positions of prominence by pushing themselves forward for places of honor at the Pharisee's house.

In response to this situation, Jesus tells them a parable. The parable is not intended to be a good piece of advice for how to get ahead socially without embarrassing oneself—it is about humility and serving others. Jesus again stresses that God wants us to humble ourselves and serve the needy. He promises that God will greatly honor in his kingdom those who humble themselves and serve. He says, "He who humbles himself will be exalted" (14:11).

Jesus then speaks directly to the Pharisee who has hosted the meal (vv. 12–14). His guests seek to promote themselves by choosing the most strategic places to sit at the meal, but the host shows the same preoccupation with his own interests by only inviting those who could advance his position and wealth in the community. He only invited those who could pay him back. He did not invite the poor, the crippled, the lame, and the blind. His love is limited.

Jesus has previously taught, "If you lend to those from whom you expect repayment, what credit is that to you? Even 'sinners' lend to 'sinners,' expecting to be repaid in full. But love your enemies, do good to them, and lend to them without expecting to get anything back. Then your reward will be great, and you will be sons of the Most High, because he is kind to the ungrateful and wicked" (6:34–35). With these words Jesus emphasizes that we are to lend and do good to others without expecting anything in return. We are to help others without a hidden agenda. This command is based on the nature of God, who is kind even to the ungrateful and wicked. This is the central command for living in the kingdom of God.

Jesus promises that those who embrace this way of life "will be repaid at the resurrection of the righteous" (6:14). Because we are only rewarded at the resurrection, it can take faith to give of our time and money to others without expecting anything in return. We need to believe what Jesus says is true—that God will honor, exalt, and repay those who follow the example of his Servant Jesus by pouring out their lives for the poor and the marginalized.

As the meal with the Pharisees continues, Jesus tells another parable (14:15–24), this one prompted by a comment made by one of the guests— "Blessed is the man who will eat at the feast in the kingdom of God." In response, Jesus tells a story about this great feast, which signifies the fulfillment of God's kingdom at the end of history. For centuries the people of Israel have envisioned the future kingdom this way. The image of a great banquet suggests festivity, food in abundance, rest, privilege, and a place in God's eternal kingdom. Jesus agrees with the Pharisees that there is a resurrection for "the righteous," but he disagrees with them regarding who is righteous and thus who will sit with him at the great feast. His parable is meant to teach them what kind of people will inherit God's kingdom.

God has sent his Messiah to proclaim to the people of Israel, "Come, for everything is now ready" (v. 17). But the Pharisees have not accepted the invitation that Jesus extends. Instead of believing Jesus and building their lives on his teaching, they make excuses. A quick reading of the parable could lead us to conclude that the excuses are legitimate, but in ancient Middle Eastern society the excuses were actually insults. For example, the first guest makes the excuse, "I have just bought a field, and I must go and see it." But no one in this culture would purchase a piece of property without first going to inspect it at great length. And once the property was purchased, there would be no need to go see it again.[62] Like the would-be guests in the story, the leaders of Israel have no excuses for not accepting Jesus and building their lives on his teaching.

The Pharisees and those who are like them will not be part of God's eternal kingdom, but their rejection of Jesus will not defeat God's plan to establish his kingdom on earth. As verse 23 shows us, God's kingdom will be full! When there are still places for many more to participate in the banquet, the servant is told, "Go out to the roads and country lanes and compel them to come in, so that my house will be full." In the same way, God sends his Servant Jesus out into the streets and alleys of the towns and villages to "bring in the poor, the crippled, the blind and the lame." Jesus invites to God's eternal banquet the very people the Pharisees do not invite to their banquets (vv. 13,21).

But who are the people that live in "the roads and country lanes"? And why must they be "compelled" to enter God's kingdom? Perhaps they are the poor, the despised, the "unclean" foreigner and the "unclean" sinners who have been made to feel shame and feel unworthy of God's love by the

---

62. H. W. Hoehner, "Herodian Dynasty," in *Dictionary of Jesus and the Gospels*, 317–64; Bailey, *Jesus through Middle Eastern Eyes*, 315.

"righteous" Pharisees. In contrast to the Pharisees, Jesus socializes with "sinners." He works to "compel them" to understand that God loves them and wants to receive them into his kingdom.

Jesus has again taught a reversal of society's expectations by revealing the kind of people who will enter God's eternal kingdom. The Pharisees and those like them will be surprised when they find themselves excluded, while "sinners" and Gentiles who received the message of God's Messiah are included. As readers of the Gospel, we are challenged to ask ourselves which group we belong to. Have we accepted the invitation to enter God's eternal kingdom?

Count the Cost before Following Jesus (14:25–35)

Jesus leaves the house of the Pharisee and continues his journey to Jerusalem. With large crowds following him, he turns and teaches them to count the cost of becoming his disciple. Most of the crowd, no doubt, believe in the One True God, the Scriptures, the prophets, and the day of judgment. Many fast and pray. But they still do not understand what it means to be a disciple of Jesus, who pours out his life in selfless service and suffering for the world.

A disciple is a person who masters his or her teacher's instruction, who carefully observes how the teacher lives, and who seeks to live the same way. Jesus, as the Messiah, is on his way to Jerusalem to suffer and die. The crowds flock to him to be healed, but are they prepared to deny themselves and pour out their lives for the good of others as Jesus does?

Because of the difference between what the crowds expect and the reality of what it means to become his disciple, Jesus uses sharp, bold words to challenge them. Speaking to the crowds, he says that they must be ready to hate their family (14:26), carry their cross (v. 27), and be willing to give up everything (v. 33) in order to become his disciple. These are strong words. How are we to understand them?

To hate one's family does not mean that a person will not emotionally love them and seek to provide for their welfare. Since Jesus teaches that we are to love everyone, how much more must he want us to love our family! But he knows that many will not receive him as the Messiah and that they will try to prevent others in their family from becoming his disciples. Thus, division will come instead of the peace God wants. When this happens, a person must put loyalty to God and his Messiah above even family loyalty. And putting love for Jesus the Messiah above love for one's family will seem like *hatred* to them and those in the community.

Jesus also says that a person must "give up everything he has" in order to be his disciple (v. 33). If a disciple is forced out of his home for following Jesus, he will lose his share of the family's wealth and be cut off from work in the community. Thus, Jesus is not exaggerating when he describes the possible consequences that someone who follows him must be ready for.

The stories Jesus tells about a man who builds a tower and a king who considers going to war (vv. 28–32) illustrate the importance of counting the cost before becoming his disciple. If the crowds think Jesus is just a great prophet who heals and amazes them with miracles, they need to stop and reconsider. There is a cost to discipleship. There is a cost to experiencing the life and love of the kingdom. One must be ready to love God completely and give up everything to follow Jesus. Jesus concludes by saying, "He who has ears to hear, let him hear." In other words, pay close attention to what Jesus says.

A FOCUS ON TAX COLLECTORS AND "SINNERS"

What comes to your mind when you hear the word "sinner"? We tend to read our own meaning into the word based on our particular cultural and religious background. But how is it used in the Gospel? At times the word "sinner" is used in the general sense of those who do not live according to God's will—robbers and murderers, dishonest business people, those who oppress the poor, those who are sexually immoral, and so on. But Jesus also often speaks of the leaders of Israel as "sinners" because they are proud and greedy and lack compassion for the needy. But their greatest sin consists in opposing God by rejecting Jesus as sent by God. Jesus is sent by God to seek out "sinners" in order to offer them God's love, peace, and forgiveness. Because he frequently eats with them in their homes, Jesus gains the reputation of being a friend of "sinners." But he maintains that he is simply showing the boundless love of God, who seeks out sinners in order to forgive them and welcome them into a relationship with him.

In glaring contrast, the Pharisees label as "sinners" all those who do not fast as they fast, all those who do not keep the Sabbath according to their particular traditions, and all those, like Jesus, who socialize with others who do not follow their traditions. Because Jesus often deliberately ignores the manmade laws of the Pharisees, they fiercely oppose him. By extending the forgiveness of God to a sinner apart from their laws and the offering of sacrifices at the temple in Jerusalem, he undermines the religious leaders' authority over the people.

All the people of Israel consider the Jewish tax collectors great "sinners" because they willingly collect taxes for their oppressors, the Romans. Furthermore, the tax collectors collect higher taxes from their fellow Jews than are required by the Romans and keep the difference for themselves. Thus their fellow Jews hate them. The tax collectors not only rob them of their hard-earned money, but they also collaborate with the idolatrous Romans, ignore the commandments of God, and oppress their countrymen in their own land.

Because tax collectors are hated and ostracized by the common people, they build their own social networks. Jesus creates considerable controversy by eating in the homes of tax collectors and "sinners," welcoming them to be part of God's kingdom. One of Jesus' closest disciples, Levi, was a tax collector from Capernaum, the small town where other disciples had a fishing business. Levi had no doubt been their enemy, excising high taxes from them. But by calling Levi to be a disciple, Jesus challenges the other disciples to learn the humility, love, and forgiveness that are central to the kingdom of God.[63]

Parables about God's Love for Lost Sinners (15:1–32)

Introduction to the Three Parables: Luke 15:1-10

As Jesus continues his journey, tax collectors and "sinners" crowd around him to hear the good news that God welcomes them to be forgiven and to have a relationship with him. When Jesus stops to celebrate God's love for

---

63. M. J. Wilkins, "Sinner," in *Dictionary of Jesus and the Gospels*, 757–60.

"sinners" by sharing a meal with them, the Pharisees and the teachers of the law grumble, "This man welcomes sinners and eats with them" (15:2).

According to the Pharisees, Jesus makes himself "unclean" by socializing with "sinners," and thus is a sinner himself. Certainly he cannot be a true prophet from God who teaches the words of God. But Jesus claims he is acting according to God's will when he seeks out "sinners" in order to show them that God loves them and wants to offer them his forgiveness and peace. So while Jesus maintains that his friendship with sinners shows that God has sent him, the Pharisees argue the exact opposite. Who is right? Who are the people to believe: the Pharisees or Jesus?

To answer this question, the Prophet Jesus tells the Pharisees and the "sinners" gathered around him three parables: the first is about a lost sheep (vv. 3–7); the second, a lost coin (vv. 8–10); and the third, a lengthier parable, a lost son (vv. 11–32). In each of the parables something of personal value is lost, a search takes place to find it, and what was lost is found. Then, as a climax, the community of friends gathers together to celebrate the finding of what was lost. With these three parables, Jesus claims that the celebrations he has in the homes of "sinners" represent the celebrations that take place in God's presence when a sinner turns to him for forgiveness.

The parables reveal the depths of God's love for "sinners." They show that God loves such people so much that he actively seeks them out in order to forgive them and welcome them into a relationship with him. The Prophet Jesus is himself the revelation of God's will as he travels from village to village to seek out the lost. When Jesus eats in their homes, it is he—and not the Pharisees, who stand outside the house and criticize him—reveals the will of God. It is Jesus who reveals what God is like, not the Pharisees.

Since there are common themes to all three parables (as noted above), the parables are to be read and understood together. In addition to the themes already mentioned, in each parable one "thing" is lost, then found. The shepherd loses one sheep among one hundred. The poor village woman loses one coin among ten. The father of the last parable loses only one of his two sons[64]—yet to lose a son is the greatest tragedy of all and thus calls for the greatest celebration!

---

64. Green, *Gospel of Luke*, 573.

The first two parables prepare us for the more detailed, climactic story of the lost son. For this reason it is important to read them even if my comments are limited to the last parable. As you read these parables, take note of the joy expressed in finding what was lost. The shepherd "calls his friends and neighbors together and says, 'Rejoice with me; I have found my lost sheep'" (15:6). The peasant woman who finds her lost coin also calls for her friends and neighbors to rejoice with her (v. 9). And the father whose wayward son returns home invites the whole village "to celebrate and be glad," because his son "was dead and is alive again; he was lost and is found" (15:32).

The Parable of the Searching Father: Luke 15:11–32

While this parable is often called the parable of the Prodigal Son, when it is read together with the two previous parables we see that it stresses more the father's search for his two lost sons than the wayward ways of the younger son. Just as the shepherd searches for his lost lamb and the woman searches diligently for her lost coin, so now the father goes out to seek both of his sons (15:20,28). As Jesus travels from village to village, seeking out lost, broken "sinners" to invite them back to life with God, he shows us the will of God: God is like the father who seeks out and celebrates the return of his lost, rebellious son.

The parable of the searching father begins by saying that a man, who apparently owned much land, had two sons. The younger son, who was unmarried and thus not more than seventeen, approached his father to ask for his share of the inheritance immediately, which he would normally receive only when his father died. In Middle Eastern culture his request would be utterly shameful, since the son was treating the father as though he were as good as dead. But the father responded with "an almost inconceivable expression of patience and love"[65] and granted the younger son his request. He divided his property between his two sons.

The younger son, of course, had a plan. Shortly after he got his money by selling his share of the family's land, he packed his belongings and traveled to a distant country. The boy continued to bring shame on his father and family as he set off to leave them for good. His destination—"a distant land"—suggests he traveled to a Gentile land (remember that

---

65. Craig L. Blomberg, *Interpreting the Parables* (Leicester, UK: Apollos, 1990), 176.

he was a young Jewish man) to be as far away from his father, life on the farm, and the restrictions of his religion as he could be. In this distant land no one knew him, so he could live exactly as he pleased. And so he did.

He spent his money on gambling and drinking and paying to sleep with prostitutes. But one day he ran out of money, and all his friends abandoned him. At the same time, a severe famine hit the land, so that he had trouble finding work. His life spiraled so far downward that he was forced to do the unthinkable for a Jew: hire himself out to feed pigs on a pig farm! By now he was starving and longed to eat the pods the workers fed the pigs. But he was not even allowed to eat pig food along with the pigs. Hungry, impoverished, and far from home, the son was truly lost.

It was only near-starvation that caused the son to come to his senses and make another plan. He remembered home. He remembered the love and generosity of his father. He realized that while he was here all alone, far from home and starving to death, back home his father's hired servants were with his family and had plenty of food to eat. At the same time, he knew he had acted shamefully toward his father and was not worthy to be called his son. So he planned to ask his father to receive him back home as a hired servant.

This time the son was not scheming. He felt genuine sorrow for his sin and wanted to live a new life. He planned to say to his father, "Father, I have sinned against heaven [i.e., God] and against you" (vv. 18,21). The son had broken the two greatest commandments by not loving God and not loving his father. He thought only of himself and his own pursuit of pleasure. But now he was ready to repent.

The son began his long journey home. He was thin and pale, clothed in rags and without sandals for his feet. Apparently someone caught sight of his pathetic appearance when he finally approached the village. Someone must have alerted the father that a boy resembling his lost son was walking toward them, for we read that his father was out searching for him! "While he was a long way off, his father saw him and was filled with compassion for him; he ran to his son, threw his arms around him and kissed him" (v. 20).

This is the dramatic moment in the story. A wealthy older man in the Middle East would never forfeit his dignity by lifting his long, flowing robe to run down the village road.[66] But this father did. Why? He ran to embrace his wayward son because he was "filled with compassion." Because of the shame and pain the son had caused him, we would not expect the father to receive the son at all. Or if he did, we would expect him to beat his son and make him a servant. But the father never stopped loving his son and longed for him to come home.

The father did not reciprocate the shame his son had caused him, but surprised the son with an extravagant display of love and compassion. The son was not even allowed to finish his planned speech! The father interrupted the son and ordered his servants, "Quick! Bring the best robe and put it on him. Put a ring on his finger and sandals on his feet. Bring the fattened calf and kill it. Let's have a feast and celebrate. For this son of mine was dead and is alive again; he was lost and is found" (vv. 22–24).

By meeting his son outside of the village, by dressing him with a splendid robe and a costly ring, and by inviting the entire village to celebrate his son's return (the fattened calf he ordered to be killed would feed seventy-five people),[67] the father protected his son from shameful comments from people in the village. For the son had not only shamed his father, he had shamed all their relatives as well. Because of his great love, the father delivered his son from shame and restored him to the community.

With this parable Jesus teaches that God is like the father who was filled with compassion and ran to his son to celebrate his return. But the main point is that Jesus himself is like God as he socializes with "sinners" and celebrates with them when they turn to God.

This parable of the lost son complements the first two parables by describing in detail the extravagant celebration that took place when the lost son returned home. An abundance of fine food was provided for the entire village. The people sang and danced. The celebration in the story, like the meals Jesus enjoys in homes as he journeys to Jerusalem, depicts the celebration that takes place in heaven when one "sinner" turns to God in repentance. Speaking about the celebration that followed the finding of the lost sheep, Jesus says, "In the same way, I tell you, there is rejoicing in the presence of the angels of God over one sinner who repents" (v. 10).

---

66. Green, *Gospel of Luke*, 583.
67. Bailey, *Jesus through Middle Eastern Eyes*, 187.

To return to the parable of the father, the entire village celebrated except for one person—the older son.

As the older son worked in the field, he learned of the celebration for his younger brother, but he refused to participate. He even refused to call him his brother, and reminded his father of the boy's shameful ways. The older son also reminded his father that though he himself had always obeyed him, his father had never given him a celebration for him and his friends. In spite of some truth in what the older son said, he acted with disrespect toward his father. Worse yet, there was no love in his words.

The older son in the parable represents the Pharisees. Just as he refused to rejoice in the return of his lost brother, so they refuse to enter the homes where Jesus celebrates the return of sinners to God. Instead, like the older son, they stand outside and criticize Jesus. The Pharisees will not accept that God seeks out sinners and welcomes them into a relationship with himself, as Jesus teaches and demonstrates. The Pharisees are so focused on what they think is right that they are blind to the beauty of love seen Jesus.[68]

In the parable, the father violated social conventions when he left the meal with village friends to go out and search for his older son. But the father's love and compassion again caused him to put aside the dignity of his position. He pleaded with his older son to join in the celebration—for he too, like his brother, was lost.

Jesus implies that the Pharisees are also lost because of their sins of pride, self-righteousness, and lack of love. They are meant to see in themselves the hardness of heart, pride, and selfishness of the older son. But God still pleads with them to turn to him in repentance. God entreats them to stop opposing Jesus and to receive his message.

Jesus Teaches about Money (16:1–18)

You may have noticed that Jesus often shows compassion for the poor and teaches the dangers of wanting to be rich. These themes continue in chapter 16. One reason Jesus teaches so often about giving to the poor is that God has special compassion for them. And Jesus often teaches about the danger of wanting to become rich because our love for money easily chokes out love for God from our hearts. The Prophet Jesus knows that

---

68. Wright, *Luke for Everyone*, 190.

we as human beings live from primary passions rooted in our hearts: either securing our own comfort, seeking our own status, and pursuing the pleasures of this world; or loving God and pursuing his kingdom purposes to remake the world for the good of all, especially the poor and oppressed.

Jesus begins his teaching on how to use money wisely by telling a story about a rich man who had a dishonest manager who wasted his possessions (vv. 1–9). When the manager was caught and learned he would be fired, he had to figure out how he would live when he was without work— so he came up with a clever plan. He contacted the people who owed his master money and drastically reduced their bills so that they would become his friends and take care of him (literally, "welcome him into their houses") when he lost his job.

The story ends with the rich master commending his manager because he acted shrewdly. It is important to note that the master praised his manager for the cleverness of his plan, not for any dishonesty. Most likely the manager simply reduced the high interest his master charged from the payments. In this way the rich master did not actually lose any money but gained honor among his business associates. He gained honor by appearing to be a good, law-abiding Jew who did not charge interest on his loans.

Then, as he often does, Jesus teaches the point of the parable after telling it. He says, "For the people of this world are more shrewd in dealing with their own kind than are the people of the light. I tell you, use worldly wealth to gain friends for yourselves, so that when it is gone, you will be welcomed into eternal dwellings" (vv. 8–9). In other words, the people of this world who do not know God know how to act shrewdly in order to get what they want from others, but the disciples are not as shrewd in practicing Jesus' teaching so as to advance in the kingdom of God. He says to his disciples, "If you have not been trustworthy in handling worldly wealth, who will trust you with true riches?" (v. 11).

There is a close parallel between verses 4 and 9. The incompetent manager used money to be welcomed into earthly homes; the disciples are to generously give to the poor so that the poor will welcome them into their eternal homes when they die. Jesus does not teach that if we simply give money to the poor we will be welcomed into God's eternal kingdom—a person needs to love and obey God from the heart. But the primary way we show our love for God is by giving to the poor.

Jesus goes on to state the root problem in regard to money. He says, "No one can serve two masters. Either he will hate the one and love the other, or he will be devoted to the one and despise the other. You cannot serve both God and money" (16:13–14). Most of us would not say that we love money or consider money a master that we serve. But many of us do devote our lives to pursuing the things money provides: a nice car, a nice house in a good neighborhood, and enough money to eat at nice restaurants and travel. People seek their own pleasure, comfort, status, and security in life. Money is simply the means for attaining those things. But Jesus teaches that we cannot set our hearts on wealth and at the same time devote ourselves to God and his purposes of bringing justice to the poor. Our hearts, quite simply, cannot be fully devoted to both serving God and serving money.

When the Pharisees overhear what Jesus has taught his disciples about money, they begin to ridicule him. They do so because they themselves love money. This is why Jesus says to them, "You are the ones who justify yourselves in the eyes of men, but God knows your hearts. What is highly valued among men is detestable in God's sight" (v. 15). The Pharisees might look righteous in the eyes of men, but God knows their hearts. The Pharisees might fool the people with their outward religious acts, but they cannot fool God, who sees into the depths of their hearts.

And what does God see in the hearts of the Pharisees and those like them? God sees the ways they scheme for positions of prominence in society. He sees their love of possessions and neglect for the poor. He sees their love for power and authority. These things, Jesus says, are "highly valued among men" but are "detestable in God's sight." These are strong words to the very leaders who have established themselves as teachers of God's ways to the people.

Jesus goes on to say that since the time of the Prophet John, "the good news of the kingdom of God is being preached, and everyone is forcing his way into it" (v. 16). Jesus welcomes and even urges everyone to enter the kingdom of God—the people of Israel, Samaritans, Gentiles, tax collectors and "sinners," prostitutes and wayward sons (15:11–32). The Scriptures predict that all who turn to God will be welcomed into his kingdom. But the Pharisees misinterpret the Scriptures and thus seek to hinder people from believing in Jesus and participating in God's kingdom.

The Beggar Lazarus (16:19–31)

The Prophet Jesus now tells a story directed at those who are devoted to money instead of loving God and living for his purposes to show compassion to the poor. It is about a rich man and a poor beggar, Lazarus, who begged outside of his gate. The story vividly illustrates the kind of person who loves a life of wealth and does not follow the command of Jesus given earlier in the chapter—"I tell you, use worldly wealth to gain friends for yourselves, so that when it is gone, you will be welcomed into eternal dwellings" (16:9). The story describes a rich man who ignored the pitiful plight of a man begging outside his gate and thus was not welcomed into God's eternal kingdom.

The story vividly contrasts its two main characters, the rich man and the beggar, Lazarus. The rich man dressed (or "covered himself") like a king, with a splendid purple robe covering the fine white linen underneath. Lazarus, the beggar, was covered only with sores. The rich man feasted daily on the finest of foods, while the beggar sat outside and longed for the crumbs that fell from the rich man's table. The rich man lived securely behind the gate of his estate, while Lazarus was laid at his gate out by the road. Street dogs licked his sores, adding to his abuse and shame. Lazarus was an unclean outcast, the kind of person the Pharisees avoid but the very kind of person Jesus, in his compassion, seeks out to heal.[69]

The time came for both the rich man and Lazarus to die. The contrast between them continues, but now their conditions are reversed! Lazarus, who only had abusive dogs for his companions, now received a new companion—the father of the faith, Abraham! God's angels carried Lazarus to the arms (literally, "chest") of Abraham. Lazarus, who had cried out to God in his poverty on earth, now received a warm and honorable welcome as he dined at the heavenly banquet at his revered ancestor's side![70] The rich man, in contrast, suffered alone in torment.

The rich man did not protest against God, for his judgment was just. He was not judged simply because he was rich, but because he devoted his life to money rather than to God and ignored the plight of the poor beggar he walked by every day at his gate. The rich man had not loved Lazarus, his neighbor, as he loved himself. Thus, he failed to live by the two

---

69. Green, *Gospel of Luke*, 605–6.
70. Tannehill, *Luke*, 252.

greatest commandments for inheriting the kingdom of God—to love God with your whole being and to love your neighbor as yourself (10:25–28). The rich man did not gain acceptance before God simply by being a descendant of Abraham. We are reminded that the Prophet John warned the people of Israel, "Produce fruit in keeping with repentance. And do not begin to say to yourselves, 'We have Abraham as our father'" (3:8).

The rich man, who had refused to offer relief to Lazarus, now asked Abraham to send Lazarus to relieve him of his thirst. Abraham answered that Lazarus could not come to him, for they were now living in permanent, irreversible places. The rich man then requested that Lazarus be sent to warn his five brothers, who also apparently devoted their lives to wealth and ignored the plight of the poor. The rich man believed that his brothers would listen to someone who had come back from the dead and would change.

Abraham answered the rich man by saying, "They have Moses and the Prophets; let them listen to them" (v. 29). The prophets repeatedly stressed the centrality of loving God and showing his compassion to the poor. If the five brothers had hardened their hearts to explain away the clear message of the prophets, they would also find a way to explain away the warning of someone who returned from the dead. It is a self-indulgent, hardened heart that keeps a person from turning to God, not a lack of evidence.

The Prophet Jesus' teaching confirms what the previous prophets spoke. When the Pharisees reject him, they show that they do not accept the message God gave to Moses and the prophets. The Prophet Jesus both confirms and fulfills the message of the previous prophets by his complete devotion to God and compassion for the poor. However, the Pharisees, who love money, neglect justice and mercy toward the poor. They are meant to see themselves in the rich man of the parable and listen to the message of the Prophet Jesus before it is too late.

Humility towards God and Others (17:1–10)

While the sayings in 17:1–10 may seem unrelated, they are connected by the overall theme of humility.[71] While in the first four verses Jesus speaks to all of his disciples, in the following six he speaks directly to

---

71. Wright, *Luke for Everyone*, 203.

the twelve apostles. Jesus teaches a large crowd out in the open (note the reference to a mulberry tree near him) with the Pharisees still present. Imagine Jesus turning to speak to different groups depending on their comments or questions.

The Prophet Jesus first warns his disciples to not be the cause of another disciple's sin (vv. 1–2). While the precise nature of the sin is not stated, due to the severity of the judgment, Jesus may have in mind the sin of no longer acknowledging him and his message.

Jesus then teaches the disciples the importance of forgiving those who sin against them daily amidst the stresses of living together (vv. 3–4). When they are constantly living and serving together, the disciples can easily and unintentionally act selfishly and speak unkindly to one other. Jesus assumes that there are many relational sins in the community of the disciples since he says they must be ready to forgive another disciple seven times a day. The disciple who sins against another must be humble to acknowledge his sin and ask for forgiveness. The person sinned against must be humble to acknowledge any part he had in the conflict, forgive the other person, and avoid mentioning the offense again. By the daily discipline of confession and forgiveness, the disciples embody the peace God sent the Messiah to bring to the world.

The twelve apostles say to Jesus, seemingly quite abruptly, "Increase our faith!" (v. 5). What is the reason for this request? From the preceding verses it appears that they have become aware of their great need to grow faith so that they will have the humility to ask another disciple for forgiveness. They do not ask for more power to do greater miracles. They ask for the power to be humble, to be honest about their failures, and to be ready to forgive another disciple over and over again.

The twelve disciples have left behind much to follow Jesus—the security of their jobs, the comforts of family and home, and their safety as they travel with a man Herod seeks to kill. Because they have given up so much, they might be subtly, unconsciously tempted to think that God is indebted to them, that he is obligated in some way to reward them for their obedience and sacrifice. This is why Jesus now tells the twelve disciples a parable to teach them humility toward God (vv. 7–10).

Jesus uses the imagery of slavery in the parable because "slaves are not wage earners who can demand pay or favors in return for performing their duty."[72] The parable depicts a small landowner with one slave who works both out on the farm and in the house.[73] The point of the parable is that the master is not in any way indebted to his slave for doing what is expected of him. In the same way, God is not obligated to reward the disciples for serving him. He will generously reward them, but he will do so out of grace, not obligation.

The Gospel reminds us that Jesus is on his way to Jerusalem and is traveling along the border between Samaria and Galilee (v. 11). You may recall that the first village he sought to enter when he began his journey was in Samaria (9:51). Now, after what seems to be many days or weeks, he is still near Galilee and Samaria! How do we account for this?

It is important to remember that it was never Jesus' intention to travel directly to Jerusalem. The purpose of the journey is to minister in many villages along the way and to take time to train the twelve disciples to continue his mission after he is raised up to God. It is also helpful to remember that the Gospel stories are often arranged logically according to specific themes and not according to a strict chronology.

THE NATURE OF GOD'S KINGDOM (17:11–19:27)

A Samaritan Leper Shows Faith (17:11–19)

As Jesus is about to enter a village near Samaria, ten men with leprosy stand outside of it, yelling to catch his attention (17:11–19). Because the lepers are contagious, they are regarded as "unclean" and are not allowed to live with their family and friends in the village. In addition to being socially isolated, they live with the stigma of being unclean lepers. But now they have a chance to be cleansed of their disease and restored to life in the community. Having heard that Jesus is coming their way, they stand together as one man and shout out to him from a distance—"Jesus, Master, have pity on us!"

As we would expect, Jesus does have pity on them. He instructs the ten lepers to go show themselves to the local priests, who will examine them in order to pronounce them clean, thus allowing them to return

---

72. Tannehill, *Luke*, 255.
73. Green, *Gospel of Luke*, 614.

to their life and family in the village. It is only on the way to see the priests that the lepers are healed. But only one of them returns to thank Jesus, praising God as he comes. Why does he return while the other nine continue on? What are we to learn from this story?

Perhaps we are to learn that God wants us to acknowledge the love and power he manifests through the Prophet Jesus. While the leper praises God for healing him, he also throws himself at the feet of Jesus to thank him. He publically acknowledges the unique power and mercy of God at work in Jesus. The other nine "were afraid to go back and identify themselves with Jesus, who by now was a marked man,"[74] but the one leper does not allow fear of the threats to kill Jesus to keep him from returning. He comes back to thank Jesus and acknowledge him as a great prophet sent by God.

Who is this bold and grateful man? It is not until the very end of the story that we learn the identity of this hero of faith: he is a Samaritan! To Jews he is the man with the wrong religion, the wrong holy book, the wrong place to worship.

Why does the story mention that the man is a Samaritan? It seems we are again being reminded that our ethnicity (in this case, being Jewish), our beliefs, and our religious practices do not in themselves secure our relationship with God. True faith consists in a personal encounter with God. True faith consists in praising God for restoring the world through his beloved Messiah Jesus. True faith consists in throwing ourselves at Jesus' feet to thank him and to acknowledge his role in defeating evil and remaking the world according to God's good purposes. Once again, we learn that all are welcomed to participate in God's kingdom—God's kingdom is not just for Israel. And once again, an outsider to the Jewish religion becomes an example of how someone can see the life of God's kingdom coming through his Servant Jesus.

Jesus Teaches When the Kingdom of God Will Come (17:20–37)

God has sent his chosen Messiah to establish his good and just kingdom on earth. Since Jesus often teaches about the kingdom of God, it is understandable that the Pharisees would ask Jesus "when the kingdom of God

---

74. Wright, *Luke for Everyone*, 206.

would come" (17:20). The Pharisees, like all the people of Israel, believe God's kingdom will come at the end of history. They believe the Messiah will be God's agent to judge the enemies of Israel and then to rule on God's behalf over a restored Israel in the land of Palestine. Since Jesus has not taught this, but rather has even suggested that the kingdom of God has in some way already arrived, the Pharisees seek clarity about when Jesus believes God's kingdom will come.

Jesus answers the Pharisees by saying, "The kingdom of God does not come with your careful observation, nor will people say, 'Here it is,' or 'There it is,' because the kingdom of God is within you" (vv. 20–21). The words translated "within you" can better be translated "here among you" or "within your grasp." The kingdom of God is not a private experience hidden within people's hearts—and it is certainly not at work within the hearts of the Pharisees.[75] Yet the Prophet Jesus teaches that the kingdom of God is still within their *grasp!* This is because God's kingdom is established through Jesus the Messiah, and its life and powers and love reside in him. To be near Jesus is to be near the kingdom.

But the Pharisees do not see this. It is sadly ironic that the Pharisees ask Jesus when the kingdom of God will come when it is already there in their midst through his ministry. Every act of compassion, every healing, every deliverance from the oppression of demons, and every lost sinner who turns to God for forgiveness is an expression of the kingdom of God at work through his beloved Messiah. The Jewish people believe the kingdom of God will come as one climactic event at the end of history, but Jesus teaches that it has already arrived through him right in the midst of history. An astonishing statement! A radical restructuring of Israel's hope! All the things humanity longs for can already be experienced in part by embracing God's Messiah, through whom his kingdom has come.

The disciples are present as the Prophet Jesus answers the Pharisees, and he now speaks directly to them instead (v. 22). He says, "The time is coming when you will long to see one of the days of the Son of Man, but you will not see it. Men will tell you, 'There he is!' or 'Here he is!' Do not go running after them" (vv. 22–23). Jesus moves from speaking of the presence of God's kingdom in him now to speaking of the time when God will send him back to earth at the end of history to bring the kingdom to

---

75. Ibid., 210.

completion. Jesus knows there will be a delay in time before his return to earth; after the events in Jerusalem, God must raise him up to be with him for a period. During this delay the disciples will continue his mission by proclaiming the good news of God's kingdom.

Because of Jesus' delay in returning, the disciples "will long to see one of the days of the Son of Man" (v. 22). In other words, they will long for the Messiah Jesus to return, because they too will suffer at the hands of evil men, they too will grieve over the sin and injustice in the world, and they too will long for the world to be made completely right. Above all, they will long to see Jesus exalted in glory in the presence of God and of all his holy angels. In short, they will long for the Messiah Jesus to return to consummate the kingdom of God that began with his first coming.

It can be hard to wait. Because of the Messiah's delay in returning to earth, the disciples might be tempted to believe false reports that God has sent him back. Some will say, "There he is!" or "Here he is" (v. 23). But such claims are lies and not to be believed. For when God sends his Messiah Jesus back, it will be clear for all on earth to see. It "will be like the lightning which flashes and lights up the sky from one end to the other" (v. 24). The return of the Messiah to establish God's kingdom in all its fullness will be "unmistakable, worldwide, sudden, inescapable, and for those who are not prepared, calamitous."[76]

If the disciples think the kingdom of God will come in all its fullness when they arrive in Jerusalem, they have not understood what Jesus has told them. He has repeatedly taught them that he must suffer, be rejected, and put to death when they come to Jerusalem. God will only raise him up to be with him, to share in his heavenly glory, after he has submitted to God's will to suffer and be put to death. The disciples must learn that God's plan to overcome evil includes suffering. Because this will be true of the Messiah, it will also be true for them.

While suffering can cause the disciples to lose faith in God, the everyday routines and distractions of life can also cause them to lose sight of the Messiah's return. Jesus teaches that when he returns, life will be just like it was in the days of the Prophet Noah (Nuh) and Lot (Lut, the nephew of the Prophet Abraham) (vv. 26–29). People will be so preoccupied with the things of this world that they will forget that there is a

---

76. Green, *Gospel of Luke*, 631.

future judgment and an eternal life to come. Jesus says that in the days of Lot, "people were eating and drinking, buying and selling, planting and building" (v. 28). These activities are gifts of God's goodness and are not wrong in themselves, but if a person devotes his life to them instead of loving God and extending the love of his kingdom, sudden disaster will await them just as it awaited people in the times of Noah and Lot.

Jesus has earlier taught that his coming will cause divisions among people—even members of a family (12:51–53). Some have embraced him and his teachings, while others have rejected him. Sadly, the division that has begun on earth will become permanent, lasting for all eternity. It is especially sad that family members and friends of the same community will be separated for all time.

Jesus teaches that as a married couple sleeps in bed, one will suddenly be taken away to judgment while the other will remain to participate in the joy of God's kingdom. As two women work together, one will suddenly be taken away to judgment while the other will remain to share in the glory of God's kingdom.

The disciples ask where this separation will occur (v. 37). Everywhere, Jesus answers. When we see vultures circling in the sky, it is clear to us that there is a dead animal below. In the same way, the Messiah's return to judge the earth will be clear and involve all the inhabitants of the earth.

The Parable of the Persistent Widow (18:1–8)

Because of the long delay before Jesus returns to consummate God's kingdom (17:22ff.), the disciples may be tempted to give up when they are treated unfairly for their allegiance to him. They will cry out to God to grant them justice. But they may lose heart when day after day and year after year he doesn't seem to hear them. Addressing this, Jesus now tells the disciples a parable intended to strengthen them so that they will not give up praying when God seems distant and unresponsive to their cries for help.

The story Jesus tells has two main characters. The first is the cold-hearted, unbelieving judge of the village. The judge flagrantly disregarded the two most important commandments of God: to live completely devoted to God and to treat others as you would want them to treat you. Twice it is emphasized that the judge neither feared God nor cared about other people (18:2,4).

In the village there was also a widow who had been cheated out of money she desperately needed to survive. The widow comes across as quite a character. In a time and place where men handled legal matters, she barged into court every day demanding justice from the judge. In fact, the Greek word used for the widow pestering the judge every day was used for boxing matches and suggests a quite humorous scene— "images of the almighty, fearless, macho judge cornered and slugged by the least powerful in society."[77] This lady will not be put off in her plea for justice, and finally wears the judge down so that he grants it.

Jesus then makes a comparison between God and the unrighteous judge. He says, "And will not God bring about justice for his chosen ones, who cry out to him day and night? Will he keep putting them off? I tell you, he will see that they get justice, and quickly" (vv. 6–8). Jesus is not saying that God is like the cold-hearted judge and will only respond to our prayers if we keep pestering him. By now we have learned that God, whom Jesus loves and obeys, is good, compassionate, and kind; Jesus has even taught his disciples that they can pray to God as if he were the best possible father (11:1–13). The point Jesus makes in this parable builds on reasoning from the "lesser" to the "greater." If a cold-hearted earthly judge who didn't fear God or care about others granted a widow (the "lesser") justice, how much more will our loving God (the "greater") grant his own people justice!

In this evil world, the disciples who are poor may remain poor. They may still hunger, weep, and be ridiculed (6:20–23). But their compassionate Father in heaven will comfort and strengthen them in their distress. Still, they will not see full and permanent justice until God sends his Messiah at the end of history to separate good from evil for all time. For now they are simply to know that God hears their every cry for justice, that he cares deeply for them, and that justice will one day be served.

The question is whether or not the disciples will continue to be loyal to Jesus in the face of persistent injustice. This appears to be the point of the penetrating question Jesus ends with. "However, when the Son of Man comes, will he find faith on the earth?" (18:8).

---

77. Ibid., 641.

Two Men Pray at the Temple (18:9–14)

The following three stories anticipate and respond to the question, "What must I do to inherit eternal life?" (18:18). Jesus first tells a story about two men who go to the temple to pray, one a Pharisee and the other a "sinner" (vv. 9–14). Then he calls children to himself and teaches his disciples, "I tell you the truth, anyone who will not receive the kingdom of God like a little child will never enter it" (v. 17). Finally, Jesus answers the question of a certain ruler who asks him, "Good teacher, what must I do to inherit eternal life?" (18:18). Let's look at how Jesus answers this question in each of the scenes.

The story Jesus tells, about two men praying in the temple, is not so much about how to pray as it is about the kind of person God forgives and accepts into his kingdom. Jesus tells the story to the entire crowd around him—to the Pharisees, the disciples, and curious bystanders. It is told to all "who were confident of their own righteousness and looked down on everybody else" (v. 9). It is told to those who are assured that their beliefs and religious practices make them acceptable to God.

The contrast between the two men who go to the temple to pray is obvious. The Pharisee strictly followed his religion's law and traditions, while the despised tax collector collaborated with the Romans, the enemies of Israel. The Pharisee stood far up front at the temple to pray, keeping himself separate from "sinners" like the tax collector, whose contact with Gentiles had made him unclean.[78] The tax collector stood far in the back, at a distance from the "holy men" who stood up front.

The Pharisee was assertive in his prayer to God, informing God of his own goodness. He spoke highly of himself—note the repetition of "I" in his prayer—while belittling others. He prayed, "God, I thank you that I am not like other men—robbers, evildoers, adulterers—or even like this tax collector" (v. 11). The tax collector, in contrast, was so conscious of his lack of worthiness before God that he would not even look up to heaven. He did not compare himself with others, as he was only conscious of the sad condition of his own heart.

The Pharisee also provided God with a short sampling of his righteous acts, which he believed made God obliged to accept him. He fasted twice a week—more than the Scriptures required—and was scrupulous

---

78. Bailey, *Jesus through Middle Eastern Eyes*, 347.

about giving a tenth of all he had earned. He focused on his outward behavior, behavior anyone could imitate, rather than the condition of his heart. He counted up his good deeds, but he didn't count on the fact that God knew the true condition of his heart.

In contrast, the tax collector knew his only chance to be accepted by God was to humble himself before God and cry out to him for mercy. He beat his breast and said, "God, have mercy on me, a sinner" (v. 13). The prescribed way to pray was to cross one's arms over the chest; instead the tax collector beat his chest, where his heart was located.[79] He knew that God desires a clean heart and humbly called out to God to cleanse him and forgive him. He knew that any good he had done could not compensate for his sinful acts or change the condition of his heart.

Jesus concludes the parable saying, "I tell you that this man, rather than the other, went home justified before God. For everyone who exalts himself will be humbled, and he who humbles himself will be exalted" (v. 14). Why was the tax collector forgiven and the Pharisee not?

The Pharisee was so focused on the practices of his religion and so confident in them that he did not see the true condition of his heart and his need for God's mercy. He was proud and judgmental towards those who did not live up to his standards. In his pride he did not realize that he was also arrogant toward God, believing God was obliged to forgive him (see also 17:6–10).

Why does Jesus say the tax collector went home a forgiven man? How could he be forgiven when he had collaborated with the Romans to exact excessive taxes from the poor Jewish farmers? He could be forgiven because he admitted his sin, was honest about the true condition of his heart, and humbly cried out to God for mercy. He did not try to compensate for his sins by acts of righteousness in order to force the hand of God to forgive him.

Sadly, the Pharisee was deceived. He believed all was well between God and himself, but it wasn't. On the other hand, the tax collector who recognized his sin left the temple a forgiven man. Once again, we may be surprised when we see who is included in God's eternal kingdom and who is not.

---

79. Ibid., 348.

Children and the Kingdom of God (18:15–17)

The context of the next scene is crucial. In the previous story Jesus has commended the faith of a tax collector who knew he could not earn acceptance from God by his spiritual diligence. Fully aware of his short-comings, he humbled himself before God and pleaded for his mercy. Jesus says that he went home justified. In the following scene, people in the crowd bring small children—even babies—to Jesus so that he will bless them and, if needed, heal them. Jesus uses this occasion to again teach his disciples of their need to embrace the values of God's kingdom. Finally, a rich, influential ruler approaches Jesus to ask him an important question (18:18) that touches on the previous two stories.

When the people bring their children to Jesus to be blessed, the disciples rebuke them. They believe Jesus has more important things to do—such as talk with a rich ruler who stands by him waiting to ask a question. To understand the action of the disciples, it is good to rid our minds of the modern, sentimental notions we can have of children. In Jesus' day children were marginalized, valued primarily for the work they could do to contribute to the family's finances—if they lived long enough to do so.

Jesus has both taught and exemplified that God has a special love for the weak and marginalized and welcomes them into his kingdom. The disciples, however, still embrace the status-seeking, power-hungry ways of the world. This is why Jesus rebukes them in the presence of the crowd, telling them to allow the children to be brought to him. After all, the kingdom of God will be made up of people who are like small children.

What is it about small children that make them an example of the qualities one needs to enter God's kingdom? Like the tax collector in the previous story, they are looked down on by society, and are socially margin-alized; they must rely completely on God's mercy to enter his kingdom.

Through his Messiah, God turns upside down the status-seeking, power-driven values of society. Jesus says, "Everyone who exalts himself will be humbled, and he who humbles himself will be exalted" (18:14). Life in the world works one way; life in the kingdom of God works another. The disciples have come to understand that the Prophet Jesus is God's Messiah (9:20), but they still struggle to understand what kind of people they are meant to become.

How to Enter God's Kingdom (18:18–30)

A rich ruler in the crowd stands by Jesus as he blesses the little children. Now he has his opportunity to ask Jesus a crucial question. He asks, "Good teacher, what must I do to inherit eternal life?" (18:18). Earlier in the Gospel a teacher of the Jewish law asked Jesus the same question. Jesus then answered that to inherit eternal life, we must love God with our whole being and treat others—even our enemies—the way we would like to be treated (10:25–37). Jesus answers the rich ruler in a similar way, but in a way that addresses the specific hindrance that keeps him from entering God's kingdom: the man's devotion to his wealth. These two stories along with many other references in the Gospel explain what it means to believe in Jesus. It means not only believing in what he teaches and what he does as the Messiah, but also above all committing oneself to practicing his ways.

Before Jesus answers the question, however, he corrects the way the rich ruler has addressed him— "Good teacher." Jesus replies that only God is good in the absolute sense. This is interesting, because we don't ever read of Jesus sinning or seeking forgiveness from God. He always lives in obedience to God. Even the demons recognize Jesus as "the Holy One of God" (4:34). Yet Jesus distinguishes himself from God, who is in heaven.

Jesus then answers the question of what one must do to inherit God's kingdom. He reminds the ruler of five of the ten most important commandments in Scripture: "Do not commit adultery, do not murder, do not steal, do not give false testimony, honor your father and mother" (18:20). These commandments are all violations of the supreme commandment, to love your neighbor as you love yourself—one of the things we must do to inherit God's kingdom. The rich ruler assures Jesus that he has kept these commandments since he was a boy, giving him hope of entering God's eternal kingdom.

Yet Jesus senses that all is not right with him. He says to him, "You still lack one thing" (v. 22). Jesus knows that he loves money—so much so that he doesn't truly love God from his heart (see 16:13). The ruler obeys God's commandments more as an expression of an external, cultural morality than out of love for God. If his obedience sprang from a heart of love for God, it would express itself in showing God's compassion for the poor.

While Jesus says that the rich ruler lacks only one thing to inherit eternal life, what he lacks is crucial: a sincere love for God with his whole being, and thus God's compassion for the helpless and hurting in the world.

Jesus reveals what it means to truly love God as he lives only for him and shows his compassion to the weak and the poor. His every word, his every act of compassion, shows us how God wants us to live. He unites love for God and love for our neighbor, showing us that love for God is the foundation and life-giving source of loving our neighbors—even our enemies.[80]

This helps us understand why Jesus commands the rich ruler to sell all he has, give to the poor, and then "come, follow me." He must follow Jesus to learn what it means to fully love God and love his fellow human beings—even his enemies. This is what is required to inherit eternal life, and Jesus shows the ruler (and us) the way to do it.

It is important to emphasize that while we are not able to love God and our fellow human beings as fully as Jesus does, we must still commit ourselves to living this way. While we will not be perfect in our obedience, we can be perfect (i.e., complete) in our commitment. The direction of Jesus the Messiah's life—pouring out his life for people damaged by sin as he journeys to Jerusalem for the culmination of his sufferings—must become the direction of our lives. One godly man called it "a long obedience in the same direction." We will often, quite often, feel that we fail; but we will continue to grow in the two great loves, love for God overflowing into love for all those around us, and so love—healing, helping, encouraging love—will characterize our lives more and more and more.

Because the rich ruler lacks love for God, as seen in his love for money rather than for the poor, Jesus now commands him to go sell all he has, give the money to the poor, and follow him. By facing this challenge he will understand that he loves his money more than God. But instead the man departs disappointed. He cannot let go of his god, his money. He illustrates what Jesus said earlier to the Pharisees, who share the same idolatry: "You cannot serve both God and money" (16:13).

The rich ruler becomes sad when he hears Jesus' answer, and I would like to think Jesus himself is sad when he looks at him and says, "How

80. Michael J. Gorman, *The Death of the Messiah and the Birth of the New Covenant: A (Not So) New Model of the Atonement* (Eugene, OR: Cascade Books, 2014), 34.

hard it is for the rich to enter the kingdom of God!" (18:24). He adds that it is harder than pushing a camel through the eye of a sowing needle!

When people in the crowd hear this they ask, "Who then can be saved?" (v. 26). The people believe, wrongly, that wealth is a sign of God's blessings and thus the wealthy have a better chance of inheriting God's kingdom than the poor. Jesus answers, "What is impossible with men is possible with God," implying that some of the rich will enter God's kingdom because God has the power and mercy to move in their hearts so that they will love him rather than money.

The story ends with Peter remarking to Jesus that the disciples have done the very thing the rich ruler refused to do. He says, "We have left all we had to follow you!" Shouldn't they then inherit God's kingdom? Jesus answers that they will (vv. 28–30).

In spite of their continued slowness to understand the nature of God's kingdom, the disciples do love God and have committed themselves to following Jesus and assisting him in rescuing and restoring the lives of the poor. Because of this, the disciples are promised the blessings and joys of already belonging to a community that follows Jesus, and are assured of inheriting eternal life.

A FOCUS ON HOW TO ENTER THE KINGDOM OF GOD

We have now read far enough in the Gospel story to summarize the main passages where the Prophet Jesus teaches how a person inherits the kingdom of God. A variety of answers to this crucial question abound both among and within the major monotheistic religions. What does the Gospel say? Here are some of the main passages in the Gospel that address this important question.

First, there are several passages that teach that we must produce the good fruit of repentance in order to escape God's judgment and enter his kingdom (3:8-14; 6:43-45; 13:6-9). For example, the Prophet John (whose teaching Jesus later affirms) says to the people of Israel who believed that simply being a descendant of the Prophet Abraham gives them favor with God, "Produce fruit in keeping with repentance. And do not begin to say to yourselves, 'We have Abraham as our father....' The ax is already at the root of the trees, and every tree that does not produce good fruit will be cut down and thrown into the fire." (3:8-9).

Then there are passages where Jesus teaches that we must put his teaching into practice if we are to enter God's kingdom (6:46,49; 8:21). In a central chapter in the Gospel, Jesus says to those who claim to believe in him but do not practice his teachings, "Why do you call me, 'Lord, Lord,' and do not do what I say?" (6:46). Jesus goes on to liken such a person to a building with no foundation that collapses when a violent flood comes (6:48,49). Those who live this way have no foundation for escaping God's judgment and entering his kingdom.

These passages lead us to ask what the nature of the fruit we must produce in our lives is in order to enter God's kingdom? Put another way, what specifically are the teachings of Jesus we must put into practice? We must try as best we can to discern what the Prophet Jesus says and avoid answering these questions based upon our own preferences. I believe Jesus teaches that it is the fruit of love as explained and practiced by him that we are required to produce in order to inherit God's kingdom. It is God's kind of love, the kind of love Jesus teaches and embodies, that we are challenged to put into practice. This love is not a vague, sweetly sentimental platitude, but a costly love objectified in concrete practices each day in all that we do. Jesus teaches that because we are motivated by love we will not commit adultery, murder, steal, or give a false witness. And we will be careful to honor our father and mother (18:20). These five important commandments are only the beginning of ways we put the love of God into practice.

In order to make God's love the characteristic quality of our lives we must first turn to God, the source of all true love, and make the commitment to practicing his love as Jesus did. Earlier in the Gospel Jesus says that in order to inherit God's kingdom (or to receive eternal life) we must love God with all our heart and with all our soul and with all our strength and with all our mind. And then Jesus adds that we must love our neighbor as ourselves (10:27), or as he says in another place, "Do to others as you would have them do to you" (6:31).

Because we can easily deceive ourselves into thinking we love God and practice his love towards others, Jesus takes great pains to both teach and demonstrate by his actions the nature of God's love. The Jewish people of Jesus' day (even his own disciples!) tended to limit their practice of love to other Jewish people, and strict Jews like the Pharisees limited their religious obligations to those who lived by their traditions.

People do the same today—people of all religions, races, political persuasions, and cultures. We tend to create our own definitions of mercy and morality in order to justify how we live. We tend to limit our acts of mercy to those within in our own social circles, and often to those from whom we can expect favors in return.

The Prophet Jesus seeks to break us out of this selective tribal mentality and calls us to join him in practicing God's mercy to people of all cultures, races, and religions. He says to his disciples, "Love your enemies, do good to those who hate you, bless those who curse you, pray for those who mistreat you" (6:27), even if they seek to oppress and kill you. And shortly after this Jesus promises, "Then your reward will be great, and you will be sons of the Most High, because he is kind to the ungrateful and wicked" (6:35).

He challenges his disciples to extend God's love towards "sinners"—corrupt persons in power, immoral people, any and all who violate God's will. Jesus challenges them to practice mercy to the heretical Samaritans and even to the idolatrous Romans, their oppressors. Above all, Jesus commands his disciples to go out to the poor, the oppressed, and the weary among them to provide for their needs and share the deliverance the Messiah provides. I suggest that nearly every story in the Gospel illustrates the nature of God's love, which Jesus embodies and calls us to practice.

Thus, when Jesus teaches that we must repent and practice the will of God in order to inherit his kingdom, he means we must turn away from our self-oriented life and reorient our life according to the way of love he teaches. He challenges us to ask ourselves every day, in any and every situation, how we can act for the good of others. While no one can perfectly love as Jesus did—in fact, we have seen how his closest disciples failed time and time again—

we can give our full allegiance to Jesus the Messiah and make a commitment to loving others as he did.

There are two final passages that speak of what we must do to inherit the kingdom of God. We have recently read that a corrupt tax collector cast himself before God and cried out, "God, have mercy on me, a sinner" (18:13). This man, Jesus says, went home forgiven by God—not the proud Pharisee who was confident of his own good deeds. From this we learn that we must always live in humility before God and cast ourselves at his mercy in order to be forgiven and inherit his kingdom.

Despite our best efforts, we will always fall short of putting God's love into practice. We will never feel we have fully measured up to the love we see in Jesus. So we must always trust in God's mercy to be accepted by him. We must avoid piling up our own acts of obedience, as the self-confident Pharisee did, and putting them on a scale with the hope that they outweigh our failures. For God knows and we know that in spite of our best efforts, we will always have fallen short of practicing his perfect will.

One final passage makes clear what is implied throughout the Gospel: we must acknowledge and honor Jesus as God's Messiah in order to enter God's kingdom. Jesus says, "I tell you, whoever acknowledges me before men, the Son of Man will also acknowledge him before the angels of God. But he who disowns me before men will be disowned before the angels of God" (12:8–9). Jesus makes the bold claim that it is not enough for us to fear the one true God and ask him for forgiveness; our faith must have a public dimension.

Because God has chosen to bring his kingdom to earth through Jesus his Messiah and appointed him as its King; because God has chosen to break the power of evil in us and grant forgiveness through Jesus his Messiah; and because Jesus faithfully fulfills the mission of God by his humble obedience to God, God commands us to honor, love, and obey Jesus. We are to give our full allegiance to him as our Teacher, Deliverer, and King. This becomes even clearer in the closing chapters of the Gospel.

While others may speak of love in ways similar to Jesus, no one else has so consistently, so compassionately, so vividly revealed the love of God to mankind. No one else has been given the authority and power to liberate us from sin and bring us peace. God has chosen to remake the world through Jesus his beloved Messiah. We must acknowledge that, honor him, obey him, and join him in remaking the world with him if we are to inherit God's kingdom.

Jesus promises his disciples that they will inherit the kingdom of God when it is culminated at the end of the ages. But he also proclaims the astonishingly good news that they can already now belong to God's kingdom. They can already now know they are forgiven, freed from the fear of death and God's judgment. They can already now be freed from the fear and the influence evil spirits. They can now be freed from the powerful seed of sin within their hearts. They can have the full assurance, the calm confidence, that they are already now accepted by God and will inherit his kingdom in all its fullness when he sends Jesus to return to earth.

Jesus Again Predicts His Death and Resurrection (18:31–34)

We will soon read that as Jesus approaches Jerusalem, "the people thought that the kingdom of God was going to appear at once" (19:11). The twelve disciples also believe that Jesus, as the Messiah, will soon establish a kingdom centered in Jerusalem for the Jewish people. Even though they know the religious authorities oppose Jesus, they are sure that as the Messiah he can call on a multitude of angelic warriors to purify Israel, defeat the nation's enemies, and set up God's kingdom. Of course, Jesus knows this is not God's plan for him. This is why he again takes the twelve disciples aside from the crowds to teach them that God's plan for him will be fulfilled through his suffering, death, and resurrection. (Jesus first spoke of his sufferings in 9:22,44, and then again in 12:50; 13:33–35; and 17:25.)

Jesus says, "We are going to Jerusalem, and everything that is written by the prophets about the Son of Man will be fulfilled. He will be handed over to the Gentiles. They will mock him, insult him, spit on him, flog him and kill him. On the third day he will rise again" (18:31–33). The death and resurrection of Jesus are so central to God's plan that everything written about him in the Prophets will now be fulfilled in Jerusalem. From this we learn that the deliverance Jesus has brought about by healing the sick, freeing the oppressed from demons, and raising the dead to life points to a greater deliverance that will take place through his death and resurrection.

In his self-denial, humility, and compassionate service to the poor, Jesus has modeled the way to live, the way God wants to make the world right. People perpetuate evil and injustice by grasping for positions of power and wealth. They also think of themselves rather than others; they limit their love to those who are like them. But the way of the Messiah will soon be supremely shown in Jerusalem. Once in the city, Jesus as God's Messiah will humble himself even to the point of enduring a horrible and dishonorable death. His submission to his sufferings and death becomes the ultimate expression of life poured out for others, which is how we are to live. As one scholar writes of Jesus, "His death was the center point of the divine-human struggle over how life is to be lived, in humility or self-glorification."[81]

The disciples "did not understand any of this" (v. 34)! Since Jesus often conveys God's word in parables, the disciples probably think Jesus is still speaking about his death and resurrection in riddles.[82] While they believe Jesus is the Messiah, they do not yet understand God's way of remaking the world for good—the way of service, and costly love- even suffering to the point of death for the good of others.

A Blind Beggar Receives His Sight (18:35–43)

At first glance, the story about Jesus healing a blind man seems like other healing stories. But the more we reflect on the details, the more we see how significant it is to the development of the entire Gospel story. Importantly, the miracle of giving sight to the blind man will be the last time Jesus publically heals someone, and it takes place shortly before Jesus enters Jerusalem.

There is another important detail to the story. The man to whom Jesus shows mercy is a blind beggar who belongs to the 5 to 10 percent of the population regarded as "expendable." With no possessions of his own, the blind man is forced to beg for food in order to survive. An embarrassment to society, he is totally marginalized.[83] The man is not only blind; he is also

---

81. Green, *Gospel of Luke*, 661.
82. Wright, *Luke for Everyone*, 219.
83. Green, *Gospel of Luke*, 663.

poor. We recall that at the beginning of his mission, Jesus said that God had sent him to give "recovery of sight for the blind" and "to preach good news to the poor" (4:18). Thus, the healing of the blind beggar in Jericho near the end of Jesus' ministry reminds us that Jesus has been faithful to fulfill the mission God gave him.

The miracle takes place as Jesus approaches Jericho, which is only twenty kilometers from Jerusalem. We will soon read that Jesus enters Jericho itself (19:1), begins to walk closer to Jerusalem (19:28), approaches Jerusalem (19:41), and finally enters the temple (19:45). These catchphrases signal that the public ministry of Jesus is approaching its end.

The news of Jesus' ministry must have already spread to Jericho, for when the blind beggar is told that "Jesus of Nazareth is passing by," he cries out to Jesus, "Jesus, Son of David, have mercy on me!" (v. 39). It is significant that the blind beggar addresses Jesus as the Son of David. We have already discussed how at the beginning of the Gospel it was said that God would give King David a son (i.e., a descendent) to rule over God's kingdom on earth (1:32–33). The people of Israel came to identify the Son of David as the Messiah, because God would anoint him with his Spirit to rule over his kingdom.

It is significant that this is the first public declaration that Jesus is the Messiah, the promised Son of David (apart from the proclamations of the evil spirits, whom Jesus commands to keep quiet). With the exception of his closest disciples, Jesus has told no one about his messianic identity up until now, because he knows that the Jewish people associate the title with a military king who will fight against their enemies and establish a kingdom centered in Jerusalem for them. If word got out that Jesus was the Messiah, the Romans would arrest and kill him for sedition. This explains why Jesus has controlled the time and manner in which his messianic identity is revealed. He needed time to teach his disciples the meaning of his messianic mission by his life and words.

There is one final point to this story. We have just read that when Jesus again spoke to his disciples about his sufferings and death, they did not understand (or "see") what he was talking about. They were not only slow to see that Jesus must be put to death; they were also slow to see that they too must be ready to lay down their lives for the good of others. The miracle of giving sight to the blind beggar suggests that it also takes a miracle for us to *see* the significance of the Messiah's death. And it takes an even greater miracle for us to reject our self-oriented ways of living and pour out our lives for the good of others.

God Saves a Wealthy Collaborator
with the Romans (19:1–10)

The story of Zacchaeus, a short, wealthy man who climbs a tree to see Jesus, is not only fun but also full of meaning. As a Jewish man collecting taxes for the Romans from his fellow Jews, he is a traitor to the Jewish cause. As the chief tax collector in the region, Zacchaeus has become quite wealthy by taking an extra cut from the tax collectors under his authority. Because the people do not know the exact amount the Romans tax them, he can demand a higher tax than required, keeping the additional money for himself. The Romans don't care. Zacchaeus is not only a despised traitor, a collaborator with the Roman enemies; he is also ruthlessly corrupt in his pursuit of wealth. His corrupt, traitorous ways explain why he needs to hide in a tree, apart from the crowd in the village, in his quest to see Jesus.

As Jesus approaches Jericho on his way to Jerusalem, Zacchaeus learns that he is passing through and exerts great effort to see him. We are not told why Zacchaeus wants to see Jesus. He is not in need of physical healing. Perhaps he has begun to feel shame for his greedy, corrupt ways and learned that Jesus can deliver him from the evil in his heart.

Normally at a public gathering the crowd would make room for a wealthy person, but not for Zacchaeus. It is not only his short stature in the crowd that will keep him from seeing Jesus; mixing with the crowd could be dangerous. The Roman authorities would not see one quick stab with a dagger by a religious zealot.

Since Zacchaeus cannot join the crowd, he plays the part of a fool and does what no man of honor would do. First he runs ahead of the crowd—in public. Then he climbs a tree, sitting on a branch, and waits for Jesus to pass through the village!

Because of its large leaves and low-hanging branches, the Jewish authorities require that a sycamore tree (the kind of tree Zacchaeus climbs) be planted at least twenty-five meters outside of a village.[84] Thus, the sycamore tree Zacchaeus sits in provides a perfect place to hide from the crowd as he seeks to get a good look at Jesus.

---

84. Bailey, *Jesus through Middle Eastern Eyes*, 178.

When Jesus approaches the tree where Zacchaeus hides, he stops and looks up at him. Their eyes meet. Zacchaeus wanted to see Jesus, but more importantly, Jesus wanted to see him! God sent his Messiah Jesus to seek out "sinners" just like Zacchaeus, offering them forgiveness and a new start in life. But when Jesus tells Zacchaeus to climb down from the tree so that he can come to his house to eat with him, the crowd reacts much like the Pharisees had reacted earlier (15:1). They mutter, "He has gone to be the guest of a 'sinner'" (19:7).

But then, with the hostile crowd listening, Zacchaeus says to Jesus, "Look, Lord! Here and now I give half of my possessions to the poor, and if I have cheated anybody out of anything, I will pay back four times the amount" (v. 8). Zacchaeus' sudden desire to be generous in the use of his wealth demonstrates that God's love now fills his heart instead of the love of money. In response to Zacchaeus' pledge to give away what would amount to almost all of his money,[85] Jesus says, "Today salvation has come to this house" (v. 9).

That's the story, but what are we to learn from it? First, the story makes the point that Zacchaeus was a wealthy ruler. We recently read that it is impossible for wealthy rulers to enter God's kingdom unless God in his great mercy makes it possible (18:23–27). This story teaches us that God *does* make it possible for some wealthy people to be part of his kingdom. What led Zacchaeus to exert so much effort to see Jesus? What led Jesus to stop on the road and look up at Zacchaeus in the tree? And what led Zacchaeus to pledge to give so generously to the poor, and to pay back those he had cheated four times the amount he owed them? I suggest it was the love of God seeking out Zacchaeus through his Messiah.

But there is more to learn from the story. This is the last story recording Jesus' public ministry before he reaches Jerusalem, and it includes many of the themes we have seen from the very beginning of the Gospel. The Prophet John warned the people of Israel that they could only be true children of Abraham if they repented and demonstrated their repentance by using their money generously and honestly (3:8–14). In this sense Zacchaeus models what true repentance looks like for the wealthy; Jesus affirms him as a son of Abraham (19:9).

---

85. Tannehill, *Luke*, 277.

The story also illustrates the profound social and economic impact the kingdom of God can have on a community. Seeds of social justice are sown in Jericho when Zacchaeus begins giving generously to the poor and graciously making restitution with those he has cheated. The oppressive, corrupt tax system is lifted from the town.[86] Imagine how different the world would be if every politician, every dishonest businessperson, every prince, and every king were to do what Zacchaeus does—put into practice the teaching of the Messiah Jesus.

Because Zacchaeus begins to love God completely from his heart and practice Jesus' teachings by living generously for others, he is forgiven and experiences the joy of salvation this very day. Jesus says to him, "Today salvation has come to this house" (v. 9). We do not need to anxiously hope for salvation when we die. The story of Zacchaeus teaches us that we can already know now the joy and peace of being accepted by God.

A FOCUS ON JESUS THE MESSIAH ESTABLISHING JUSTICE AND RIGHTEOUSNESS

The prophets repeated time and time again that the Messiah would establish justice and righteousness on the earth. In many places we read of the Messiah that "he will reign on David's throne and over his kingdom, establishing and upholding it with justice and righteousness" (Isaiah 9:7), and that "with righteous he will judge the needy, with justice he will give decisions for the poor of the earth" (Isaiah 11:4). This raises the question of how we see justice and righteousness established on earth through the life and teaching of Jesus the Messiah. How are justice and righteousness expressed by Jesus when we read the Gospel story?

It is important to note that in the Scriptures, justice and righteousness always go together and extend to every area of life on earth. The tendency for many people in the secular West to speak out for specific just causes in the world (a good thing in itself), but to largely ignore God's commands in their personal lives, shows a failure to understand that how we live personally inevitably affects others, either for good or for ill. For example, lying creates

---

86. Bailey, *Jesus through Middle Eastern Eyes*, 184.

distrust, hardness, and alienation in a community. A man who commits adultery breaks the bond of trust with his wife, leaving her and their children broken and betrayed, drifting in an insecure world, where the family was meant to be a strong haven for safety.

Morality is never a private matter. How we live will always affect those around us—for good or for ill. This may be why Jesus says, "He who is not with me is against me, and he who does not gather with me, scatters" (11:23). With self as the center of our lives, we scatter—we contribute to the fragmentation of society. With self-denying love, thinking first about the good of others, we gather—we contribute to a healthy and whole society. God's commandments are an expression of his love, meant to protect us, to cause us to thrive, and to experience the life he intends for us. In short, a just and righteous world will emanate from the Source of love.

Jesus teaches his disciples, "Do to others as you would have them do to you" (6:31). He teaches them to love all people, even their enemies. He unleashes God's love as a constant, creative, life-giving power that always looks out for the good of others. Love is a commandment that is meant to be lived out at every moment of every day towards every person—even our enemies. Love, God's love, the kind of love seen in Jesus, establishes justice and righteousness wherever it is practiced. Life will be good. We will be at peace with God, ourselves, and those around us.

When a hated, corrupt official vows to give half of his possessions to the poor and pay back four times the amount to all he has cheated, his expression of love brings about justice and righteousness in his village. What would happen if the mayor of a Jewish settlement built by bulldozing Palestinian houses learned of the way of love shown by the Messiah Jesus, and vowed to give half of his possessions to those the government had made homeless and to build for them new houses? This is God's politics of justice, and where it is practiced, it works.[87]

---

87. S. McKnight, "Justice and Righteousness," in *Dictionary of Jesus and the Gospels*, 411–16.

Jesus Will Be Made King (19:11–27)

Jesus is still near Jericho when he tells another parable to the crowd, which includes his disciples. They have just heard Jesus declare to Zacchaeus, "Today salvation has come to this house." Because they believe God's salvation will come to Israel through his Messiah-King, and because Jesus is very close to Jerusalem, where the Messiah will reign as King, the crowd's expectation is "that the kingdom of God was going to appear at once" (19:11).

The Jewish people expect the kingdom of God to come as one event at the end of history when God will judge their enemies and give them salvation in their land. But Jesus knows that he will not establish an earthly, political kingdom for Israel in the land of Palestine when he comes to Jerusalem; instead he will suffer and die, be raised by God from the dead, and be exalted by God to his presence in heaven. There he will remain until God sends him back to hold people accountable for how they have responded to him and to the message God gave him. Because of the false expectations of the crowd and the disciples, Jesus tells a parable challenging them to be faithful in serving him until God sends him back at the end of history.

As we read this parable, it is good to remember what Jesus' parables are—stories based on everyday life in the land of Palestine at the time. These are stories that *could* have really happened but didn't. The stories teach a few main points about the coming of the Messiah and the kingdom of God, and they are not to be taken literally in every detail.

In this particular parable Jesus speaks of a nobleman who was made king; his servants, who were directed to serve him as king; and his subjects, who rejected him as king. He says, "A man of noble birth went to a distant country to have himself appointed king and then return. So he called ten of his servants and gave them ten minas. 'Put this money to work,' he said, 'until I come back.' But his subjects hated him and sent a delegation after him to say, 'We don't want this man to be our king.' He was made king, however, and returned home" (vv. 12–15).

A story such as this would sound familiar to the people of Galilee. Aspiring kings in regions of the Roman Empire travelled to Rome to have their positions as client-kings confirmed. And the brutal slaughter of the enemies of the king's rule in the story (v. 27) would sound familiar in the world of ancient politics. For example, the enemies of King Herod were brutally killed.[88] However, while such events provide general background for this parable, we should not interpret the parable literally in every detail. How then shall we understand it?

Jesus is the man of noble birth, whom God has sent to be King. God, of course, is the sovereign Ruler of the world. But he has appointed Jesus, as his Messiah, to represent him and rule as his King on earth. By now we know that the leaders of Israel will not accept Jesus as their King when he comes to Jerusalem. But even though they will cause the Messiah to suffer and die in Jerusalem, God will raise him from the dead after three days, exalt him to his presence as King, and send him back at the end of history to hold everyone accountable for how they have responded to the coming of God's kingdom through him.

The servants whom the nobleman puts to work until he is sent back (v. 13) represent Jesus' disciples. Jesus has spoken often to them about the kingdom of God; they have experienced the life, love, and powers of the kingdom of God; and a few of them have significant wealth. They are to use this training and these gifts to extend God's good and gracious way on earth. Those who are faithful in their service will be richly rewarded, while those who are idle will suffer loss. Zacchaeus is a good example of someone who faithfully invests his life to extend the kingdom of God. He humbles himself before God, gives generously to the poor, and becomes honest in his business affairs. For this reason he can expect Jesus to say to him, "Well done, my good servant!" when he returns (v. 17).

The subjects in the parable, who hate the king and say, "We don't want this man to be our king" (v. 14), are people like the Pharisees and the leaders in Jerusalem, who reject Jesus as God's appointed King. Jesus therefore ends the parable with sobering words directed at them: "But those enemies of mine who did not want me to be king over them—bring them here and kill them in front of me" (v. 27).

How are we to understand this? As stated earlier, we should take care not to press the details of the parable for how Jesus will carry out his role as God's Judge at the end of history. Still, these are sobering words to all who oppose the way of God's good and just kingdom. To reject the Messiah and his message is to reject God and the message God gave him.

---

88. Tannehill, *Luke*, 280.

And to reject God means we will not partake in his kingdom either now or in eternity.

SUMMARY OF THE WAY OF JESUS THE MESSIAH

God has sent Jesus his Messiah not only to establish his kingdom but also to show us the way we are to live, so that his kingdom grows and flourishes on earth. Jesus is portrayed as the true humanity, the very model of how God intended human beings to live and behave. He is the new Adam, showing us what it means to love and obey God where the first Adam failed. Jesus is also portrayed as the true Israelite who is loyal in his love for God when tempted.

There is tension between various characters in the story—not only between Jesus and the leaders of Israel, but also between Jesus and his disciples. In spite of their loyalty to Jesus, the disciples are slow to understand, accept, and emulate his selfless service and suffering for the good of others, which includes even his enemies.

Thus, on the journey to Jerusalem Jesus has focused his attention on teaching the disciples the way of life in God's kingdom. The religious leaders, along with the rich and the rulers of the world, have often been portrayed in glaring contrast to the way God wants us to live.

By word and by deed Jesus has often taught his disciples to follow

- the way of humility rather than seeking positions of authority;
- the way of self-denial and giving of oneself for the good of others rather than using others for one's own gain;
- the way of serving rather than being served;
- the way of accepting suffering for the good of others rather than seeking security and comfort at all costs;
- the way of seeking justice and mercy for all people rather than for only our own people;
- the way of befriending the poor and the ostracized rather than those who can help us succeed;
- the way of loving in order to make peace with other "tribes" and religions rather than fighting for our own "tribe" and religion;
- and the way of forgiveness rather than bitterness and revenge.

This is what it means to believe in Jesus as the Messiah, to live for God in his kingdom.

A Focus on Jerusalem at the Time of Jesus

Jesus does not appear to have ministered in Jerusalem to any great extent until his last days on earth. However, we can assume that during the thirty-three years of his life he at times journeyed to Jerusalem for Jewish festivals and observed how the leaders of Israel lived and maintained worship in the temple. We have already read that he was there as a boy during the Passover (2:41–46). But because he knew that his message of the kingdom of God coming through him as the Messiah would lead to direct clashes with the Jewish leaders in Jerusalem (as did in fact happen), he ministered primarily in Galilee during the three years of his public ministry.

When the city of Jerusalem is mentioned in the Gospel, it often stands for much more than just the political and religious capital of Israel. Jerusalem often stands for the nation's collective opposition to God's prophets throughout its history, culminating in its opposition to the Prophet Jesus. At the same time, Jerusalem represents the destination of Jesus the Messiah as he purposely travels there with his disciples to fulfill God's will—the things predicted of him in the ancient prophets. Jerusalem comes to represent the place of rejection, suffering, and death, in which we see God's mysterious way to remake the world.

Archaeological surveys estimate that around 60,000 people lived in Jerusalem during the time of Jesus. During the great Jewish festivals such as the Passover, the city could swell to some 180,000, with Jewish pilgrims traveling there from throughout Palestine and across the Roman Empire. While Aramaic and Greek were the most commonly spoken languages in Jerusalem, during festival seasons all kinds of languages could be heard among the pilgrims who had traveled from distant lands. Yet even in times of celebration, the fact that Roman soldiers were stationed at the temple was a reminder that the Jews were a subject people in an occupied land.

The city itself consisted of two parts, Upper and Lower Jerusalem. Upper Jerusalem was located on the hill just west of the temple. Here lived the leaders of Israel in splendid houses, with a splendid view of the magnificent edifice. There too lived the Roman prefect when he was in the city. It was to this Roman palace that the leaders of Israel brought Jesus, where he would stand trial before Pilate, the Roman prefect at the time.

In Lower Jerusalem, which was also the older part, lived the working class. Because most of the artisans and unskilled workers of the Lower City would have labored at building and maintaining the temple structure, they too would have been critical of Jesus' pronouncements of judgment against the temple. Thus, they were easily swayed by their leaders to join them in calling for the Messiah Jesus to be crucified.[89]

---

89. Witherington III, *New Testament History*, 138–39.

PART FIVE

JESUS, GOD'S MESSIAH, COMPLETES HIS MISSION IN JERUSALEM (19:28–24:53)

Jesus now reaches his destination—Jerusalem, the destination God has planned for him from the very beginning. Because his journey has been long, and because he has repeatedly taught his closest disciples that he will suffer and die in the city, we, as readers of the Gospel, are right to be apprehensive. How will the people of Jerusalem receive him? Why will the leaders of Israel put God's Messiah to death? How will his disciples respond when they see the one they have put their hope in brutally killed by Roman soldiers?

The Messiah's intense confrontation with the leaders of Israel in Jerusalem now becomes the focus of the final part of the Gospel story. The Pharisees and teachers of the law increasingly opposed Jesus when he spoke the word of God in Galilee. It is safe to assume that they have informed the leaders in Jerusalem of his teaching and lack of conformity to their traditions. Now the time has come for the leaders in Jerusalem themselves to hear God's Servant teach and to deal with him directly.

It is significant that Jesus no longer teaches in the towns and villages of Galilee, but now in the temple in Jerusalem, the focal point of Jewish belief and culture (19:47–20:1). He continues to proclaim the good news that God's kingdom has begun with his ministry. Because the leaders of Israel reject him as God's Messiah, he says, they are not part of God's kingdom. They do not understand the purposes of God revealed in the very Scriptures they read and revere! Jesus continues to claim that he reveals the purposes of God for Israel and the nations, and that by opposing him, the leaders of Israel oppose God himself!

To demonstrate how the leaders of Israel misrepresent the way God wants people to live, Jesus engages in a prophetic act: he forcefully drives out of the temple the merchants, who make the selling of animals for sacrifice a means for making money. Jesus disrupts worship in the temple for the entire day! With tens of thousands of pilgrims at the temple to offer sacrifices to God, the chaos Jesus causes does not go unnoticed. Just before this Jesus again predicted God's impending judgment on Jerusalem and its temple (19:41–44). Now he cleanses the temple as if he owned it, as if he, not Israel's leaders, had authority over it as its Lord. Thus, the conflict with Israel's leaders that has increased throughout the Gospel now reaches its climax.

It is important to recall that most of the leaders of Israel live in fine, spacious houses very near the temple. And they profit financially, politically, and socially from their authority to oversee the sacrifices and prayers. But more importantly, by their administration of the temple the leaders of Israel control the faith of Jews scattered throughout the empire. Jerusalem, with its splendid place of worship, is the center of the world for the Jewish people. From its priestly overseers and elite scholars, Jewish beliefs and practices are dispersed throughout Palestine and the Roman Empire. In short, the temple in Jerusalem holds everything together for the Jewish people; it serves "a world-ordering function."[90] Without the temple, who would they be?

Thus, by predicting the destruction of Jerusalem and the temple and by claiming authority over it through his prophetic acts, Jesus is creating a revolution—the unraveling of all that holds the people of Israel together, of all they build their identity on and long for. Where will God manifest his presence on earth if not here? Where will the people hear the priest pronounce the forgiveness of their sins if they cannot sacrifice here? And how will the Gentiles learn the ways of God from the people of Israel if they cannot come to Jerusalem to learn from the Jewish leaders? Many onlookers are wondering, *Who is this Jesus, this son of a common laborer with a rural Galilean accent, from an obscure village in Galilee, a so-called teacher and prophet of God with no formal training in Jerusalem? Who is he to come to Jerusalem and teach us about God, his kingdom, and God's judgment on the temple, the center of our world?*

The Gospel answers that he is God's Servant and Messiah, sent by God to create a new world order according to what God has revealed in the Scriptures. The new way for ordering the world is the kingdom of God, and its focal point is God's Messiah Jesus. The peoples of the world will no longer come to Jerusalem to learn the ways of God, but instead the

---

90. Green, *Gospel of Luke*, 681–82.

Messiah will direct his disciples to move out from Jerusalem to teach the nations of the world. And God will no longer manifest his presence in the temple in Jerusalem, but instead, just as he has revealed his presence in the Messiah through his Spirit, so now he will be present through his Spirit in the disciples. Forgiveness of sins will no longer be pronounced by a priest in Jerusalem but will be received directly from God to anyone, anywhere, who trusts his Messiah for the forgiveness of his sins and commits to his way of living. This new way of ordering the world according to God's plan is briefly summarized at the very end of the Gospel (24:46–49).

The time of Jesus' arrival in Jerusalem coincides with the celebration of the Passover, the festival when Israel remembers God's mighty, merciful act in delivering them from bondage in Egypt and providing a sacrifice lamb so that their sins are passed over. Thus, the timing of Jesus' coming to Jerusalem "contributes to the drama . . . by locating Jesus' death squarely within the highly charged environment of Israel's celebration of its own identity."[91]

So the Gospel will reach its climax with the crucifixion of Jesus. This final section records the determined efforts of Israel's leaders to have Jesus killed; his explanation of why it is God's will for him to suffer and die; the disciples' disillusionment after his death; and their joy when God raises Jesus from the dead.

The Gospel ends on a note of fulfillment and triumph, with God's obedient Servant Jesus having won the victory. God confirms the identity of Jesus as his beloved Messiah by raising him from the dead and exalting him to his very presence in heaven. His slow and unperceiving disciples remain in Jerusalem—near the very leaders who had Jesus put to death. We cannot help but wonder what will happen to them.

JESUS ARRIVES IN JERUSALEM (19:28–48)

Jesus Approaches Jerusalem as God's Chosen King (19:28–40)

The story of the Gospel intensifies as the Prophet Jesus approaches two villages on the Mount of Olives, just three kilometers east of Jerusalem.

---

91. Ibid., 744–45.

Until recently, when the blind beggar from Jericho shouted out, "Son of David, have mercy on me!" (18:39), Jesus did not allow anyone to publically declare that he is the Messiah. He did not allow this because he knew people would misunderstand God's reason for sending him if he used this title. But now as he comes to Jerusalem, where he will soon suffer and die, it doesn't matter.

It is important to remember that even if we, as readers of the Gospel, know that Jesus will suffer and die in Jerusalem, none of his disciples understand this yet. The disciples still believe Jesus will defeat Israel's enemies in some miraculous way and establish a visible political kingdom for Israel, centered in Jerusalem. Events move quickly now. Jesus enters Jerusalem as its King, weeps over the people's unbelief, enters the temple to drive out those who use it as a place for profit instead of prayer, and evades attempts by the leaders of Jerusalem to kill him (19:28–48).

Jesus has just told a parable in Jericho about the subjects of a kingdom who rejected their king (vv. 11–27). He now leads the way to Jerusalem, knowing that this story is his story. He approaches the climax in Jerusalem with resolve: his sufferings and death will not catch him by surprise. He will not die as a helpless victim but as God's obedient Servant. Walking ahead of the crowd of disciples, Jesus orchestrates his entrance into the city on the colt of a donkey.

Jesus could have continued to walk all the way to Jerusalem, but as King he knows he must ride into the city. That's what kings do in these days. However, they always ride in on a magnificent horse, not on a donkey's colt! Jesus' choice of a donkey suggests that he comes as a triumphant yet humble King.[92]

As a Prophet, Jesus knows where the colt of a donkey is tied up in the village ahead of them, so he directs two of his disciples to get it for him to ride into Jerusalem. When the donkey's owner asks the two disciples why they are taking his colt, they only need to reply, "The Lord needs it" (vv. 31,34).

As Jesus rides down from the Mount of Olives with Jerusalem in full sight, he receives the messianic welcome from the crowd, who praise God in loud voices, saying, "Blessed is the king who comes in the name of the Lord!" "Peace in heaven and glory in the highest!" (v. 38). Jesus now

---

92. Ibid., 685.

openly presents himself as Israel's promised Messiah-King, the way to peace on earth.

But some of the Pharisees in the crowd don't approve. They say to Jesus, "Teacher, rebuke your disciples!" (19:39). They don't believe Jesus is the Messiah. They don't believe in the kind of kingdom he proclaims. The clash of kingdoms and outlooks, the clash of two different ways of understandings God's will and working in the world, will soon come to a climax.

A FOCUS ON JESUS THE PATH TO GOD'S PEACE

The word "peace" in the English language is often used to refer to the absence of war, inner tranquility (what some call "peace of mind"), or harmony in our relationships. These meanings are included when the Gospel speaks of the peace of God that comes to earth with the arrival of his Messiah. Yet like most words and concepts, the meaning of "peace" builds on how it was used by the ancient prophets. So, for example, when Jesus encourages a leper he has healed to "go in peace," he means much more than "You may now go with peace of mind."

The prophets used the Hebrew word *shalom*, which we translate "peace," to describe a person's (and a community's) complete well-being, including "health, prosperity, security, friendship, and salvation" from enemies.[93] One could say *shalom* refers to life as we would all like to experience it: absent of poverty, sickness, loneliness, fear, anxiety, shame, and guilt. To imagine it more concretely, *shalom* means good health, food and shelter, inner tranquility, peace in the home and neighborhood, belonging to a community where one is loved and valued, living without the fear of violence, and above all, experiencing the love and presence of God. This is what is meant when it is prophesied that the Messiah Jesus will "guide our feet into the path of peace" (1:79). This is what is meant when Jesus heals a sick women, isolated from her community for twelve long years, and says to her, "Go in peace. (8:48). "

---

93. T. J. Geddert, "Peace," in *Dictionary of Jesus and the Gospels*, 604; Gorman, *Death of the Messiah*, 147–49.

The prophets spoke of the Messiah as "the Prince of Peace" (Isaiah 9:6) through whom God would introduce an eternal age of peace, or a covenant of peace (Isaiah 54:10; Ezekiel 34:25; 37:26). By reading, for example, the prophets Isaiah and Ezekiel we learn that the age of peace will be characterized by

- the peaceful rule of God through his chosen King, a descendant of King David;
- a reconciled relationship with God;
- deliverance from and defeat of the enemies of God's people;
- the inclusion of all the nations of the earth in God's salvation;
- living in harmony with one's neighbors;
- the absence of violence;
- the establishment of justice and righteousness;
- the renewal of all creation in joyful abundance for all;
- God's Spirit enabling his people to live in peace with one another.[94]

If these points summarize the age of peace that God would bring about when he sent his Messiah, and if Jesus was in fact God's Messiah, we must then ask how Jesus brought into being the "shalom vision" portrayed by the prophets. Obviously God's rule of peace was not established the way the people of Israel had envisioned it. They continued to fight the Romans and live under oppression until the Romans finally destroyed Jerusalem and drove them from the land.

At the same time, the Gospel teaches that God's reign of peace actually begins with the coming of the Messiah Jesus. So again we must ask, in what way does peace come into the world through the mission of Jesus the Messiah?

Jesus repeatedly speaks peace into the lives of those who participate in the kingdom of God by following him. Peace comes into the world, for example, when he protects a despised prostitute, a "sinner" who has embraced the love and forgiveness offered

94. Ibid., 140.

through Jesus, from hostile, self-righteous Pharisees at a meal. Jesus pronounces the woman's sins forgiven; invites her to join the community of disciples, where she will be valued and accepted; and above all, enables her to know the love and acceptance of God. All this and more is included when Jesus says to the woman, "Your faith has saved you; go in peace" (7:50). There are many other examples of Jesus bringing peace. Often after healing people and delivering them from disease and demons (the dark enemies of God), Jesus restores them to life in their community and encourages them with the same words—"Go in peace."

Jesus, God's Messiah, refuses to use violence; he welcomes the ostracized into a loving community; he gives honor to those who live in shame; he heals the sick; he cleanses the dirty; he gives the power to forgive and live in peace with others; he frees people from the fear of death, giving them hope beyond their short life on earth; he invites them to join him in his mission of remaking the world according to God's eternal purposes of peace; and above all, he brings people close to God. All this and much more is meant when the Prophet Jesus says to the people of Israel, "If you, even you, had only known on this day what would bring you peace" (19:42).

God's way of peace, achieved by his suffering Servant Jesus, differed sharply from the famous Pax Romana, the way of peace envisioned by the Romans. The Romans sought to establish a golden age of peace, world prominence, and security from their enemies. But it was "achieved and maintained by military victory and power over enemies," and then Roman law and culture were imposed on the conquered, all by the power and with the approval of their gods.[95] This way of peace sounds all too familiar in the history of humankind.

Jesus taught and demonstrated in his life a different way of peace, claiming it was God's way, the way God wants us all to live. It was the way of praying for, doing good to, and even suffering for the good of our enemies; the way of pouring out our lives every day for the weak, the poor, the alien, and those who hate us.

---

95. Ibid., 179.

Jesus did this even to the point of allowing himself to be put to a violent, humiliating death on a cross. The way of peace Jesus practiced and taught his disciples challenged the Roman way of "peace" and power, and it was rejected by both the people of Israel and the Romans.[96] Many Christians, Muslims, and Jews, along with followers of other religions and political ideologies, still fail to understand the power of love, sacrifice, and humility as the way to peace. And the world still suffers because of it.

Those who embrace Jesus as God's Prophet, Servant, and Messiah are called to not only experience God's peace but practice it in the world. Jesus journeyed to Jerusalem to pour out his life for the peace of the world. But all along the way he loved, served, forgave, healed, and taught the way of peace. As the Prince of Peace, Jesus is "defined by how and why he goes to Jerusalem. He goes in peace to make peace, and he instructs his disciples to follow."[97] Like his first disciples, the new community he formed on the way to Jerusalem, those who say they embrace Jesus as the Messiah today are to be defined by his life. They are to join him on his journey and in turn pour out their lives for the good of others all along the way. Peace comes where the ways of Jesus are practiced.

Jesus Weeps for Jerusalem (19:41–44)

As Jesus rides the donkey down the Mount of Olives just east of Jerusalem, he sees the city of Jerusalem in all its splendor. The crowd that has followed him here from Galilee has welcomed him as Israel's King, but where are the leaders of Israel? Why haven't they led the people from Jerusalem out to welcome their King? Sadly, Jerusalem (again, representing all the people of Israel) is not here to receive him as God's Messiah and thus receive the peace that belongs to God's kingdom. Jesus says, "If you, even you, had only known on this day what would bring you peace—but now it is hidden from your eyes" (19:42). Jesus weeps. The mood shifts sharply from the rejoicing of the crowd (vv. 37–38) to Jesus the Messiah-King weeping.

---

96. T. J. Geddert, "Peace," in *Dictionary of Jesus and the Gospels*, 604–5.
97. Gorman, *Death of the Messiah*, 180.

What kind of king weeps when his subjects reject him? Is he weak? If not, why doesn't he mobilize an army to destroy them? Why does Jesus weep? He does not weep from being rejected or for his impending sufferings; he weeps for the people of Israel. He weeps because they do not know that this very day, the day he enters Jerusalem, is the day they could find the way to peace. Zechariah, the father of the Prophet John, said that Jesus the Messiah was the one who would guide their "feet into the path of peace" (1:79). And shortly after that, a great host of angels praised God for now bringing his peace to earth with the birth of Jesus, saying, "Glory to God in the highest, and on earth peace to men on whom his favor rests" (2:14).

The praise of the crowd as Jesus approaches Jerusalem toward the end of his life—"Peace in heaven and glory in the highest" (19:38)—reminds us of the angels' praise at his birth. These two outpourings of praises form literary "bookends" in the Gospel story, suggesting that everything Jesus says and does during his life on earth teaches us the way to peace. We recall that often after Jesus healed people, delivered them from evil spirits, and pronounced the forgiveness of sins to them, he would then encourage them by saying, "Go in peace."

Seeing Jesus approach Jerusalem, the crowd praises God for his heavenly peace now coming to earth through his Messiah. This final praise, coupled with Jesus saying that he offers peace as he enters Jerusalem to suffer and die, suggests that somehow God's offer of peace culminates in the death of his Messiah. "The good news of peace Jesus was born to bring is being brought to a new level, a fuller conclusion, with his imminent death."[98]

Jesus has come to teach the people how they can have peace with God and peace with one another. But what he wants, what God wants, does not happen. The people reject God's Prophet and Messiah, the source of peace. "We don't want this man to be our king," cried the rebellious subjects in the parable (v. 14). That parable now becomes a reality.

In great sorrow Jesus, God's Prophet and Messiah, pronounces God's judgment on the city of Jerusalem and the nation of Israel. Israel's enemies, the Romans, will encircle the city of Jerusalem and tear down its walls. The people will not be judged because they did not believe in God,

---

98. Ibid., 164.

read the Scriptures, or pray and fast but because they "did not recognize the time of God's coming" to them (v. 44).

How did God come to them? He came to them through Jesus, his beloved Messiah. God had given Jesus his Spirit, with all its power and authority, to establish his kingdom of peace on earth.[99] Sadly, the people of Israel—chiefly their leaders—did not recognize God's presence in Jesus offering them his kingdom of peace. The ambitions of Israel's leaders, fueled by their pride and hunger for wealth and power, kept them from seeing it. The way of peace is hidden from the proud and powerful and revealed to the humble and contrite in spirit (see 10:21).

Jesus Claims Authority over the Temple (19:45–48)

As soon as Jesus enters Jerusalem, he goes straight to the temple and begins to drive out merchants who are selling sacrificial animals at exorbitant prices. He says that by making a profit at the expense of the poor pilgrims who have come to Jerusalem for the Passover, they have made the temple "a den of robbers" (19:46). The temple was intended to be a place for prayer, not a place for greedy and unjust business transactions.

The disruption Jesus causes at the temple does not go unnoticed by the leaders of Israel, who are guardians of the temple. He has disrupted worship and the offering of sacrifices at the temple for the entire day.

After this incident Jesus comes to the temple every day, teaching the people and preaching to them about the kingdom of God, adding to the growing tension between him and Israel's leaders. They are present to hear every word he says, becoming increasingly jealous and fearful of him. His cleansing of the temple and his teaching about the kingdom of God are a direct threat to their authority.

The chief priests, teachers of the law, and leaders want to kill Jesus, but they are not able to because of the people, who act as a buffer between him and them. Jesus is so popular with the people that they would cause a riot if the leaders tried to kill him. The Gospel says that "all the people hung on his words" during his teaching in the temple (v. 48).

The leaders' reasons for having Jesus put to death will become even clearer as we continue to read the Gospel. But already we begin to see that

---

99. Green, *Gospel of Luke*, 690.

he is a threat to their power over the people, their status as religious leaders, and their wealth—all derived from their authority over the temple.[100]

What right does Jesus, a man from Galilee, a man who is not a priest with any connection to the temple, a man with no official religious education, a poor wandering prophet—what right does he have to enter their temple, violently disrupt worship for the day, call them "robbers," and return daily, claiming to speak the words of God? How dare he proclaim that God's kingdom has arrived through him! As far as the leaders of Israel are concerned, Jesus is an outsider from a backward province who leads the people down the wrong path with his teaching. His message threatens to unravel the delicate balance of power they have with the Roman authorities and disrupt their secure, comfortable life. He must be stopped.

A FOCUS ON THE JEWISH GOVERNING COUNCIL (SANHEDRIN)

Shortly before Jesus begins his journey to Jerusalem, he says to his twelve closest disciples, "The Son of Man must suffer many things and be rejected by the elders, chief priests and teachers of the law, and he must be killed and on the third day be raised to life" (9:22). When Jesus finally approaches Jerusalem, the people enthusiastically welcome him as Israel's king. He then goes straight to the temple and drives out all who are exploiting the people by selling animal sacrifices at exorbitant prices.

This provocative prophetic act of claiming authority over Israel's temple, along with his popularity with the people, who eagerly listen to him teach each day in the temple, brings Jesus into direct confrontation with the leaders in Jerusalem. Threatened by his authority and jealous of his popularity, "the chief priests, the teachers of the law and the leaders among the people" look for ways to kill Jesus (19:47). This group of leaders in Jerusalem is often referred to as the Council, or the Sanhedrin. By understanding the makeup and functions of the Council, we can better understand why they so fiercely opposed Jesus and sought to have him killed.

---

100.   Ibid., 699.

The Council consisted of seventy-one men who governed the affairs of all the Jews in the entire land (22:66; 23:50). The Council consisted of the high priest and his family; leading scribes, who were the prominent interpreters of the Jewish law; and the "elders," who came from prominent, wealthy families in the region of Jerusalem.

As president of the Council, the high priest possessed immense power and wealth. He and his family derived much of it from the high priest's control of the temple treasury. By collecting taxes and payment for sacrifices, the temple accumulated enormous wealth, making it the most significant single element in the economic life of Palestine. In addition, the high priest wielded great authority by overseeing the temple, its personnel, and its religious functions.[101]

The high priestly family, together with other members of the Jewish council, lived in spacious houses overlooking the temple. Archaeological excavations today reveal to us the grandeur of these houses and the wealth of the leaders of Israel; they also enable us to envision the trial of the Messiah Jesus as he stood surrounded by the Sanhedrin in a spacious room in the high priest's house.

Only the high priest could enter the most sacred part of the temple, called the "holy of holies"—and that only once a year to offer a sacrifice to God for the forgiveness of the people's sins. Even though the people of Israel generally despised the high priest and the council of Israel, they held a distant respect for them because of their position, their education in religious matters, and the religious rituals they performed for the welfare of the nation.

The priests offered sacrifices each day for the people, collected taxes for the treasury, and determined where in the temple people could worship based on gender, ethnicity, and the amount of money they paid for their sacrifice. While common priests in the countryside (such as Zechariah, the father of John the Baptist) were respected among the people, the high priest and the ruling council were often loathed because they collaborated with the Roman occupiers in order to maintain their power and wealth.

---

101.   Porter, *Jesus Christ*, 28–29.

The leaders of Israel would even use violence against their own people in order to keep the status quo.

It was Jesus' popularity among the people and his message of the good news of God's kingdom that led the leaders of Israel to want to kill him out of fear and jealousy. His teaching and the way he lived and led undermined their teaching, their lives, and their authority over the people. They feared that his popularity in Jerusalem would escalate into riots and end their privileged status as collaborators with the Roman authorities. Ironically, the council of leaders was killed by the Romans and ceased to exist when Jerusalem and the temple were destroyed nearly forty years later—just as Jesus had predicted. He, of course, was raised up to God to live forever.[102]

THE LEADERS OF ISRAEL TRY TO TRICK JESUS (20:1–21:4)

The Leaders of Israel Challenge Jesus' Authority (20:1–8)

Jesus now spends every day at the temple in Jerusalem, teaching the people and proclaiming the good news that God's kingdom has come, helping the poor and liberating those in bondage. The leaders of Israel who reside in Jerusalem now replace the Pharisees as Jesus' chief opponents. They are anxious about the influence Jesus has over the people, who gather at the temple each day to hear him teach. The temple is their territory; they are to be the ones teaching the people. But now the people gather around Jesus, hanging on his every word. Because of Jesus' popularity, the leaders are unable to kill him. So they seek to minimize his influence by discrediting him in the presence of the people.

Their collective authority lies in being descendants of other priests, being formally educated as scribes, and belonging to families of wealth and influence as elders.[103] Who is Jesus to enter Jerusalem as the Messiah with

---

102. Witherington III, *New Testament History*, 148–50; L. D. Hurst and J. B. Green, "Priest, Priesthood," in *Dictionary of Jesus and the Gospels*, 633–36; Twelftree, "Sanhedrin," in *Dictionary of Jesus and the Gospels*, 728–32.

103. Green, *Gospel of Luke*, 700.

the blessing of the crowds, to cause chaos at the temple, and now to teach there every day, undermining their teaching and authority? To grasp the enormity of the strained and tense atmosphere, imagine a young Muslim from rural America, with no formal education in the Quran, entering Mecca for the haj to tell the mullahs of Mecca they have misunderstood the Quran and are not properly submitting to the message of the prophets!

The leaders of Israel stand to lose everything—their privileged positions and wealth, their power over the people, their very identity as Israel's leaders—if this continues. At question is who speaks for God and who represents his authority to the people: the leaders of Israel or Jesus? If they can marginalize Jesus' influence in full view of the people at the temple, they will keep their positions of power.

So on one of the days Jesus is teaching the people, the leaders push through the crowd and interrupt him with a challenging question: "Tell us by what authority You are doing these things, or who is the one who gave You this authority?" (20:2). Who gave him the authority to cleanse the temple, to preach that the kingdom of God has arrived? Because Jesus is not a priest with any official position at the temple, they feel it should be fairly easy to expose his lack of authority to speak for God.

But since the leaders of Israel do not know who Jesus is, they underestimate his wisdom and power. Instead of answering their question, Jesus outwits the Jewish leadership by asking them a question in return. "Tell me: John's baptism- was it from heaven, or of human origin?" (vv. 3, 4). In essence Jesus asks them, "Do you believe John spoke the words of God as a prophet sent by God, or do you believe he spoke on his own authority and thus misled the people?"

The Prophet John preached that all of Israel must turn to God with their whole being to live good lives and give themselves generously for the poor. Simply relying on being Jewish, being a descendent of Abraham, would not guarantee entrance to God's kingdom and escape from his judgment. More importantly, the Prophet John said his role was to prepare the people of Israel to receive the Messiah—whom he then identified as Jesus (3:3–22)!

The chief priests, teachers of the law, and elders quickly huddle together to discuss how they will answer Jesus. They realize their dilemma. Jesus has outwitted them. The people who stand around them all believe John was a prophet sent by God. If the leaders deny this, the people can accuse them of blasphemy and stone them for insulting one of God's prophets.[104]

On the other hand, if the leaders acknowledge John as a true prophet, they know Jesus can reasonably ask why they didn't repent and practice his message. The Prophet John prepared the way for Jesus as the Messiah. Why haven't they led the people of Jerusalem out to welcome him as such?

Right in the temple, before all the people and Jesus, the leaders of Israel must shamefully admit that they don't know if John spoke with authority from God![105] This admission allows Jesus to say that he will then not reveal his authority to them.

Jesus Exposes the Hearts of the Leaders (20:9–19)

The people along with the leaders of Israel still stand around Jesus in the temple, where he teaches. Jesus now turns from the leaders who have challenged him to the people to tell them a parable. While Jesus tells the parable to the people, the leaders of Israel also hear it. Read without any context, the parable could be confusing. But in light of the history of Israel and what we have learned about Jesus as the Messiah sent by God, the parable is clear. It is certainly clear for the Jewish authorities, who know that Jesus speaks the parable against them (20:19)! As we read the parable, it is helpful to ask why Jesus tells it at this precise moment to the people who have welcomed him to Jerusalem as the Messiah.

The parable is about a man who planted a vineyard, was away traveling for a long time, and later sent his servants to receive the fruit of the vineyard. The people of Israel—especially the leaders, who study the Scriptures diligently—know this story well. One of God's prophets had long ago told another story in which Israel is represented by a vineyard, planted by God for the purpose of producing the good fruit of righteousness and justice to be spread throughout the world (Isaiah 5:1–7). However, the people of Israel continually fail to obey God by blessing the world with the fruit of righteousness and justice.

Building on the same imagery, Jesus tells a parable about a landowner who planted a vineyard and rented it out to a group of farmers to cultivate. The owner of the vineyard represents God, and the farmers charged to

---

104.   Ibid., 702n17.

105.   Tannehill, *Luke*, 288.

produce fruit from the vineyard represent the leaders of Israel, both past and present.

The servants the owner sent to gather fruit from the vineyard, one after another, represent the many prophets God has sent to Israel to warn them against worshipping idols and to remind them to love only him and practice justice and righteousness as a light for the whole world. In the parable the farmers mistreated the servants the owner had sent and drove them away empty-handed. They returned with no fruit to offer their master. By and large, this is how the people of Israel have treated the prophets God has sent them (Luke 11:47–50).

In the parable the owner of the vineyard asked himself, "What shall I do? I will send my son, whom I love; perhaps they will respect him" (20:13). We have read earlier in the Gospel that Jesus is the chosen Messiah to whom God says, "You are my Son, whom I love; with you I am well pleased" (3:22). As God's beloved Messiah, the Prophet Jesus speaks the message of all the previous prophets: to love and worship only God and to practice justice and mercy towards others, even one's enemies. If they did this, God's light and love would spread beyond the people of Israel to the whole world.

But Jesus is not just another prophet sent to call a wayward people back to God. As God's Servant-Messiah, he is sent to defeat God's enemies and establish his just and righteous ways on earth. And God has given his Messiah the authority to rule as his King on earth. In the parable the farmers believed they would rule over the vineyard if they killed the owner's son. Even though the leaders of Israel do not believe Jesus is the Messiah who will rule over God's kingdom, they do believe that his popularity with the people threatens their authority over the people of Israel. And it is these leaders who will turn Jesus over to the Roman authorities to be put to death.

Is the owner of the vineyard defeated when the farmers kill his son? No. Will God be defeated when the leaders of Israel have his beloved Messiah killed? No! God has all power and infinite wisdom. His purposes can never be defeated. He will judge Israel's corrupt leaders and give leadership over his kingdom to others (20:16). Jesus will soon say to his disciples, "I confer on you a kingdom, just as my Father conferred one on me, so that you may eat and drink at my table in my kingdom and sit on thrones, judging the twelve tribes of Israel." (22:29–30). God's kingdom will come through his chosen Messiah, but those who will participate and lead in the kingdom comes as a surprise.

When the people hear that Jesus, whom they recently welcomed to Jerusalem as God's Messiah, will be killed, they say, "May it never be!" (20:16). They have no mental category for a Messiah who is killed by his enemies; the Messiah is supposed to kill the enemies of God.

When Jesus entered Jerusalem, the people praised God from a song of King David, saying, "Blessed is the king who comes in the name of the Lord!" (19:38). They fully expect him to drive the Romans out of Israel and establish a kingdom centered in Jerusalem. So Jesus must now remind the people of another line in the same song: "The stone the builders rejected has become the cornerstone" (20:17). He adds soberly, "Everyone who falls on that stone will be broken to pieces; anyone on whom it falls will be crushed" (v. 18).

By quoting David, Jesus teaches that Israel's leadership will reject him as King. He is the stone that is rejected by the builders. But even though he will be rejected and killed, God will raise him from the dead and exalt him as his King. In this way Jesus the Messiah becomes the "cornerstone," the choicest stone in the building, selected by God. And ultimately he will judge ("crush") the leaders of Israel and all who reject him.

We conclude by returning to the question we initially asked: why does Jesus now teach this parable to the people who believe he is the Messiah? He does so to prepare them for his rejection and death. When their hope is shaken by the terrible events of the next few days, they need to know that God will accomplish his purposes through Jesus' sufferings and raise him from the dead as his King. And they need to distance themselves from Israel's leaders so that they will not share in their judgment.

The leaders of Israel, of course, understand that the parable is about them, so they seek to silence Jesus by arresting him. But they cannot. Jesus is so popular with the people that arresting him would lead to a riot. Instead, the leaders will keep a close eye on Jesus and silence him some other way (v. 20).

Jesus Outwits the Leaders of Israel (20:20–26)

Because Jesus is so popular with the people, the leaders cannot kill him (19:47–48). If they use any force against him, the people might riot, causing so much commotion that the Roman governor, Pilate, could brutally suppress the crowds and diminish the power of the leaders. The leaders are in a bind. They cannot stop Jesus by using force, but if the crowds in Jerusalem continue to be fascinated with his teaching and follow him, the leaders' authority over the people and their income from the temple will rapidly diminish. So for now they seek to trick Jesus with cleverly planned questions in order to expose him as a false prophet, or to give them grounds for handing him over to the Roman governor as a seditious revolutionary against Caesar and the Empire.

The leaders in Jerusalem were recently humiliated in public when they asked Jesus the source of his authority (20:1–8). They will not risk this happening again. So they devise a clever plan: they will select some men and send them as spies to trip Jesus up with a trick question. They don't have to kill Jesus themselves. If they can trick him into speaking openly against the authority of Caesar, then he can be charged with sedition and put to death.

The spies approach Jesus pretending to be sincere inquirers of the will of God. In an attempt to make him lower his guard, they flatter him by commenting on his fearless, impartial manner of speaking of the ways of God. Then they ask the trick question the leaders have given them to ask: "Is it right for us [as Jewish people] to pay taxes to Caesar or not?" (v. 22). And indeed, it is a clever question. If Jesus answers that the Jews should pay taxes to Caesar, he will lose his popularity with the people. After all, they believe he is the Messiah who will overthrow the Romans, not bow down in subjection to them by paying unjust taxes. But if Jesus answers no, as the leaders expect him to, they can hand him over to the governor for sedition. Either way the leaders will have silenced Jesus. How will he evade this clever plot?

Jesus directs the spies to show him a Roman coin. One of them takes from his pocket a coin bearing the inscription "Tiberius Caesar," with the emperor's portrait on it. Tiberius is the son of the Emperor Augustus, honored as divine in the Roman world. Jesus then asks, "Whose portrait and inscription are on it?"[106] In asking this question, Jesus shows their hypocrisy: Why do they have such blasphemous coins in their pockets?[107]

---

106.   Ibid., 293.

107.   Wright, *Luke for Everyone*, 241.

Do they revere Augustus as a god and Tiberius as the son of a god? Clearly they are not as pious and sincere as they pretend to be.

When the deceitful spies acknowledge it is Caesar's portrait on the coin, Jesus answers them, saying, "Then give back to Caesar what is Caesar's" (v. 25). How does this answer enable Jesus to evade their trap?

The rulers of Israel are themselves responsible for collecting taxes to give to the Roman authorities. They do so in order to appease the Romans, but it also means that they maintain control of the temple as a source of wealth.[108] Since they collect and use Caesar's coins, they can't object to Jesus saying they should return them to Caesar as the rightful owner.[109] In this way Jesus avoids giving an answer that could leave him open to the charge of sedition, and for the time being he also maintains his popularity with the people.

In a subtle way Jesus further exposes the failure of Israel's leadership. For he continues, "Give . . . to God what is God's" (20:25). With these words Jesus implies that the leaders have failed to give God their lives and thus failed to lead his people in his way—the way of humility, mercy, and justice towards all people. They have failed to make the temple in Jerusalem a place of prayer and instead have used it as a place for their own profit.

The spies are astonished and silenced by the authority of Jesus and the wisdom of his answer. Since this exchange of words takes place in public, we can assume that the people remain enthusiastic in their support of Jesus. The division between the people and their leaders continues to grow. What will the leaders do next to try to discredit Jesus?

The Leaders Question Jesus about the Resurrection (20:27–40)

The leadership of Israel continues to meet behind the scenes to find ways to silence Jesus. They now send some Sadducees from among their leadership in order to discredit him with a trick question. The Sadducees are from wealthy families related to the chief priests and live in spacious houses near the temple. They too regard Jesus as a threat to their control over the temple and the income it provides for them. Even though they address Jesus as teacher, they are not at all interested in being taught by him.

---

108.   Green, *Gospel of Luke*, 712.
109.   Tannehill, *Luke*, 293.

The question they challenge Jesus with is based on belief in the dead rising at the end of the ages. While the Pharisees believe in the resurrection from the dead, the Sadducees deny it. Because they know Jesus believes in the resurrection, they create an incredible scenario in which a woman has been married to seven different men, each of whom has died without providing her a child to carry on the family name. The Sadducees then ask Jesus, "Now then, at the resurrection whose wife will she be, since the seven were married to her?" (20:33). Their question is based on the law of Moses, which requires a man to marry the wife of a deceased brother in the hope of producing a child to carry on his name. But it is also based on belief in resurrection, a belief they flatly deny. They know that since Jesus believes in the resurrection, their question will make him look foolish and discredit him in the presence of the people.

Jesus demonstrates his wisdom once again. He points out that their question is based on the false assumption that resurrection life in the age to come will be exactly like life as it is now on earth. Jesus doesn't describe it as some kind of otherworldly experience, but he does say that our bodies will be different than they are now, and that we will become like angels in that we will not deteriorate and die again. We will also be like angels in the sense that we will not marry.

The leaders of Israel finally give up trying to trick Jesus with dialogue and questions. His wisdom and knowledge of the Scriptures far exceeds theirs. They will have to find another way to silence him.

Jesus Teaches He is King Davis's Lord! (20:41–44)

The leaders have finally given up trying to trap Jesus with questions in order to discredit him before the people. Jesus now directs a question to them in the presence of the crowds (20:45) to teach that the Messiah will be much greater than the Jewish people expect.[110] Since the day for Jesus' death is drawing near, he now reveals more of his full identity and his future position.

Jesus teaches that he is more than an earthly king or lord. After his death God will exalt him to his presence at his right hand—the position of highest authority and honor. Jesus will not be enthroned on earth in Jerusalem, as his disciples still expect, but in heaven in God's presence. From

---

110.   Wright, *Luke for Everyone*, 248.

heaven he will continue to extend God's kingdom until the enemies of God's kingdom are defeated. Ironically, the rulers of Israel who now seek to kill Jesus are among the enemies of the kingdom God will subdue![111]

Jesus quotes from a well-known psalm of King David to illustrate how the Scriptures teach that the Messiah will be more than a king on earth for Israel. In it David says, "The Lord said to my Lord: 'Sit at my right hand until I make your enemies a footstool for your feet'" (Psalm 110:1). David calls the Messiah his Lord! This shows that the Messiah will be more than a descendant of David and a king on earth over Israel. He will be David's Lord and will reign over earth at God's right hand, not in Jerusalem.

This revelation should be no surprise for us as readers of the Gospel. Jesus has repeatedly referred to himself as the Son of Man who is given an eternal kingdom when he is escorted into the presence of God by God's holy angels.

While the Gospel does not record how the leaders of Israel respond to Jesus making this claim, it is likely that they are filled with rage. Jesus implies that they are God's enemies, whom God will make a footstool for the feet of Jesus!

Wealthy Leaders and a Poor Widow (20:45–21:4)

By now we know that Jesus is critical of Israel's leaders. However, it is not their beliefs he criticizes so much as the way they live. They believe, as does Jesus, in praying to the One True God, in reading the Scriptures he has revealed through his prophets, in a future day of judgment, and similar beliefs central to the Jewish faith. Nevertheless, Jesus severely criticizes the leaders of Israel for their failure to understand and practice the central truths of God's revelation given through the prophets—to love God with one's whole being and to humbly obey him by practicing mercy and justice for others, regardless of their ethnicity or status in society.

Because the leaders of Israel (in this passage, the teachers of the law) are self-absorbed and fail to practice the love and compassion of God, Jesus once again warns his disciples not to be like them. The disciples have observed Jesus model humble, selfless service to the poor. They have seen

---

111.   How the Messiah becomes Lord and extends God's kingdom on earth from heaven becomes clearer in the book of Acts, the sequel to the Gospel of Luke.

him extend God's mercy and forgiveness to those Israel considers their enemies. And Jesus has repeatedly taught his disciples to also serve the needy instead of seeking greatness for themselves. But sadly, after all this time and all Jesus' teaching, they still need to be warned not to emulate Israel's leaders. Apparently the desire for positions of prominence and the desire for possessions reside deeply in the human heart.

The teachers of the law seek to impress the common people with their great knowledge of the Scriptures, but they don't practice Scripture's central commands. Jesus says they "like to walk around in flowing robes and love to be greeted in the marketplaces and have the most important seats in the synagogues and the places of honor at banquets" (20:46). In addition, they love to make a show of their lengthy prayers. Everywhere they go, everywhere—whether it is the marketplace, the synagogue, or banquets—they take their haughty hearts with them and look for praise from the people.[112]

Imagine Israel's leaders walking the streets of Jerusalem in their long flowing robes with their heads held high. Imagine the people stepping aside to make way for them and greeting them with words of praise. Imagine them standing up front during public prayer, praying profoundly and at great length to impress the people. If we can imagine that, we can imagine the kind of religion God hates and sent the Prophet Jesus to expose. People like this, says Jesus, "will be punished most severely" (v. 47).

Because these leaders are so consumed with self-importance, they fail to see the needy around them and act with compassion. As interpreters of Scripture they know they are responsible to care for widows—the weakest, most vulnerable members of society. But not only do they not care for them; they go so far as to use their legal skills to find ways to cheat widows out of money left to them by their deceased husbands. Jesus says, "they devour widow's houses" (v. 47). Using religion to make money from worship at the temple is bad, but using it to cheat poor widows out of their money is about as low as one can get. It is worth repeating Jesus' stern pronouncement of judgment on such people, whatever their religion: they "will be punished most severely."

At the same moment Jesus warns his disciples not to imitate the teachers of the law, he looks up and sees a perfect example of what he has

---

112.   Green, *Gospel of Luke*, 727.

just taught (21:1–4). He sees the rich putting large amounts of money (but a small portion of their total wealth) into the temple treasury. They typify the rich scribes in the previous verses who love to be seen in their display of religion. Jesus also sees a poor widow giving two small copper coins. (A common worker would receive 132 such coins for one day's work!) Possibly the two copper coins are all the poor widow has left after being cheated by the scribes' clever legal maneuverings. The poor widow, then, may exemplify the widows of the previous verses whose houses are devoured by the teachers of the law.

What is the point Jesus is making by comparing the giving of the rich with the giving of the poor widow? Jesus seems to be encouraging his many poor disciples by reminding them that God values the sacrificial heart from which they give, not the amount they give. While their gifts may be small, they and their gifts are significant to God because they give sacrificially out of their poverty.

But Jesus probably intends to teach more than this. Again, his observation contains a criticism of the leaders of Israel for not taking care of the poor and for publically flaunting their religious practices. The leaders are responsible for showing the people how to practice mercy and justice toward the poor. Instead they resist the coming of God's just and compassionate kingdom, manifest in his Messiah.

A FOCUS ON THE TEMPLE IN JERUSALEM

The Temple Mount in Jerusalem at the time of Jesus occupied an area of thirty-five acres (approximately 30 soccer fields). The facade of the temple itself was covered with gold plates, and the upper part built with pure white marble, so that on a clear day the brilliance of the temple could be marveled at from far away as pilgrims approached the city. Its splendor was spoken of throughout the entire Roman Empire.

It was King Herod who had torn down the previous, less impressive temple built five hundred years earlier to replace it with his own magnificent temple in order to create a lasting legacy from his rule. He began building it about twenty years before Jesus was born (20/19 BC) and completed the basic structure in ten years. Yet artisans and laborers continued to adorn the temple throughout the life of Jesus, so that it was only finally completed about AD 66. Then it was destroyed four years later, just as Jesus had predicted.

Herod was a man of great ambition, with grand building projects. He doubled the area for the Temple Mount from the time of King Solomon and reshaped the topography of Jerusalem by filling in the valleys around the temple structure. It proved to be the most impressive religious structure in all the Roman Empire; but he heavily taxed the people in order to build it, and they resented him for this injustice.

The people of Israel would flock to the temple to offer sacrifices to God. But it also contained rooms where scribes studied the Scriptures, copied them, and instructed their students. The temple became a place for political and religious debate. It was here as a boy of twelve that Jesus amazed the religious scholars of Jerusalem with his wisdom and understanding of the Scriptures.

The people believed that God revealed his presence in a unique way in the temple, making it the meeting place between heaven and earth. They also saw it as a sign that God had chosen them to be a special people from among the nations, and that one day the nations of the world would stream to Jerusalem to worship at their temple. The size of the temple, its splendor, and the many hopes associated with it created in most Jewish people a supernatural awe, a reverence for their beliefs. Yet by the time of Jesus' ministry, many had become increasingly critical towards how worship was led under the supervision of the leaders of Israel.

Thus, when Jesus enters the temple area in the last week of his life to drive out those who are using it as a place of commerce, many of the people would sympathize with his actions. They hear him cry out that the temple is to be a place for prayer, not the den of robbers that Israel's leaders have made it (19:46). By driving out those doing business, Jesus engages in a prophetic act that signifies God's rejection of Israel's leaders for exploiting the people. The way they require the common people to pay taxes and tributes to the temple treasury is oppressive. Jesus declares that Israel's leaders are the true bandits of the day, not hiding out in caves in the wilderness outside of Jerusalem but operating in the temple itself, in the very center of Jerusalem.

God's judgment on Jerusalem and the corrupt temple enter-prise occurred just as the Prophet Jesus had predicted. In AD 70, Titus, the son of the emperor, approached Jerusalem with 20,000-foot soldiers and 500 cavalry to attack it from the north, its most vulnerable side. The temple itself was set on fire and all of its walls demolished, except for the western retaining wall, which still stands today and is now called the Wailing Wall by the Jewish people. Many of the large temple stones toppled by this attack can be seen near the Wailing Wall today.

Previously when God judged the people of Israel for their idolatry and disobedience by making them captives in a foreign land, he raised up prophets who promised that God would restore them to their own land. But God gives no such promise through the Prophet Jesus! God has manifested his presence through his chosen Servant Jesus the Messiah. Heaven and earth now meet in the Messiah, not at the temple in Jerusalem, from which God has judged and withdrawn his presence. In addition, the land of Palestine will no longer belong to Israel for rejecting God's Messiah as the way to peace. The people of God who embrace Jesus as the Messiah will come to include peoples from all the nations of the earth. And the Prophet Jesus promises them that they will inherit the earth and dwell in a new Jerusalem, not made by human hands.[113]

THE DESTRUCTION OF JERUSALEM AND JESUS' COMING AT THE END OF THE AGE (21:5–38)

As readers of the Gospel, we know Jesus the Messiah will soon be betrayed, suffer, and die according to the plan of God. We also know God will raise him from the dead after three days to show that he was indeed his Messiah. But no one in the Gospel understands this now, not even Jesus' twelve closest disciples. They too believe that Jesus will drive the

---

113.   Witherington III, *New Testament History*, 358–63; M. O. Wise, "Temple," in *Dictionary of Jesus and the Gospels*, 811–17; W. R. Herzog II, "Temple Cleansing," in *Dictionary of Jesus and the Gospels*, 817– 21; Porter, *Jesus Christ*, 110.

Romans from the land and reign from Jerusalem as God's appointed King over Israel. Thus the disciples must be baffled to now hear the Prophet Jesus predict the destruction of the temple and Jerusalem by their Roman enemies! Equally puzzling would be his statement that soon they will not see him until he comes as the Son of Man "in a cloud with power and great glory" (21:27). They do not expect him to leave, so why would he speak of coming back? Even though the disciples do not now understand all that Jesus is saying at this time, after he has risen from the dead they will understand and find encouragement from the words of his prophecy.

Jesus has earlier taught his disciples about his coming at the end of history to usher in God's kingdom in all its fullness (17:22–37). He now adds to his earlier teaching the signs that will precede his return, along with exhortations for his disciples to be prepared. This teaching is a response to comments made by some of his disciples about the splendor of the temple, where they have gathered to hear Jesus teach. Whereas earlier Jesus cleansed the temple as a sign of its coming destruction (19:45–46), he now speaks of it directly: "As for what you see here, the time will come when not one stone will be left on another; every one of them will be thrown down" (21:6).

Jesus predicts two separate events in this passage: first the destruction of Jerusalem and the temple by the Romans (vv. 8–24), and then his return at the end of history for the entire world to see (vv. 25–36). While the disciples ask when the temple will be destroyed and what the signs will be to show when it will happen, Jesus stresses their need to be alert and prepared for his coming. He replies, "Watch out that you are not deceived. For many will come in my name, claiming, 'I am he,' and, 'The time is near.' Do not follow them" (v. 8). False prophets and messianic pretenders have appeared before Jesus, and he knows that more will come after him—even when he exalted to be with God. In times of social upheaval, people will be easily deceived into believing strong and eloquent leaders who make great promises. The disciples must be alert. They must not to be fooled into following them.

In verses 12–17, Jesus warns his disciples that they too will suffer and be betrayed. They will suffer because of their allegiance to him as the Messiah. But God will use their sufferings to extend his just and righteous ways on earth. They will be bold and effective witnesses of the salvation that has come through Jesus when they are arrested and put on trial for their faith. Remarkably, Jesus promises that he himself will be with them in their time of trial, giving them boldness. He says, "I will give you words and wisdom that none of your adversaries will be able to resist or contradict" (v. 15). The Prophet Jesus knows that he will be alive in the presence of God and able to strengthen them.

Sadly, Jesus says that even members of the disciples' own families will betray them. But if they stand firm in their allegiance to him during such tragic times, they will gain eternal life in God's kingdom. Jesus says, "You will be betrayed even by your parents, brothers, relatives and friends, and they will put some of you to death. All men will hate you because of me. But not a hair of your head will perish. By standing firm you will gain life" (vv. 16–19).

When Jesus says the disciples will not lose a hair from their heads (v. 18), he does not mean they will not suffer and even be killed for their faith (John the Baptist lost his whole head for his faith in God!). Jesus means that no one can separate them from God's care or keep them from entering his kingdom.

Apparently many of the disciples will stay in Jerusalem after Jesus is raised to God's presence, for they will "see Jerusalem surrounded by armies" (v. 20). Jesus has earlier wept when speaking of the coming judgment of Israel. He knew the heart of God and spoke the heart of God when he said, "Jerusalem, Jerusalem, you who kill the prophets and stone those sent to you, how often I have longed to gather your children together, as a hen gathers her chicks under her wings, and you were not willing" (13:34). Israel will be judged for rejecting God's coming to the world through his Messiah with the message that brings peace.

The people of Israel, who mistreated and killed the prophets God previously sent to them, will also mistreat and kill his beloved Messiah Jesus. He has been sent to offer his life as the means of deliverance, forgiveness, and peace. But since Israel's leaders and most of the people will reject him, Jesus the Prophet predicts that their Roman oppressors will drive them out of the land of Palestine into exile among the Gentiles. Israel was previously driven into exile to Assyria and Babylon when they rejected the warnings of God's prophets. Sadly, Jesus predicts the same for his hearers—with no promise of return. The people will lose their capital (Jerusalem), their land (Palestine), and their temple for rejecting their Messiah.

After describing the signs and events related to the coming destruction of Jerusalem (21:8–24), Jesus then speaks of signs and events that will come upon the whole earth at the end of time (vv. 25–36). When Jesus speaks of "signs in the sun, moon, and stars" along with "the tossing of the sea" and the shaking of "heavenly bodies" (21:25–27), he is using language commonly employed to describe the future time when God will bring an end to history as we now know it, ushering in his kingdom of righteousness and peace over the whole world. The vivid imagery is not meant to be understood with absolute literalism but to teach that the whole world will see the coming of Jesus as the Son of Man to consummate God's eternal kingdom.

When God again sends his Messiah back to earth, all those who live on earth will see him as "the Son of Man coming in a cloud with power and great glory" (v. 27). We have seen in the Gospel how Jesus comes in humble obedience to God and how he suffers rejection and humiliation. He speaks God's word predominantly among the people of Israel, in a tiny corner of the earth, during a period of only a few years.

But when God sends him back again he will come as the mighty Ruler of an eternal kingdom over all the earth, for all the peoples of the earth to see. Jesus again claims that he will fulfill the words of the Prophet Daniel, who prophesied of "one like a Son of Man coming with the clouds of heaven" who is led into the presence of God and "given authority, glory and sovereign power" over all people (Daniel 7:13–14).

Because Jesus' prophecy about the destruction of Jerusalem was fulfilled some forty years later just as he predicted, we can be assured that what he said concerning his future coming to earth again with great power and glory will also be fulfilled. Jesus assures us that his "words will never pass away" (21:33).

When Jesus speaks of "this generation" not passing away until the events of verse 32 have happened, he is not referring to a specific time and people such as that generation of Jewish people. The word "generation" often connotes people in their opposition to God. Thus, Jesus teaches that evil will persist and evil people will continue to resist the way of God's kingdom until he returns at the end of the ages to separate good from evil and to create a world filled with love, peace, and justice.[114]

---

114.   Green, *Gospel of Luke*, 742.

In conclusion, while the disciples are more interested in the signs of future events, Jesus is more concerned with challenging them to stand firm and remain true to him in the midst of opposition and disappointments. He knows his return could be delayed (obviously, from today's standpoint, it has been) and they could easily become discouraged. A heavy heart can quickly turn to short-term comforts and release in loose living and drinking. So the disciples are challenged to be careful so that they don't give up and are not caught off guard by Jesus' return. He challenges them by saying, "Be always on the watch, and pray . . . that you may be able to stand before the Son of Man" (v. 36).

JESUS TEACHES HIS DISCIPLES AT THE PASSOVER MEAL (22:1–38)

A Disciple Agrees to Betray Jesus (22:1–6)

The leaders of Israel have wanted to kill or discredit Jesus since he entered Jerusalem a short time ago. When they could not kill Jesus because of the crowds who surround him, listening to him teach, they sent spies to trip him up with questions and discredit him before the people. None of this has worked. So we now read that they continued to look for some way to get rid of Jesus.

The leaders fear his growing popularity with the people as crowds flock to hear him teach in the temple each day. They are especially fearful now because one of the main Jewish festivals, the Passover, is approaching, with tens of thousands of Jewish pilgrims coming to Jerusalem from all over the Roman Empire to celebrate how God delivered his people from oppression in Egypt centuries earlier. Expectations, passions, and longings for deliverance will run high. Jesus has already created a great commotion by forcefully cleansing the temple, disrupting worship and sacrifices for an entire day. If tens of thousands of zealous pilgrims come to believe Jesus is the Messiah, Israel's King, they could cause a riot leading to war with the Romans. While we as readers know that Jesus will not use force to establish God's rule, we must once again remember that no one else knows this. The leaders "were afraid of the people" (22:2) because a riot would threaten the positions of power they hold through cooperation with the Roman authorities.

While the leaders of Israel have thus far been unable to silence Jesus, we now read with surprise and sadness that one of Jesus' closest companions, Judas, approaches them, suggesting a way to catch Jesus when he is alone apart from the crowds. Judas knows where Jesus spends his nights with the twelve disciples—on the hill called the Mount of Olives just across from the Temple Mount. There Judas will soon lead the chief priests and their guards to arrest Jesus (vv. 39–53).

We do not know exactly why Judas betrays Jesus. Money is involved, but more than money. It is hard to believe that Judas, as one of the twelve closest disciples who have always been with Jesus, does not see that God is with him. So many miracles. So much love. Yet it seems that Judas never fully opened his heart to God and to following Jesus whatever the cost. Is he fearful of the continued attempts to kill Jesus? If Jesus were killed, he as a close companion would also be killed. Perhaps he plans to return to the safety of Galilee to start over again with the money he receives from betraying Jesus?

When we read that "Satan entered Judas" (v. 3), we are not to think that Judas is not accountable for his actions. He gives into Satan's temptation to be disloyal to God and his Messiah. Jesus, on the other hand, remained loyal to God when tempted by Satan (4:1–13), and he exhorts his other disciples to pray so that they will not fall into temptation as Judas did (22:40,46).

Verse 3 also reminds us that Jesus has been sent to wage a war of cosmic proportions against the forces of evil. Satan has sought to derail Jesus from his mission from the very beginning, but he has failed. After failing, Satan "left him until an opportune time" (4:13). Throughout his ministry Jesus has rescued thousands of people from the evil, oppressive darkness of Satan. And Satan has fought back, primarily through the opposition of Israel's religious leaders.

The time has now come for Satan to launch a full-scale counterattack against Jesus by working through the hearts of the greedy, power-hungry leaders of Israel who live in Jerusalem. Satan works in Judas' heart and theirs. The common response of the people as they embrace the love and liberty that comes with the kingdom of God has been joy. In sad irony we read that the leaders "were delighted" (or rejoiced) in now finding a way to arrest Jesus and hopefully put him to death. They are confident of their ability to control Jesus—but they do not realize they are mere puppets in the hands of Satan, and God will outwit both them and the devil.

Jesus Explains the Meaning of his Death (22:7–20)

The Context of Jesus' Explanation

Jesus' betrayal by Judas reminds us that Jesus has journeyed to Jerusalem to die. Even though he has spoken of his death many times, his disciples do not seem to understand him. Therefore, it is not surprising that Jesus waits until the day before he dies to explain *why* he will die. It is doubtful they understand him even now, but later they will. Jesus knows he will die according to God's plan; his death will not be his defeat, his failure to accomplish his mission, but his glory in winning the victory of God. After God raises him from the dead, Jesus will more fully explain to his disciples what his death achieved.

If we assume, as the Gospel records, that the death of Jesus is central to why God sent him, then other references to why he was sent may illuminate what Jesus now teaches about his death. While Jesus now speaks more clearly about the meaning of his death, I suggest the Gospel has hinted at its meaning throughout. Thus, it may be especially helpful to recall some of the main reasons the Gospel gives for why God sent Jesus as his Messiah and to see how they may coincide with what we now learn.

- He will baptize with the Holy Spirit.
- He will provide salvation.
- He will release the oppressed.
- He must preach the good news of God's kingdom.
- He will call sinners to turn to God, pronouncing them forgiven.
- He will heal the sick and free those oppressed by evil spirits.
- He will restore the broken, sending them away with peace.
- His death will bring about a new exodus comparable to Israel's deliverance from oppression in Egypt.

These are the reasons God sends Jesus as his Messiah, and these statements summarize in large part what we see Jesus doing as he walks from village to village proclaiming the kingdom of God. I suggest that all of this and more are connected to Jesus' dying and then being raised from the dead by God. If the Messiah's death is the climax of his coming, the end of the path he has walked, all that came before should help explain its meaning. At the same time, the explanation Jesus now gives for the meaning of his death should correspond with all he has previously said and done. This is indeed the case.

All of the healings, all the deliverances from the demonic, and all the peacemaking and restoring to community are not only signs that Jesus is God's Messiah, but much more—they are signs of the great deliverance that he will bring about through his death. The death of Jesus the Messiah is the culmination of all he has previously said and done. The healings, battles, and deliverances from evil in the early part of the Gospel prefigure the great battle and deliverance that will take place at his death.

The power of evil in us and all around us is broken by the death of God's Messiah so that we can be freed to walk the path he walked. Because of Jesus' death, his disciples are liberated to continue his mission of rescuing and restoring the broken, to establish justice and peace, and to announce that we can be cleansed and forgiven.

The Gospel emphasizes the Passover as the time of Jesus' death (22:1,7,14). Jesus sends two of his disciples, Peter and John, into Jerusalem to make preparations for the traditional meal. The preparations "would have involved the purchase of an unblemished lamb and the other food necessary for the meal, the sacrifice of the lamb in the temple, roasting the lamb, and the arrangement of the room."[115]

We can assume that Jesus celebrated the Passover with his family as he grew up. Perhaps he went on occasions with his father to the temple in Jerusalem to purchase the sacrificial lamb and watch as the men took its life in preparation for the meal. Then as Jesus gathered with his family around the table for the meal, he would listen to his father explain the meaning of the Passover and why they had sacrificed a lamb.

When God delivered the people of Israel from their oppression and slavery in the land of Egypt, he commanded each Israelite family to sacrifice an unblemished lamb and apply its blood to the doorposts of their houses so that their firstborn would be spared (Exodus 12:1–14). Because the people of Israel obeyed God in this, they were spared from judgment (Exodus 12). Their homes were "passed over" by the angels God sent to judge the Egyptians. But the Passover meal was not only a celebration remembering God's great mercy and power in delivering the Israelites; it

---

115.   Ibid., 755.

had also become a time to look forward to God once again rescuing his people from oppression through his Messiah.

The Explanation of Jesus' Death

This background enables us to better understand why Jesus now says that he will pour out his body in death for the sake of the disciples (22:19). He, as the Messiah, will be God's Passover Lamb—that is why he must die. Jesus—God's holy Servant, God's powerful Prophet, God's Messiah—is sent to die! He must die for us; neither the sacrifice of a lamb nor any other deed done by man can cleanse and deliver us from sin.

So instead of retelling the story of Israel's deliverance from Egypt centuries ago, as the Jewish people have done at every Passover celebration, Jesus tells his own story. Israel's story has become his story. Jesus makes his death the climax and fulfillment of the story of Israel's deliverance from bondage and oppression in Egypt. By his great power and mercy God will bring about a new deliverance—a deliverance far more powerful, so much further reaching, than the deliverance from Pharaoh and the Egyptians. God will deliver mankind from the enslaving, dehumanizing power of Satan and from our own twisted, broken hearts. Through his death the Messiah will deliver us from the forces of evil at work within us, in our homes, and in the structures of society.

It is important to point out once again that Jesus willingly suffers and dies in obedience to God. His death will not take him by surprise or be his defeat. He knows his death will bring about the victory God, planned by God and achieved by him, the Messiah.

We must also note that Jesus rejects the use of violence in bringing about God's rule on earth. He is prepared to pour out his own blood rather than take the blood of his enemies. Instead of inflicting violence on them, he allows them to inflict violence on him.[116] He is the Prophet of Peace, the Prince of Peace, who conquers his enemies by love; who through loving them makes them his friends; who brings peace by pouring out his life for the good of those who hate him.

The kingdom of God is a kingdom of peace. If God were to establish his kingdom by violence it would not be his kingdom. It would be like the kingdoms of this world. Why would the Romans, the Greeks,

---

116.   Gorman, *Death of the Messiah*, 180.

the Persians, the Arabs, or any other great people love and submit to the God of Jesus if Jesus his Messiah subdued them by violence?

Speaking of his approaching death, Jesus says to his disciples, "This is my body given for you" (v. 19). At the time, the language of giving one's body (which Jesus would do in dying) was a forceful image used "for giving one's life (in battle) for the sake of one's people."[117] Thus, part of the meaning of Jesus' statement is that there will be war and violence when the Messiah dies. He will allow himself to be brutally killed, and in this way wage war against Satan and sin. In ways we do not fully understand, by dying for us he releases us from the oppression of sin and Satan so that we can live in freedom and experience God's love and peace.

Up until now Jesus has taught that his death will fulfill the meaning of the Passover by bringing about a deliverance from the oppression of sin and the forces of evil. But now he says that by pouring out his life in death he will bring about a new way of relating to God, which he calls a new covenant. Referring to his blood that will soon be shed, Jesus says, "This cup is the new covenant in my blood, which is poured out for you" (v. 20)."

God originally made a covenant with his people so that they could relate to him and belong to him in a unique way among the peoples of the earth. When that covenant was renewed at the time of Moses, it was secured by the sacrifice of young bulls. After the sacrifice Moses said to the people, "This is the blood of the covenant that the Lord has made with you in accordance with all these words" (Exodus 24:8). Jesus has these words in mind when he says his blood will be poured out to secure a new covenant with God.

The promise of God to make a new covenant with those who love and obey him was foretold by the prophets. One of the prophets described the new covenant in the following way. God said, "I will cleanse you from all your impurities and from all your idols. I will give you a new heart and put a new spirit in you; I will remove from you your heart of stone and give you a heart of flesh. And I will put my Spirit in you and move you to follow my decrees and to be careful to keep my laws" (Ezekiel 36:25–27).

The Prophet Jeremiah described the new covenant in a similar way: "'This is the covenant I will make with the house of Israel after that time,'

---

117.   Green, *Gospel of Luke*, 761.

declares the Lord. 'I will put my law in their minds and write it on their hearts. I will be their God, and they will be my people. No longer will a man teach his neighbor, or a man his brother, saying, "Know the Lord," because they will all know me, from the least of them to the greatest, for I will forgive their wickedness and will remember their sins no more'" (Jeremiah 31:33–34).

From these and other prophecies we learn that when God brings into effect the new covenant with his people,

- they will be completely cleansed and forgiven of all their shame and misdeeds;
- they will experience liberation, a new exodus from oppression and slavery;
- they will live in unity as one people;
- they will experience *shalom*, peace with God, peace with their enemies, and life in its fullness as God always intended it to be;
- they will know God in a personal, intimate relationship of mutual love; and
- they will be given God's Spirit so that they have power and delight in obeying God from their hearts.

We have read throughout the Gospel how most of these promises have partly begun to come true in the ministry of Jesus. At times he tells people that their sins are forgiven, frees people from disease and demons, and after healing them, tells them to go in peace. These are signs of the new covenant. Yet we continue to read of selfishness, pride, strife and division even among Jesus' closest disciples. How do we explain this lack of a "new covenant life" in the midst of his own followers?

Part of the explanation is that the promises of the new covenant will not be established until Jesus dies, and he has not yet died. The disciples' continued preoccupation with power and prestige will not be conquered until his death for them. However, equally important is the fact that Jesus has not yet poured out God's Spirit on his disciples as John the Baptist and, long before him, the Prophet Ezekiel prophesied (Luke 3:16; Ezekiel 36:27). After God raises Jesus his Messiah to his right hand in heaven, he will give his Spirit to Jesus to pour out on the disciples (Acts 2:33). Then they will finally begin to live as obedient people of peace, striving after unity and enjoying the favor of all the people (Acts 2:42–47).

By way of summary, Jesus the Messiah has made the bold claim that by his death his disciples will be able to participate in all of the promises of the new covenant. In a way we cannot fully understand, his death *for us* defeats sin *over us* and *in us* so that we are freed to experience the presence, power, and peace of God. To reduce the purpose of the Messiah's death to just one of the blessings of the new covenant—such as the forgiveness of sins, as great a blessing as that is—is to miss out on the fullness of life that God has planned for us, and to minimize the meaning of the Messiah's sufferings and death for us. It is to live weakly in a world that so needs to see a people who live like Jesus.

Jesus Continues to Prepare His Disciples for Their Mission (22:21–38)

The presence of Judas, who will betray Jesus and thus seek to save his life, stands in stark contrast to Jesus, who will selflessly pour out his life in death for others (22:21–23). Jesus says, "The Son of Man will go as it has been decreed, but woe to that man who betrays him" (v. 22). It is part of God's plan that Jesus will die as his Messiah, but Judas is still responsible for the betrayal. This is an example of the mysterious relationship between God's sovereign authority over humanity and humanity's choices for their actions.

At the Passover meal the other disciples again begin to argue among themselves over which of them is the greatest (vv. 24–27). This is so hard to read! They too stand in stark contrast to their Teacher, who models selfless service for others. Jesus' teaching about the kind of life that characterizes the kingdom of God has not yet penetrated their passion for power and greatness.

How can the disciples be so insensitive to Jesus and so blind to the way he lives and the way he teaches them to live? He has once again told them he will die, and this time he explains why. Yet they seem to ignore what he has said—and abruptly change the subject to which of them should have the highest position of honor in God's kingdom!

This isn't the first time the disciples have argued about positions of greatness, and it is at least the seventh time Jesus has taught them that humility and selfless service are the high marks of following him. It is both remarkable and sad that the disciples show so little progress in patterning their lives according to Jesus' teaching and example. As stated above, the disciples will only fully begin to emulate the life of Jesus after his death, resurrection and the giving of the Spirit.

And yet, as on previous occasions, Jesus responds to his disciples' immaturity with patience. He teaches them his way once again: The leaders of the world like to lord it over others, be in charge, and get to the top—"but you are not to be like that" (v. 26). As one interpreter says, "To pursue honor at the expense of others, or in any way to dominate them in a quest for personal power," is to act like those who do not know God.[118]

Instead, the disciples are to pattern their lives after Jesus' life of service. He teaches them, "The greatest among you should be like the youngest, and the one who rules like the one who serves. For who is greater, the one who is at the table or the one who serves? Is it not the one who is at the table? But I am among you as one who serves" (vv. 26–27).

Jesus again practices what he teaches. While he is the Master and Teacher of the disciples, the one who sits at the table and who should be served by his disciples, he demonstrates true greatness by getting up from the table to serve them instead (v. 27). This is the kind of leader he is. He is the self-giving Servant, the best example of how God wants us to live and lead others by pouring out his life for the good of others. This outpouring reaches its climax, showing the greatest act of servanthood, when Jesus allows himself to be crucified.

This is the way of God's kingdom that his disciples have still not embraced. They must learn to embrace him as the Suffering Servant of God, as the Messiah who humbles himself in death for others. And they must learn to make his life their life. To not do so is to disbelieve who he is and instead believe in a Messiah of their own choosing. To chase after positions and power is to betray him, as Judas will soon do; to minimize the way of the cross is to deny him, as Peter and the other disciples will soon do. But in God's mercy, Peter and the other disciples will return to Jesus and learn his ways.

It is important to note that Jesus does not negate strength in leadership. Nor does he deny our desire for significance, to make an impact on the world. But he redirects our desire for greatness and redefines how it is achieved. Acting out of strength, the disciples are to choose to be like servants in a household, who do the most menial tasks. Their ambition

---

118.   Gorman, *Death of the Messiah*, 116.

for greatness can be fulfilled in becoming the servants of all. In a society where children and servants occupy the lowest status, lacking power and honor, Jesus calls his disciples to lower themselves and serve others in hidden and seemingly insignificant ways.[119]

Jesus then says to the disciples, "You are those who have stood by me in my trials. And I confer on you a kingdom, just as my Father conferred one on me" (v. 29). If the disciples have not yet understood and committed themselves to the way of Jesus, the way of humble service, how can he confer on them a kingdom? How can he promise that they will share in his rule over it? It is because they have stood by Jesus in his trials. While they still struggle to understand and practice the true meaning of discipleship, of true greatness, they have remained loyal to Jesus when others have turned away. Faith is a commitment, not perfect obedience.

But how can Jesus grant the disciples a kingdom when the kingdom is God's and God's alone? While the kingdom is God's, he has granted his Messiah the authority to rule over it, so Jesus has authority to let his faithful followers share in his rule. It is important to note that Jesus does not confer on the disciples a kingdom separate from God's. God is one and his kingdom is one. The awesome reality is that the disciples are given the right to participate in *God's* kingdom.

Jesus has earlier said to all of his disciples, "Do not be afraid, little flock, for your Father has been pleased to give you the kingdom" (12:32). Thus, what Jesus now says to his closest disciples is true for all of them. All of them are granted two privileges: First, they will eat and drink with Jesus at his table in God's kingdom (22:30). The image of sharing a meal with Jesus—which we have seen throughout the Gospel—suggests the disciples' joy, the overflow of love, life, and peace in their hearts from being near Jesus, their King. Second, the disciples are given a share in ruling over God's kingdom. Not only has Jesus said this outright, but the image of them sitting on thrones reinforces his promise. One way they will exercise their rule will be by "judging the twelve tribes of Israel." Ironically, the disciples will become the new leaders of God's true people and will judge the very leaders of Israel who now judge Jesus and seek to have him sentenced to death. It is also ironic that they are promised positions of greatness in the kingdom when Jesus has just rebuked them for

---

119.   Tannehill, *Luke*, 317.

seeking their own greatness! But he knows that they will change and learn to suffer and serve as he has.

Although the disciples will join Jesus in his future kingdom, the way there will not be easy for them (vv. 31–34). Just as Jesus battled against the temptations of Satan, so must they. Satan has succeeded in getting Judas to betray Jesus, so he now seeks to shake the faith of the remaining eleven disciples. He does not yet know that Jesus' death will cause his defeat, so he still believes he can stop the growth of God's power and love in the world by tempting the other disciples to deny Jesus. Satan believes that when Jesus' closest companions deny him and scatter, and when Jesus is put to death, the rest of those who have followed Jesus to Jerusalem will also give up and go back to Galilee.

While Peter (originally called Simon) is the focus of the spiritual battle, "you" in verse 31 is plural in the Greek text, indicating that all the disciples are the targets of Satan's attack. As wheat is violently shaken to separate it from the chaff, so Satan will seek to shake the faith of the disciples to separate them from Jesus. Satan will attack the disciples, but Jesus will pray for them—and his prayers will prevail! For the disciples will return to Jesus all the stronger after their failure and strengthen those who also waver in their faith.

At the end of the meal Jesus gives his disciples new instructions for how they are to carry out their mission. In light of his rejection by the leaders of Israel and subsequent death, the circumstances in which they conduct their mission will change. Instead of hospitality they will meet increased hostility. Previously when they had traveled with Jesus, many of the people believed he was a great prophet sent to liberate them from the Romans and establish a kingdom centered in Jerusalem. Instead, their leaders will reject him and put him to death as a false prophet, a false messiah. Why would the people welcome to their villages the disciples of a man who died the shameful death of a common criminal?

Previously the disciples did not need to take provisions with them, for almost everyone welcomed them into their villages. But after Jesus death' they may face a hostile, even violent reception. So now they need to take food and extra clothing along to sleep out in the cold if necessary. Jesus also tells his disciples, "if you don't have a sword, sell your cloak and buy one" (22:36). This is hard to understand in light of Jesus' teaching that the kingdom of God is not advanced by force, by warring against the Roman occupiers, but by the power of love and forgiveness. Why then does Jesus now tell his disciples to purchase swords?

It is suggested that Jesus uses strong, figurative language in order to alert his disciples to the harsh, violent times they will now face. Jesus is not abrogating his extensive and emphatic teaching that loving one's enemies is the way to achieve peace (e.g., 6:35). But the disciples point to two literal swords in their possession. (Perhaps in light of the increased sense of danger in Jerusalem, several of the disciples-unknowns to Jesus—had recently procured two swords.) To this Jesus replies as an expression of exasperation,[120] "That is enough." He means something like, "That is enough of this conversation. Do you think I would want you to literally purchase swords"?[121]

In conclusion, it is interesting that though Jesus knows he will die, he also knows his disciples will continue the mission after his death! Because he knows that his death will be the victory of God and that God will raise him from the dead, he continues with great confidence and intentionality to prepare his disciples for their mission after his resurrection.

JESUS IS ARRESTED AND PUT ON TRIAL (22:39–23:25)

Jesus Prays as He Anticipates His Imminent Sufferings (22:39–46)

Jesus again passes through the gates of Jerusalem to spend the night with his disciples on the Mount of Olives, just across from the Temple Mount. It will not be a restful night for Jesus, for he knows the intense suffering he is about to face. How will he respond now that his most severe torment is upon him? Will he continue to submit to God? Knowing all that will happen, what does Jesus do? He prays!

Just before Jesus began his mission—to rescue and restore broken, bound, and weary souls—Satan sought to derail him from obeying God. Satan now launches a final, full-scale attack on Jesus and the remaining eleven disciples. Satan tempts them to deny Jesus just as Judas did. This

---

120.   Green, *Gospel of Luke*, 775.
121.   Marshall, *The Gospel of Luke*, 827.

will be an hour "when darkness reigns," says Jesus. So he challenges the disciples, "Pray that you will not fall into temptation" (22:40). But the disciples, "exhausted from sorrow" (v. 45), sleep rather than pray.

Apparently the disciples have finally understood that Jesus will in fact die. They now realize that he was not speaking in riddles when he spoke to them of his betrayal, sufferings, and death. Now the disciples are overwhelmed with fear and uncertainty. Questions flood their minds. If Jesus is put to death, how could he be the Messiah? And what will happen to them—what about their dreams of sharing in his glorious kingdom in Jerusalem? Which one of them will betray Jesus? How could any of them betray the one who has shown them so much love? And how could Peter deny Jesus?

All these questions and more have left the disciples mentally exhausted, so it is understandable that they sleep instead of pray. But because they sleep, they will not be prepared when Jesus is arrested and led away by the leaders of Israel.

While the disciples fail to meet their time of trial with prayer, Jesus does. Three times we read that he prays. He struggles so profoundly in prayer that his sweat looks like blood falling to the ground.[122] Why is Jesus, God's Righteous Warrior, in such anguish? Why does he feel so weak? Because he dreads "the cup" (v. 42) that will be poured out over him in death, he prays, "Father, if you are willing, take this cup from me; yet not my will, but yours be done." The cup symbolizes God's just judgment for the sins of the world that will be poured out on Jesus as he dies. What Jesus dreads is not so much the physical pain done to his body as the cosmic assault from sin and Satan that he must submit to in death.

Jesus will not die as one more zealous Jew fighting to liberate Israel from their enemies. Never before has anyone died as he will die; never will anyone die in this way again. In ways we cannot fully comprehend, Jesus' death as Messiah will be God's way of delivering us from the forces of darkness. The torment and anguish he will experience in death will go far beyond his physical and emotional suffering. No one will ever know what Jesus suffered but Jesus.

But we do know why he chooses to embrace his suffering. It is because of his love and loyalty to God, whom he knows intimately as Father. His

---

122. Green, *Gospel of Luke*, 780.

love for God, his resolve to fulfill God's will, leads him to pray, "Not my will, but yours be done" (v. 42). Although Jesus demonstrates resolve in obeying God, he dreads the nature of his death and wishes there were some other way for God to defeat the forces of evil and the tyranny of sin. But there isn't. Knowing this, Jesus continues to labor in prayer, asking God to strengthen him. God cannot remove the cup of suffering from Jesus—Jesus knows that; but God will strengthen and comfort his Servant in his sufferings. So God sends an angel from his very presence to strengthen Jesus in his anguish. We do not know how the angel strengthens Jesus, but we read that Jesus "rose from prayer" (v. 45) stronger, ready to face his sufferings as God's Servant-Warrior. He has cast himself in humble dependence on God and is now determined to meet the forces of darkness that approach him. He has prayed and thus remained strong and obedient to the very end. Jesus shows us that "the way to remain triumphant (measured as persistent obedience to the divine will) in the time of trial is through persistent, earnest, submissive prayer."[123]

A FOCUS ON JESUS THE SERVANT OF GOD

The prophets often referred to the people of Israel collectively as God's servant. They challenged Israel to obey the Lord and to teach the nations to obey him as the One True God. But time and time again the people of Israel failed to fulfill their calling; they worshipped idols from the nations around them instead of showing the nations the way to life in the One True God. Thus, in time God promised through the prophets to raise up a Servant who would do what the nation of Israel had failed to do.

In the Gospel we see that Jesus is conscious of being not only the Messiah but also God's chosen Servant with a unique task to fulfill. As God's Servant, Jesus submits to God perfectly. By his humble obedience he fulfills the mission God gave to Israel—namely, to be a light to the nations of the world. Thus Jesus believed the prophet Isaiah spoke of him when he said:

And now the Lord says—
he who formed me in the womb to be his servant,

123.   Green, *Gospel of Luke*, 778.

to bring Jacob back to him
and gather Israel to himself,
for I am honored in the eyes of the Lord

and my God has been my strength—
he says:

"It is too small a thing for you to be my servant
to restore the tribes of Jacob
and bring back those of Israel I have kept.
I will also make you a light for the Gentiles,
that you may bring my salvation
to the ends of the earth." (Isaiah 49:5–6)

In another place the Prophet Isaiah says of the sufferings and death of God's Servant,

He was despised and rejected by men,
a man of sorrows, and familiar with suffering. . . .
But he was pierced for our transgressions,
he was crushed for our iniquities;
the punishment that brought us peace was upon him,
and by his wounds we are healed. . . .
After the suffering of his soul,
he will see the light of life and be satisfied;
by his knowledge my righteous servant
will justify many,
and he will bear their iniquities. (Isaiah 53:3,5,11)

But God promised his Servant would be raised to life and exalted after his sufferings. "See, my servant will act wisely; he will be raised and lifted up and highly exalted" (Isaiah 52:13).

Jesus knows he is chosen by God to fulfill the task of the Suffering Servant. He knows that his obedience to God entails rejection, suffering, and death—but after that, resurrection and exaltation to God's right hand.

When God speaks from heaven at Jesus' baptism, saying that he delights in his Servant Jesus and will give him his Spirit to accomplish the mission, it echoes another prophecy from Isaiah:

> Here is my servant, whom I uphold,
> my chosen one in whom I delight;
>
> I will put my Spirit on him,
> and he will bring justice to the nations.
> (Isaiah 42:1)

Jesus received God's Spirit at his baptism and heard God's voice from heaven saying, "You are my Son, whom I love; with you I am well pleased" (Luke 3:22). He knows that God has a special love for him as his beloved Messiah, but he also knows that he must suffer as God's Servant before God exalted him. Jesus understands what has to happen, because the role of God's suffering Servant is interwoven with his mission as the Messiah. And Jesus never acts on his own initiative, but always in submission to the will of God revealed for him through the prophets.

But it is not until after God raises Jesus from the dead that the disciples understand that he, as the Messiah, has fulfilled God's will by becoming the Suffering Servant. In their sermons and prayers after his resurrection, they speak of Jesus as God's Servant. After God exalts his Servant Jesus to his presence in heaven, Peter preaches to a crowd in Jerusalem and says that the God of Abraham has "glorified his servant Jesus" (Acts 3:13). And later in the same sermon Peter preaches that God has sent "his servant" Jesus first to the Jews, teaching them to turn from their wicked ways (Acts 3:26). Later still, all the disciples speak of how the rulers of Jerusalem conspired against God's "holy servant Jesus," whom he anointed with his Spirit. They then pray that God would continue to do miracles among them through his "holy servant Jesus" (Acts 4:27,30). Exalted as Lord to the presence of God, King Jesus nonetheless remains the Servant of God. His beauty is seen in his humble submission.[124]

---

124.   R. T. France, "Servant of Yahweh," in *Dictionary of Jesus and the Gospels*, 744–47.

The Leaders of Israel Arrest Jesus (22:47–53)

With tens of thousands of pilgrims in Jerusalem for the Feast of the Passover, it is easy for Jesus to mix into the crowd at the temple and leave Jerusalem undetected to the Mount of Olives each night. But now the leaders in Jerusalem have Judas, an informant from among the twelve disciples, who can easily lead them to the place where Jesus sleeps. Because the crowd will not be there surrounding Jesus, it will be easy to arrest him without causing a commotion—provided his disciples don't put up a fight.

As Jesus speaks to the disciples about the urgency of praying, Judas leads the hostile parties to Jesus. Unknowingly, the leaders of Israel have become agents of Satan, unleashing the powers of darkness upon Jesus, God's Messiah (22:53). It is tragic to read that Judas is now called simply "the man," no longer a disciple. It is even sadder to read that he is leading the crowd. The one Jesus led in the way of love, light, and peace now betrays Jesus and leads to him the very people who want to kill him. In the darkness Judas spots Jesus from among the disciples, and he approaches Jesus to greet him with a kiss, thus identifying him for the leaders of Israel who come to arrest him.

"When rebel leaders were rounded up, their associates were frequently captured, tortured and killed along with them."[125] As far as Judas knows, his eleven companions will be brutalized and killed along with Jesus. It is hard to understand how Judas could have developed such a cruel, cowardly, deceptive heart that he would betray his friends and, above all, the one he has followed as his Master. He betrays Jesus with a kiss, the customary way of greeting a friend in the Near East.

Jesus shows himself to be the true leader, the man with spiritual power, even when he is arrested in the middle of the night. He has risen from wrestling in prayer: he is strong, composed, and bold to face his enemies. Except for the brief question from the disciples about using their swords (v. 49), no one but Jesus speaks during his arrest.[126] And he speaks with spiritual authority—simultaneously challenging Judas, the other eleven disciples, and the leaders of Israel who come to arrest him in the secrecy of the night.

---

125. Wright, *Luke for Everyone*, 269.
126. Green, *Gospel of Luke*, 782.

Because the disciples have not been diligent in prayer but instead slept, they respond impulsively and ignorantly in this time of trial. Still groggy from their sleep, they look up in the darkness to see their companion Judas leading the very men who have sought to kill Jesus straight to him. Forgetting all that Jesus has taught them about responding with love to one's enemies, forgetting his repeated statement that he will be rejected and suffer at the hands of Israel's leaders, the disciples ask Jesus if they should resist the arresting soldiers with the two swords they still have in their possession (v. 38).

One of the disciples doesn't wait for an answer and strikes the servant of the high priest with a sword. But apparently he misses the servant's head and manages to only cut off his ear. At this Jesus yells out, "No more of this!" No more violence! Violence only breeds more violence. He then heals the ear of the man, an enemy, to once again model for his disciples the way of the kingdom of God: love for one's enemies to break the endless, senseless cycle of vengeance and violence in the world.

Jesus then turns to speak directly to the leaders of Israel, who have come to capture him with swords and clubs in the middle of the night. He asks, "Am I leading a rebellion, that you have come with swords and clubs? Every day I was with you in the temple courts, and you did not lay a hand on me. But this is your hour—when darkness reigns" (vv. 52–53). They have heard him speak in the temple of the power of love and the way of peace. They know he is not a violent man leading a rebellion with soldiers and swords to force the kingdom of God upon others. For such a kingdom would not be God's kingdom; such a kingdom would not bring peace.

Jesus stands face to face with his enemies, boldly challenging them. He knows God's heart. He knows God's will. And because he knows that the will of God for him is to defeat sin and death by submitting to death, he will allow himself to be taken. "This is your hour—when darkness reigns" (v. 53)—for a brief time, a time decreed by God, God has allowed the leaders to seize his Servant and cause him to suffer. As one commentator writes, "From this point on, Satan as well as Jesus' enemies appear to hold Jesus in their power."[127] But it is only an appearance. In reality God is in control, attacking and defeating sin and the forces of evil through the sufferings and death of his Servant. Satan and the Jewish leaders don't

---

127.   Tannehill, *Luke*, 326.

understand this. They will delight in Jesus' death only to later discover that God in his great power and wisdom has outwitted them.

Peter Disowns Jesus (22:54–65)

Jesus has stood face to face with the leaders of Israel and their soldiers, challenging them. Now he allows himself to be seized and led away. From now on we will read of Jesus being led about from place to place like a criminal (22:66; 23:1), mocked as if he were nothing more than a false prophet with the delusion of being God's Messiah.

But we know that Jesus allows all this because he is submitting to God's will for him. Even in this story, when Jesus is held captive at the high priest's house, his status as God's Prophet is highlighted.[128] Everything he predicted about Peter's denial comes to pass exactly as he said it would. And when the soldiers guarding him beat and mock him, demanding that he prophesy for them, they only fulfill what he already predicted—for he prophesied of himself that he would be mocked, insulted, spit on, flogged, and killed (18:32).

When Jesus is arrested, ten of the disciples flee for their lives into the night. We will not read of them again until we learn that they stand at a distance watching as Jesus dies (23:49). But one of the disciples, Peter, does not flee. He promised Jesus he would go to prison with him—even die with him if it came down to that (22:33). So Peter cautiously follows Jesus at a distance as the soldiers lead him through the darkness of the night, the darkness of the time, down the Mount of Olives and up to the palace of the high priest near the temple. While Peter is courageous in following Jesus (after all, he tried to cut off the head of the high priest's servant with a sword!), he is not as strong as he imagines. Three times in the coming hours Peter will deny any connection with Jesus.

As Jesus sits bound by a fire in the high priest's courtyard in the cold of the night, Peter joins them. But he sits too close to the fire. When the flames flash his way, a servant girl recognizes him as one of Jesus' disciples—"This man was with him," the girl says, but Peter denies it. "Woman, I don't know him," he responds (22:57). Peter then denies knowing Jesus two more times in quick succession, fulfilling Jesus' prediction.

---

128.   Green, *Gospel of Luke*, 786.

Jesus earlier taught Peter to fear God alone, and not to fear those who can kill the body but not the soul (12:4,5). Jesus challenged Peter and the other disciples not to cave in to fear and deny him as God's Messiah when they are dragged before hostile rulers to be questioned, but instead, gripped by fear and panic, Peter denies knowing Jesus. His desertion during Jesus' time of trial shows us how weak we can be in ourselves. But Peter will be restored. His transformation into a bold, respected leader among the disciples shows us the patient understanding and mercy of God.

At the very moment Peter denies Jesus for the third time we read, "The Lord turned and looked straight at him" (22:61). When Peter sees the expression on Jesus' face he remembers the words of Jesus—and runs out into the darkness weeping bitterly. What does Peter see in the face of Jesus? I believe he sees understanding and love. And this is why he weeps. But the tears of contrition are the beginning of the way back. That too Jesus has predicted!

Jesus is now left all alone in his time of great trial. The guards begin to mock and beat him. The rulers of Israel are meant to lead the people in welcoming God's Messiah, but instead they allow their guards to abuse him. Blindfolding and hitting Jesus, the guards play a cruel game, demanding that he prophesy which one of them struck him. But Jesus will not play their game. He could destroy them with a word, but he knows the time has come for him to enter into his sufferings for the world—for these very men who beat him.

The Trial of Jesus

The leaders of Israel will have to twist the truth and make Jesus look like an enemy of the Empire to get him sentenced to death by the Romans. The trial of Jesus contains four scenes. First he is led before the entire council of Israel, who succeed in getting him to openly confess that he believes he is the Messiah (22:66–71). This is all they need to hear to drag him before the Roman governor, Pilate, so that he can be tried for treason (23:1–5). When Pilate finds no legal basis for sentencing Jesus to death and learns that he is from Galilee, he sends him to Herod, who governs Galilee. Herod earlier sought to kill Jesus, and he happens to be at his palace in Jerusalem at the time (23:8–12). When Herod also finds Jesus innocent of any crime, he sends him back to Pilate, who finally gives in to the frenzied shouts of the crowd to have Jesus crucified (23:13–25).

Scene One: Jesus before the High
Council of Israel (22:66–71)

At daybreak Jesus is led from the high priest's courtyard into his palace, where the council of Israel's leaders has gathered. The Council's goal will be to get Jesus to say with his very own lips that he believes he is Israel's Messiah. (As we have already seen, while Jesus knows he is God's chosen Messiah, he has avoided using this title because of the political expectations it conjures up for the people.) Since the Messiah is supposed to be sent by God to rule over his kingdom as King, if the Council can get Jesus to openly say he believes he is God's promised Messiah, they can use this as the basis for turning him over to the Romans for sedition. The Roman authorities will not tolerate another king who challenges their authority.

Several prominent titles are used for Jesus as the leaders interrogate him and accuse him before Pilate. Jesus is referred to as the Christ (i.e., the Messiah), the Son of Man, the Son of God, and a king, or "the king of the Jews." It is important to follow the dialogue in the trial of Jesus closely in order to understand the meaning and significance of each title. This will reinforce what we have earlier learned about the meaning of these titles.

As the leaders of Israel interrogate Jesus, they demand, "If you are the Christ, tell us" (22:67). Jesus stands before the Council bound and beaten, but his spirit is strong because he has prayed, and God is with him. So as he faces his accusers, he answers them boldly. He does not answer their initial question directly because he knows they do not sincerely seek the truth. They would not submit to his way of the kingdom of God or to him as the true Messiah. So he boldly declares, "From now on, the Son of Man will be seated at the right hand of the mighty God" (v. 69). Jesus identifies himself as the Son of Man from Daniel's prophecy who will soon be exalted to the place of highest authority and honor in heaven.

The leaders know the prophecy in Daniel (Daniel 7:13). They understand that because the Son of Man is given an eternal kingdom to rule over, and because Jesus is calling himself by that name, he is making a direct claim to be the Messiah. And since the Messiah is also called the Son of God, a title equivalent in meaning, they now ask Jesus, "Are you then the Son of God?" By this they mean, "So you say you are the Messiah?" To this question Jesus now gives a direct answer: "You say that I am" (22:70).

The leaders of Israel have heard from Jesus' own lips the answer to their original question in verse 67—Is he the Christ? This is all they need to have Jesus put to death. They will lead Jesus before Pilate and then Herod, pressing for his execution because he "claims to be Christ, a king" and—so they claim—will incite a rebellion that threatens the peace and stability of the Roman Empire (23:2,14).

While Jesus' claim to be the Messiah makes the leaders fearful of losing their power, it is his claim to be the Son of Man that enrages them, so it is worth revisiting to find out why. Jesus has often told his disciples that as the Son of Man he will suffer and be killed, but then be raised from the dead and sent back to earth again in great glory. But the claim he makes to the leaders of Israel is even more dramatic. "Jesus in effect is claiming the right to go directly into God's presence and be seated with him in heaven."[129] In other words, Jesus not only claims to be God's Messiah, who will reign as his King on earth; he claims he will be exalted to the very presence of God to share in his power, glory, and authority!

Why does this enrage the leaders? While the people of Israel believe that God inhabits the highest heavens, they also believe that he manifests his presence in the innermost part of the temple, called the holy of holies. Because this is the most holy place that exists, the meeting place of heaven and earth, no one but the high priest is permitted to enter it—and him only once a year, on the Day of Passover, to offer a sacrifice for the sin of the people.

If Jesus, a man from Galilee and not even a priest, much less the high priest, had sought to enter the holy of holies while he was teaching in the temple, he would have been mobbed, charged with defiling God's holy place, and most likely killed in a riot. But now Jesus, this so-called prophet from Galilee, this messianic pretender, makes the astonishing claim that the mighty God will honor him and exalt him to his very presence in heaven! This is blasphemy and cannot be tolerated.

To the leaders of Israel, Jesus is not only speaking blasphemy but also challenging the very institutions of their religion—the temple, the teaching of the law for sacrifices, and the priestly order. Jesus stands before the high priest and the combined political and religious authority of all of Israel, and in effect says to them, "*I* am the one whom God has chosen

---

129.   Bock, *Luke*, 578.

to enter his presence to cleanse the people of their sins. My body will be sacrificed to remove the sins of the world; the sacrifice of an animal by the high priest could never fully and forever remove sin. And after this I will be exalted to God's right hand to share in his power and authority."

While the leaders are enraged by Jesus' claims, they are satisfied that they have now managed to get him to openly say he is the Messiah. This is all they need to lead him before Pilate and have him charged with sedition, and put to death.

Scene Two: Jesus before Pilate (23:1–7)

While the leaders in Jerusalem do not for one second believe Jesus is God's Messiah, they have now succeeded in getting him to publically say so. So they now lead Jesus a short walk up the hill from the high priest's palace to Pilate's. When they arrive they tell Pilate, "We have found this man subverting our nation. He opposes payment of taxes to Caesar and claims to be Christ, a king" (23:2).

It is true that Jesus has challenged the way the leaders of Israel and the leaders of the world rule over their people. It is true that he has exposed their corruption and injustices, subverting their proud, hierarchical, wealth-grabbing ways by modeling and proclaiming the way of God's kingdom—the way of mercy, justice, and humility. And it is true that Jesus has now openly claimed to be the Messiah, a king. But it is not true that he is a man of violence, openly inciting the people to take up arms to overthrow the rule of the Romans. Jesus would use other means both to bring them down and to lift up the humble (1:52).

But the leaders of Israel are desperate to convince Pilate that Jesus is stirring up rebellion. There are tens of thousands of pilgrims in Jerusalem for the Passover, all of whom long for God to deliver them from their Roman oppressors. Many of them have eagerly listened to Jesus every day as he has taught in the temple about another kingdom. Pilate surely understands how easily things can get out of hand. The unrest they now experience could quickly spill over into riots if they don't get rid of Jesus. If Jesus' teaching leads to riots, the emperor in Rome will hold Pilate responsible as governor of the region.

Pilate listens, but now he looks at Jesus, who is bound and beaten, and asks him, "Are you the king of the Jews?" Jesus replies, "Yes, it is as you say" (v. 3). Again, Jesus openly claims to be the Messiah whom God has sent to rule over his kingdom. But Pilate doesn't take Jesus' claim seriously. Jesus stands before him alone, fettered, and severely beaten. His closest followers—hardly an army—were only armed with two swords and offered little resistance when Jesus was arrested. Now they have all abandoned him. And Jesus makes no threats, offers no resistance; he hardly says a word.[130]

As Pilate looks at Jesus he perhaps thinks, "If this man believes he is a king, he is deluded and not to be taken seriously." He finds no basis for the charge of sedition against the Roman Empire. He finds Jesus innocent of any crimes and states that he does not care to involve himself in Jewish squabbles concerning a man who is not a threat, insignificant.

But the leaders of Israel persist. Now that they have Jesus, they are not about to let him be released. They tell Pilate, "He stirs up the people all over Judea by his teaching. He started in Galilee and has come all the way here" (v. 5). When Pilate hears that Jesus comes from Galilee, he asks if he is a Galilean. Learning that he is, Pilate finds an easy way out of his dilemma. He will send Jesus to Herod, who rules over Galilee but is in Jerusalem at present. Jesus will become Herod's problem, not his. So he has Jesus led off to the man who has wanted to see him for such a long time.

Scene Three: Jesus before Herod (23:8–12)

It has been some time since we read about Herod, the ruthless ruler of Galilee, where Jesus spent most of his life and began to proclaim the good news of God. You may remember that Herod imprisoned Jesus' cousin, John the Baptist (3:19,20), and later attempted to see Jesus when he learned about his proclamation and ministry (9:1–9). Then, not too long before Jesus arrived in Jerusalem, he was warned that Herod wanted to kill him. Hearing this, Jesus sent messengers back to tell Herod—"that fox," as he called him—to say that he would only die at God's appointed time and in God's appointed place, not out on a road in Galilee at the hands of Herod.

In light of all this, we would expect Herod to beat Jesus and put him to death, as Israel has done with most of their prophets. But seeing Jesus alone in Jerusalem, already bound and beaten, Herod realizes that he is no longer a threat to his rule in Galilee. Now Herod seems more driven by

---

130.   Wright, *Luke for Everyone*, 276.

an insane desire to be amused, asking Jesus to perform a miracle for him (23:8). When Jesus refuses to provide Herod with a miracle, Herod presses him with many questions. We don't know what he asks, but perhaps it is along these lines: "So did you really raise a girl from the dead? Where do you get your power to heal people? Is it true you claim to be Israel's King? If so, where are your people? You don't look like much of a King. Just how do you plan to establish your kingdom?" Such questions would amuse Herod and the cruel crowd that surrounds Jesus as he stands alone before his captors.

Jesus refuses to answer Herod's questions; Jesus remains silent. Why speak the words of God to one who will not listen?

The leaders of Israel failed to get Pilate to sentence Jesus to death, so having followed Jesus as he is led to Herod; they now step forward and again vehemently accuse Jesus of sedition. But Herod, like Pilate, finds Jesus innocent of any crime (vv. 14–15). Before he sends Jesus back to Pilate, however, he must get full enjoyment out of this man who calls himself a King. Unable to get Jesus to perform a miracle for him, unable to amuse himself with answers to his many questions, Herod begins to ridicule and mock Jesus. He has Jesus dressed in an elegant robe, thereby mocking Jesus' claim to be a King. Herod is so absorbed in his mockery of Jesus that he degrades himself as a ruler, standing alongside his soldiers to mock the would-be King. The entire scene depicts the willingness of God's Servant Jesus to suffer ridicule, dishonor, and humiliation as he obeys God's will.

There is powerful irony when Herod finally meets the Prophet Jesus— God will soon exalt his Servant Jesus to his presence as King because of his humble obedience, while the ruthless Herod, who mocks Jesus and schemes to become a king himself, will be humiliated when he is deposed and banished from the land he sought to be king over. As the Prophet Jesus has taught, God exalts the humble but humbles the proud.

The story ends by saying, "That day Herod and Pilate became friends—before this they had been enemies" (v. 12). Jesus has been sent to bring peace between warring factions, but in sad, cruel irony, Herod and Pilate, who have been enemies up until now, become friends through their common rejection of Jesus and his message. Jesus' trial before Herod shows how everyone—Jews and non-Jews, representatives of different social classes, and people of different political and religious persuasions—unites in their ridicule and rejection of the Messiah Jesus, who is himself God's way of peace. Throughout his ministry Jesus has sought to bring together Jews and Gentiles; he has welcomed people of different social classes into God's kingdom; and he has even ushered in those of different religious backgrounds. The kingdom of God is the great equalizer. But Herod and Pilate, united in their apathy and their blindness to see who Jesus is, fail to join it. They hold on to their paltry kingdoms, which will one day come to an end.

The Final Scene: Pilate Allows Jesus to be Crucified (23:13–25)

When Jesus is led back to Pilate, the governor calls together the leaders and the people of Israel and says to them, "You brought me this man as one who was inciting the people to rebellion. I have examined him in your presence and have found no basis for your charges against him" (23:14). Pilate goes on to note that Herod also found Jesus innocent of any wrongdoing and not deserving of death.

This final scene in the trial clearly demonstrates Pilate's belief that Jesus is innocent of the charges against him and should be released. But evidence and reason do not prevail. Jesus is not released.

What happens next is beyond belief. Some of the very same people who welcomed Jesus to Jerusalem as the Messiah, who listened intently to him as he taught in the temple each day, have now turned against him. How could they have changed their minds so suddenly?

It helps to again recall what the people of Israel hope the Messiah will do. Their expectation was that Jesus would deliver them from Roman occupation. They now feel he has failed them. He has not taken up the sword to fight against the Romans. He has not even prayed for God to destroy them. Added to these unmet expectations, his closest followers have now abandoned him, so the people conclude that Jesus must not be the Messiah after all.

In addition, the leaders of the people insist that Jesus is a false prophet, a deluded messianic pretender who must be put to death. They have told the people that Jesus has blasphemed by saying he will soon share in God's rule, seated at God's right hand in heaven. But it is not only disappointment and the accusations of their leaders that cause the people's sudden hostility toward Jesus; it is also fear.[131] If they continue to support Jesus, and their leaders convince Pilate to crucify him, they may be crucified along with him for being his followers.

Thus, while the people of Israel now join their leaders in calling for Jesus to be crucified, they do not share the same deep-rooted hostility and jealousy as these men who have wanted to kill Jesus since he first came to Jerusalem (19:47–48). We will read shortly that the people come to realize and regret their mistake in calling for Jesus to be crucified. Overall, "Jesus' death is the consequence of the relentless and overpowering presence of the Jewish leadership."[132]

But for now the people of Israel unite with their leaders in crying out with one voice, "Away with this man! Crucify him! Crucify him! Release Barabbas to us" (23:18,20). Barabbas, an insurrectionist and a murderer, was seized by Roman soldiers in Jerusalem for his crimes. It is possible that he and his followers believed he was a king God had raised up to liberate Israel from the Romans.[133]

Pilate has made it a custom to release a prisoner to the crowds during the Passover each year. Clearly he wants to release Jesus, but the crowd's shouting prevails. He releases Barabbas instead. The crowd's demand exposes their reasoning: Jesus failed to deliver them the way they wanted. Barabbas, at least, had taken up his sword and made an attempt to liberate them. He fought for Israel, so he should be released. Jesus—a false prophet, a messianic pretender—should be crucified. The people prefer the release of a man guilty of insurrection and murder over that of Jesus, the Innocent and Holy One of God. "Either Barabbas or Jesus must die; either the one who stands for violent revolution, which Jesus has opposed from the beginning, or the one who has offered and urged the way of peace."[134]

Throughout the Gospel we have read of how Jesus has selflessly given himself in love to rescue and restore lost people. Now Jesus will go so far as to give himself up in death. The people believe he is a sinner, a blasphemer, a deluded false prophet. In reality he is the Holy One of God. Jesus doesn't die as a sinner; he dies instead of the sinner Barabbas. He dies instead

---

131. Ibid., 280.
132. Green, *Gospel of Luke*, 791.
133. Wright, *Luke for Everyone*, 279.
134. Ibid.

of all who are sinners. He dies for all of us. When Jesus explained the meaning of his death at the Passover meal with his disciples, he said he would offer his life in death so that others could live—that they would be free and forgiven.

When Barabbas is released, he receives a new chance to believe in the one who died for him. All of us are invited to see ourselves "in the figure of Barabbas; and, as we do, we discover in this story that Jesus comes to take our place, under condemnation for sins and wickednesses great and small."[135]

JESUS IS CRUCIFIED AND BURIED (23:26–56)

Jesus Is Led Away to Be Crucified (23:26–31)

The trial of Jesus is over; the people's voices have prevailed. Jesus is now led away to be crucified. He often told his twelve closest disciples that he would be put to death, but we have only recently learned that it would be by crucifixion. Crucifixion was such a heinous, horrific form of execution that it was rarely described in ancient literature. But those who lived in a place like Jerusalem at the time of Jesus were well aware of what it entailed. The leaders of Israel, many of the people, the Roman soldiers, and many of Jesus' disciples see him crucified. Its horror is not hidden from them, nor should it be from us. What do they see?

A FOCUS ON CRUCIFIXION

"Crucifixion included a flogging beforehand, with victims often required to carry their own crossbeams to the site of the execution, where they were nailed or bound to the cross with arms extended, raised up, and perhaps seated on a small wooden peg."[136] The victim normally died slowly as he hung on the cross for several days. Death finally came about by shock or asphyxiation, as the muscles used in breathing suffered increasing fatigue. But for the onlookers, the victim's death did not end the horror and

---

135.   Ibid.
136.   Ibid., 280.

humiliation of crucifixion. "The corpse of the crucified was typically left on the tree to rot or as food for scavenging birds."[137]

Political rebels, criminals, and others were crucified near busy crossroads so that people would see and be warned not to rebel against Roman power. "The victim was subjected to savage ridicule by frequent passersby, while the general populace was given a grim reminder of the fate of those who asserted themselves against the authority of the state."[138]

This background information on crucifixion helps us better understand the Gospel story. We now read that Jesus is led through the streets of Jerusalem and out the city gates to be crucified, with many people present. Jesus has been viciously flogged (22:63). When flogged, the pieces of bone and lead embedded near the ends of the leather strips cut into the flesh, often causing the victim to die. Because of this flogging and additional abuse from Herod and his soldiers, Jesus is too weak to carry the heavy crucifixion crossbeam to the place of his execution. So the Roman soldiers seize a random man entering Jerusalem and force him to carry Jesus' cross.

Even though Jesus suffers great agony as he struggles to walk through the streets, he is still filled with compassion; he still speaks the word of God and warns the people of the judgment that will soon come upon them. As Jesus stumbles along he hears a group of women wailing behind him. He turns to them and says, "Daughters of Jerusalem, do not weep for me; weep for yourselves and for your children. . . . For if men do these things when the tree is green, what will happen when it is dry?" (23:28,31).

Jesus seems to mean if the Romans would brutally crucify him, God's Righteous Servant (i.e., when the tree is green), what will they do when unrighteous rebels revolt against Rome in reckless, brutal acts of terror? This will be the time when the tree is dry and ready for burning. This will be the time (in AD 70) when the Romans surround Jerusalem and burn it to the ground.

The people of Israel have shouted out for Jesus to be crucified. He is barely alive after his vicious floggings; he has remained mostly silent during his trial. Why does he now speak? Why does he bother to warn them once more of the approaching judgment? Because of love. Even

---

137.   Green, *Gospel of Luke*, 810.
138.   J. B. Green, "Death of Jesus," in *Dictionary of Jesus and the Gospels*, 146–63.

though the nation of Israel will be destroyed and the people displaced from the land, Jesus entreats them to turn to God and participate in the eternal kingdom he establishes through his Servant Jesus.

God's Messiah is Crucified (23:32–43)

The soldiers lead Jesus and two criminals to the place outside of the city wall where they will be crucified. The place is called the Skull because of the shape of the rock that protrudes from the ground.[139] The rulers of Israel, who took the lead in having Jesus put to death, stand closest to the cross to ensure that he is executed according to plan. Next to them are the Roman soldiers who will carry out the crucifixion. Behind them are the people the leaders persuaded to cry out for Jesus to be crucified. At a distance stand Jesus' disciples (23:49), watching along with the passersby on the road.

Knowing the physical, mental, and spiritual agony he would endure in dying, Jesus prayed the night before, overwhelmed with anguish. So we may wonder now how he will respond to the horror and humiliation he experiences as he hangs on the cross. Normally those crucified curse the soldiers who nail them to their cross. Many even curse God, disillusioned by their failed attempt to deliver Israel from its enemies. Will Jesus curse his enemies? Will he become disillusioned with God?

No, Jesus knows his God is still with him, even on the cross—especially on the cross—and will strengthen him to fulfill his will. God is referred to at least five times while Jesus is crucified,[140] reminding us that God has not abandoned his chosen Servant in his sufferings—even if it seems so to those who stand watching him hang there in disgraceful agony. On the contrary, God is present and working through his beloved Messiah as never before. If Jesus is fearful at any point, he did not give in to his fear. He continues to think of others and trust in God from the cross. "Jesus emerges as more than a hapless victim; he is ever in control and his trust in God never waivers."[141]

As in Galilee, so also now in Jerusalem: it is the ostracized, the poor, and those on the margins of society who respond in faith to Jesus. While

---

139. Bock, *Luke*, 595.
140. Green, *Gospel of Luke*, 812.
141. Ibid.

the leaders of Jerusalem continue to mock him (v. 35), some women mourn for him (v. 27), a criminal crucified next to him comes to believe he is God's chosen Servant (v. 42), and finally a Gentile soldier, watching how Jesus suffers and dies, praises God and says of Jesus, "Surely this was a righteous man" (v. 47).

Even in his agony, Jesus continues to care for and pray for others. He said little during his trial and remained completely silent during the latter part of it. But now on the cross he speaks again. So we now read that Jesus is the first to speak as his crucifiers pound the nails through his wrists to fasten him to the cross. Jesus prays, "Father, forgive them, for they do not know what they are doing" (v. 34). He prays not only for the Roman soldiers who drive the nails deeper and deeper into the cross, but also for the leaders of Israel, who have orchestrated his trial and execution, and for all his enemies, all who shouted out, "Away with this man!" (v.18).

To the very end, and now to the uttermost, Jesus shows us the depths of God's love as he seeks out sinners and suffers for them so that they may be forgiven and live. Even in his suffering Jesus continues to love, pray for, and do good to his enemies, just as he taught his disciples to do (6:27–36). He does good to them by not cursing them, by not calling upon God to destroy them, by staying on the cross to take the judgment for their sins upon himself. Instead of saving himself and destroying them, he allows himself to be destroyed in their place so that they may live and find peace. If only they will see and believe.

Now Jesus becomes silent again while his enemies mock him both verbally and in cruel acts of ridicule. He is verbally mocked three times. The leaders of Israel sneer at him, saying, "He saved others; let him save himself if he is the Christ of God, the Chosen One" (v. 35). Then the Roman soldiers join in the taunting, saying, "If you are the king of the Jews, save yourself" (v. 37). Emboldened by these words, even one of the criminals crucified beside Jesus joins in saying, "Aren't you the Christ? Save yourself and us!" (v. 39). The whole world, it seems, has gathered to mock the man God sent to save it.

Along with the three verbal taunts hurled at Jesus, we read of three acts of humiliation carried out by the Roman soldiers. First they strip Jesus of his clothing to nail him naked to the cross (v. 34). "To be stripped of clothing signified gross indignity and the loss of personal identity."[142] Jesus is shamefully humiliated and treated as if he were a nonperson. Then the soldiers offer Jesus wine vinegar to drink (v. 36). This too is mockery, for Jesus is offered the sour wine of poor people rather than wine that suits a king.[143] Finally, the Roman soldiers write a mocking notice and fasten it to the cross. It reads, "THIS IS THE KING OF THE JEWS" (v. 38). All who stand there (except the disciples), all who pass by, will laugh in derision at a man who claimed to be a king but hangs naked on a cross.

Jesus was given authority to save people from the powers of evil, even death. Hadn't he raised the dead? If Jesus really is the Messiah, a King with the power to save, why doesn't he save himself? Why doesn't he heal himself on the cross and come down? Why?

Jesus stays on the cross, enduring the suffering and shame, because he knows that his demise is God's way to deliver the world from its bondage to the tyranny of sin and death. What those who taunt do not know is that Jesus has willingly submitted to death to make salvation possible—even for them. What his enemies do not know, and what his disciples will only later understand, is that Jesus shows the love and power of God precisely by staying on the cross. By suffering for his enemies rather than saving his life and seeking revenge, Jesus shows us all the way to break the endless cycle of hatred, revenge, and violence. Most importantly, by undergoing the agony and suffering in our place, Jesus frees us all from fear, shame, and bondage to sin—if we will only believe and receive this gift.

Jesus knows that his suffering on the cross is the climax of his obedience to God as his Servant-Messiah. He knows that his death will not be the failure of his messianic mission but its fulfillment.

We then read that when one of the criminals crucified next to Jesus hurls insults at him, the other rebukes the man for not fearing God. He then implores Jesus, "Remember me when you come into your kingdom." Jesus answers him; "Today you will be with me in paradise"! (vv. 42–43). Knowing who he is and knowing that God will rescue him from death, Jesus promises the criminal being crucified that he will join him this very day in the presence of God!

---

142.   Ibid., 820.

143.   Wright, *Luke for Everyone*, 284.

This criminal, this murderer deserving to die—this man hanging naked on a cross who will die this very day—will also be saved this very day. He turned to Jesus with a contrite heart and believed. So he will be received. Jesus has looked beyond his suffering and death, knowing he will soon be exalted to the very presence of God, where he will share in God's rule (22:69). Now he enables the criminal to see beyond his own sufferings, to see beyond his dying. This very day, after dying together, they will still be together—together in heaven with God.

This criminal is the first to believe that Jesus' death will not be the end of him. It is not the end of the kingdom Jesus has proclaimed but the way to it. This man is the first to believe that though Jesus will die, God will rescue him from death. His contrite confession of faith in Jesus to save him stands in stark contrast to the words of the leaders of Israel and the onlookers, who in their unbelief mock Jesus as a messianic pretender, a false prophet, and a poor fool who cannot even save himself.

Jesus, though not a criminal, dies like a criminal for a criminal. Jesus, though not a rebel, dies like a rebel for a rebel. Jesus the Righteous One, Jesus the Innocent One, takes upon himself the sins of this offender. In Jesus the criminal has seen "the meaning of kingship, the meaning of the kingdom itself."[144] He has seen a King who rules by love, not by retaliation; he has looked at Jesus and seen a King who humbles himself, even suffers, for the good of others. He has seen a King like no other king. And he wants Jesus to be his King. So "like a king on his way to enthronement, Jesus promises a place of honor and bliss to the one who requests it."[145]

The disciples abandoned Jesus, fleeing in fear for their lives. But Jesus does not suffer and die alone after all. God chose a criminal crucified beside Jesus to die with him and then join him at once in paradise. Can you imagine that?

The Death of Jesus (23:44–49)

We now read of Jesus' last hours on the cross. His trust in God, who has loved him and cared for him, remains strong until his last breath, when he cries out, "Father, into your hands I commit my spirit" (23:46). Jesus has

---

144.   Ibid.
145.   Ibid.

repeatedly prophesied that God will raise him from the dead; now as he dies he trusts in him to do so.

We have read in the Gospel how Jesus' death will bring about the defeat of the dark, evil forces led by Satan. So it should not surprise us that the battle between light and darkness intensifies in the last hours before Jesus dies. We read that "darkness came over the whole land until the ninth hour, for the sun stopped shining" (v. 44). Darkness engulfs the region from noon to 3 p.m. (according to the Jewish way of calculating time). From the moment Satan led Judas to hand Jesus over to the leaders in Jerusalem, the forces of evil have increased.

When Jesus was arrested he told the leaders of Israel, "This is your hour—when darkness reigns" (22:53). Satan is allowed for a short time to have his way with God's chosen Messiah, but he does not fully understand the power and wisdom of God. Satan foolishly believes he will maintain his control over humanity by working through the governing rulers to have Jesus put to death. Similarly, the Jewish leaders believe they will finally be rid of Jesus, who for them has been a menacing messianic pretender undermining their power and authority with the people. But Satan, the leaders, the people, and the Roman rulers will all be surprised. In the midst of the darkness, God is present accomplishing his purposes. His Servant will be killed but then raised to life as God's King. No one can outmaneuver God.

When Jesus dies, God responds by tearing the heavy curtain in the temple in two (23:45). This huge cloth divider kept people from entering the innermost part of the temple, where God revealed his presence. Jesus did predict the destruction of the temple, so it is possible that the tearing of the curtain symbolizes the coming judgment. But more likely it symbolizes that the temple will no longer be the place where God reveals himself and receives sacrifices for the forgiveness of sin—Jesus will be. No longer will the leaders of Israel be the guardians of the holy place and the mediators of God's presence—Jesus has replaced them for all time.

And because the entire temple system segregated priests from ordinary people, men from women, Jews from Gentiles, and those who considered themselves righteous from those who threw themselves at the mercy of God, the tearing of the curtain signifies that Jesus' death has opened the way for all people to freely enter the presence of God, regardless of religious positions, sex, or ethnicity.

In his mission Jesus often ignored the classifications created by society and sought to remove them. By sharing meals with sinners, the Pharisees, non-Jewish people, and especially the poor and the marginalized, Jesus sought to bring them together at one table as a new people living in love and peace with one another. Now by his death Jesus forever breaks the formidable boundaries created by man, expressed in the physical space of the temple. Because of his death, any and all can be forgiven, cleansed, and received into God's presence.

The way Jesus dies and the events surrounding his death do not go unnoticed. We read of three different responses to "what took place" (vv. 47–49). The Gentile Roman soldiers, the people of Israel, and Jesus' disciples all respond differently to his death. Interestingly, nothing is said about how the leaders of Israel respond. We can speculate about their joy and relief in finally getting rid of this menacing prophet from Galilee, and how they return to Jerusalem once they are assured he is dead, but the Gospel is silent about it.

What is it the people see as they watch Jesus die? They see how Jesus asks God to forgive those who have crucified him rather than cursing them. Instead of calling down retribution, Jesus prays for them. They see how Jesus, in spite of his own agony, turns to the criminal crucified beside him and assures him of salvation this very day. They witness the cloud of darkness that covers the land. They learn from those back within the walls of Jerusalem that the curtain in the temple has suddenly been torn in two. And they see how Jesus continues to trust in God in his agony, and how he dies in peace. Observing all these things, they sense that God is somehow at work in the darkness of Jesus' death.

It is a Roman soldier who first responds to Jesus' death. Seeing what has happened, he praises God, saying, "Surely this man was a righteous man" (v. 47). His words imply more than that he believes Jesus to be innocent of any crime. As a Gentile, the Roman soldier probably does not know the prophecies concerning the righteous Messiah in the Jewish Scriptures. But God leads him to speak words that echo what was said of the coming Messiah. The Scriptures said that the Messiah would be "a righteous Branch, a King who will reign wisely and do what is just and right" (Jeremiah 23:5). God also spoke through one of his prophets saying of the Messiah, "See, your king comes to you, righteous and having salvation, gentle and riding on a donkey, on a colt, the foal of a donkey" (Zechariah 9:9).

After the soldier's response, we read of the people of Israel beating their chests when they see how Jesus has died at the hands of their leaders. This is an expression of sorrow. The people initially welcomed Jesus to Jerusalem as the Messiah, their King, but then joined their leaders in calling for him to be crucified. We have already seen signs that they have begun to realize their mistake (23:27). Now as they witness the events of the crucifixion, they pour out their grief and regret over their mistake. Though they do not know it yet, we know that they will have the opportunity to right their wrong and believe.

Finally we read of the response by Jesus' disciples. Except for Peter, the disciples have not been mentioned since they fled for their lives when Jesus was arrested. Even now they seem fearful and weak in faith as they stand at a distance, watching their Master die. They believed he was the Messiah who would rescue them from their enemies. They believed they would sit beside him on thrones as he ruled the kingdom from Jerusalem. As the story continues we will learn more about the mental state of the disciples, who have followed Jesus from Galilee to Jerusalem only to see him arrested and crucified. For now we read only that they stand far back from the cross and watch as Jesus dies. We can presume that they are shocked, disillusioned, and overwhelmed by grief.

Throughout Israel's history their leaders have mocked and killed the prophets God sent to them. But now they have killed one who was more than a prophet. He was God's Messiah, sent to rescue Israel. The Messiah cannot be killed! The Messiah was to kill Israel's enemies, not be killed by them. God would send him to deliver, not to die. So as the disciples see Jesus on the cross, he who healed so many people by the power of God, they too must be asking themselves, "If he is the Messiah, the Chosen One, why doesn't he heal himself, come down from the cross, destroy our enemies, and establish God's kingdom for Israel?" In time they will understand why; they will understand the mystery, power, and love of God.

Jesus Receives an Honorable Burial (23:50–56)

As readers of the Gospel, we have learned to honor God's Servant Jesus as Prophet and Messiah. Thus we would expect him to receive an honorable burial. But the leaders of Israel do not honor him, and while Pilate did not believe Jesus was guilty of any crime, Jesus means nothing to him. The Romans believe that Jesus is just another common criminal, and a "decent burial is not something that the families of executed criminals could count on. The bodies could be left for the carrion birds and scavenger animals to eat or could be thrown into a common grave."[146] Even the Jews, who took care to bury their dead, would place the corpse of a criminal in a common grave. In light of all this, it is surprising that Jesus is buried at all. It is even more surprising that he receives such an honorable burial.[147]

But if we remember that Mighty God controls the events surrounding the life and death of his Messiah, it should not surprise us that Jesus receives an honorable burial. Just as God earlier worked through good and upright people who longed for the kingdom of God (e.g., Zechariah, Elizabeth, Simeon, and Anna in 1:5–6; 2:25,36–38), so also now he works through a man named Joseph, "a good and upright man . . . who was waiting for the kingdom of God" (23:50–51). Even though Joseph is a member of the council of leaders in Jerusalem that condemned Jesus to death, he "had not consented to their decision and action" (v. 51). They aren't all bad—and Joseph is one of the exceptions. He has already risked being ostracized by the other leaders through his openness to Jesus' teaching, and now he risks again by giving Jesus an honorable burial.

So Jesus' body is not left on the cross to rot and satisfy the appetites of wild animals, nor is it thrown into a common grave for criminals. Joseph carefully takes his body down from the cross, wraps it in clean linen cloth, and places it in a tomb that he owns, one that is "cut in the rock, one in which no one had yet been laid" (v. 53). Jesus' body is also prepared with spices and perfumes to dispel the stench of dead flesh (v. 54).

In the midst of the horror and tragedy, God has been at work to provide Jesus, his beloved Messiah, with an honorable burial. More importantly, God is at work to ensure that there are witnesses at Jesus' death and burial to confirm that he, the Messiah, is the very same Jesus who proclaimed the arrival of God's kingdom, the very same Jesus who died, and the very same Jesus who was buried alone in an unused tomb. It is Joseph, who also watched Jesus die, who now takes his body down from the cross and wraps it in linen cloth, and places it in a privately owned, unused tomb. Since

---

146.   Tannehill, *Luke*, 348.
147.   Green, *Gospel of Luke*, 831.

Jesus' body is not placed in a common tomb among other corpses, there could be no mistake in confusing his body with other decaying corpses.[148]

But Joseph is not the only witness. Some women who knew and served Jesus in Galilee also witnessed him die on the cross (v. 49), and they remained at the crucifixion site after the crowds had left to see Joseph take the body of Jesus down. They then followed Joseph to see the tomb where he had laid him (v. 55). They too could attest that it was the same Jesus.

We recall that the Gospel was carefully recorded so that we may know "the certainty of the things" that took place (Luke 1:4). Because Jesus repeatedly stressed the centrality of his death and resurrection to his mission in bringing God's kingdom to earth, it is essential that we know that the very same Jesus who proclaimed God's kingdom was crucified and buried, but then raised from the dead.

JESUS IS RAISED FROM THE DEAD AND APPEARS TO HIS DISCIPLES (24:1–53)

Angels Appear to the Women at Jesus' Empty Tomb (24:1–12)

Jesus repeatedly told his closest disciples that God's plan for him as the Messiah was to be put to death in Jerusalem but then to be raised from the dead. So when we read of how slow the disciples are to believe that Jesus is alive, we tend to judge them as being spiritually slower than they really are. It is very difficult for us, living after the fact, to understand the shock—no, the impossibility—of a crucified Messiah for the Jewish mindset. It is equally shocking, for the disciples and those they later tell, that Jesus has been raised from the dead. Why is it so hard for the disciples to believe that Jesus is now alive?

The disciples are shattered by the crucifixion of Jesus. Throughout Israel's history the prophets God sent were rejected, shamefully treated, and most often killed. But this would not happen to the Messiah, the King who would liberate Israel from her enemies. The closest disciples gradually came to understand that Jesus was more than a great prophet;

---

148.   Wright, *Luke for Everyone*, 287.

he was the Messiah sent to liberate them from the Romans and rule over God's righteous kingdom from Jerusalem.

This is why the disciples are so stunned by Jesus' crucifixion at the hands of their enemies. They have seen so much of God's power and love at work in Jesus. There is no denying that he was a great prophet of God. But now they are forced to conclude that Jesus must have been mistaken in believing he was the Messiah, that he was more than a prophet. Jesus is dead. Dead. They have to deal with that.

Shocked, disillusioned, and still struggling with how Jesus, their hope for deliverance, could have been so shamefully, cruelly crucified, the disciples cast aside a report that he is alive as sheer nonsense (24:11). For according to their belief as Jews, the resurrection of the dead will not occur until the very end of history, and at that time all the righteous will be raised from the dead, not just one man. As one scholar says, "It was simply that nobody had ever dreamed that one single person would be killed stone dead and then raised to a new sort of bodily life the other side of the grave, while the rest of the world carried on as before."[149]

The startling fact with the resurrection of Jesus is that God raises him to a completely new kind of existence—resurrection existence with a body, but a *transformed* body. And God does this right in the middle of our carrying on with life, apparently to show what he will do at the end of time. While God and his Servant Jesus previously raised people from the dead, they all died again. But God raises Jesus from the dead with a transformed body, never to die again. This is an unexpected, completely new way of existence for a human being.

In short, even though Jesus often told his disciples he would die and rise again, they have no mental category, no place in their belief system, for a Messiah who comes and is killed only to then be raised from the dead. What will it take for them to believe that God has raised Jesus from the dead?

The first disciples to receive the honor of learning that Jesus is alive are women: Mary Magdalene, whom Jesus delivered from seven demons; Joanna, the wife of the man who manages Herod's palace; and several other women who faithfully, selflessly served Jesus in Galilee and bravely followed him to Jerusalem (23:55; 24:10). After seeing Joseph take Jesus'

---

149. Ibid., 290.

body down from the cross, they "followed Joseph and saw the tomb and how his body was laid in it" (23:55).

Now the women return to the tomb in order to apply spices and perfumes to the body of Jesus, to cover the stench of his decaying flesh. Jesus' body is the first to be placed in Joseph's tomb, but others' bodies could follow in the coming months. The central area of the tomb is high enough to stand in, and more bodies will be laid on shelves dug into the rock on the sides of the tomb.[150] So in order to make the smell of the tomb bearable for those who will later enter it carrying other corpses, the women bring spices and perfumes to put on Jesus' body.[151]

But when they come to the tomb, they find that the large stone used to seal the entrance has been rolled away. Perhaps Joseph, the owner of the tomb, has already come to apply spices and perfumes to the body. Alarmed, curious, they step through the low doorway. But when the women enter the dark chamber, the body of Jesus is not there!

As they stand stunned, wondering what could have happened to the body of Jesus, two angels suddenly appear beside them and say, "Why do you look for the living among the dead? He is not here; he is risen! Remember how he told you, while he was still with you in Galilee: 'The Son of Man must be delivered into the hands of sinful men, be crucified and on the third day be raised again'" (24:5–7). Then it all comes back to them—all that Jesus said and promised. This is it. Jesus has been raised from the dead.

What enables the women to believe that Jesus is alive? The signs of his resurrection surround them: Here is the massive stone used by the Romans to seal the tomb and prevent entry, which has somehow been rolled back. Here is the tomb itself, empty of everything but the linen used to wrap the body of Jesus. But above all, here stand two angels sent by God to appear to the women, reminding them that Jesus often predicted both his death and his resurrection.

Thus Mary Magdalene, Joanna, Mary the mother of James, and a few other women become the first to know that God had raised Jesus from the dead. When they saw the stone rolled away from the tomb, they could have run back to tell the other disciples so that Peter and the other men

---

150.   Ibid., 287.

151.   Green, *Gospel of Luke*, 830.

would have encountered the angels instead. But God chose to honor these faithful women by making them the first to know that Jesus is alive.

In their joy and excitement, the women run back from the tomb and tell the eleven and all the other disciples what has happened. Perhaps in their excitement they hastily jumble their words: "He's not there . . . we saw angels . . . but first we saw the stone rolled away and . . . the angels, they said Jesus is alive . . . but we didn't see him . . . still, the angels said we should remember what he said. Do you remember?"

Whatever the women's exact words, the other disciples do not believe them—not for a second (v. 11). The women's words seem to them like useless chatter, nonsense. But perhaps we should not be too hard on the other disciples for so quickly dismissing the news. For as we noted previously, a crucified Messiah and the resurrection of one person from the dead in the midst of history are concepts completely foreign to the Jewish mind at this time. And the angels have not appeared to the other disciples as they have to the women. In addition, at this time in history the testimony of women is not considered credible.[152] That's just the way the world is in the disciples' day.

The women, like all of them, have lost much sleep, still in shock over the cruel, humiliating crucifixion of Jesus—so the male disciples probably reason that the women's emotions are still running high, and their ability to judge reality low. Perhaps in their tiredness and sorrow the women went to the wrong tomb and, wishing for Jesus still to be with them, imagined seeing angels who told them that Jesus was alive.

Peter, however, seems to believe that there is something to the women's report, for he gets up and runs to the tomb where Jesus was buried. He looks in and finds it empty, just as the women said. But he still does not believe the women's report. Peter simply wonders what has happened to the body of Jesus.

What will it take for Peter and the remaining disciples to believe that God has raised Jesus from the dead?

---

152.   Wright, *Luke for Everyone*, 290.

Jesus Appears to Two Disciples
Leaving Jerusalem (24:13–35)

Despondent and confused, two of the disciples leave Jerusalem. As they walk they discuss all that happened to Jesus over the past few days in Jerusalem. They believed he was not only a great prophet but also the Messiah who would rescue them from their enemies. But instead their enemies killed him! So now, downcast and defeated, they walk to the village of Emmaus, about ten kilometers west of Jerusalem.

Is Emmaus their home? Are they leaving the community of disciples Jesus formed to start over again where they were before? We are not told. But their departure from Jerusalem may signal the beginning of the disintegration of the community Jesus gathered around himself.[153] Jesus' crucifixion by the Romans dashed their hopes of him establishing God's kingdom. What is there to do but go back home and start where they left off?

They know Jesus was a good man, a prophet powerful in all he said and did. But now they see that he must have been mistaken to believe he was God's chosen Messiah. What is there to do but accept the fact that they placed their faith in the wrong man, good as he was? Yes, he was a prophet powerful in word and deed—but not the Messiah. For he was crucified.

Yet the conversation of the two disciples on their journey suggests that they hold on to some undefined hope that God may still be at work among them. They have not completely ruled out the report of the women who found Jesus' tomb empty. Did angels actually appear to the women saying that God had raised his Servant from the dead just as Jesus had predicted?

Only one of the two persons on the road is named, a man called Cleopas. The other may be his wife, a son, a daughter, or another male disciple.[154] Perhaps the identity of the other disciple is left open-ended so that any one of us can place ourselves in the story, knowing that Jesus is now alive and wants to guide us through our own doubts and fears. In any event, walking and talking with a close friend is a good way to process life's events—especially when we discover that Jesus is present.

Suddenly, as the two disciples discuss all that happened in Jerusalem, a stranger joins them on their journey. As readers of the Gospel, we know that the "stranger" is Jesus, now raised from the dead. But for some unexplained

---

153.   Green, *Gospel of Luke*, 844.
154.   Wright, *Luke for Everyone*, 293.

reason the disciples "were kept from recognizing him" (24:16). While it is the very same Jesus they have known, his body has been transformed at his resurrection. Perhaps Jesus also disguises his physical appearance until it is time for him to reveal his true identity as the risen Messiah.

As Jesus walks with the two disciples he asks them what they are discussing. He already knows, of course. But with a bold stroke of irony, the Gospel records how the two disciples challenge the "stranger" for being the only person visiting Jerusalem who does not know that a Prophet from Nazareth, who many believed to be the Messiah, was arrested by the leaders of Israel and handed over to Pilate to be crucified.

As Jesus continues to conceal his identity, the two disciples proceed to tell him all about the Prophet Jesus. Oh, the irony! They teach Jesus about Jesus! They inform him that Jesus "was a prophet, powerful in word and deed before God and all the people. The chief priests and our rulers handed him over to be sentenced to death, and they crucified him; but we had hoped that he was the one who was going to redeem Israel. And what is more, it is the third day since all this took place" (vv. 19–21). They then go on to inform Jesus that some of the women had found the tomb of Jesus empty and were told by angels that he was alive. Imagine—they are telling all this to Jesus! Perhaps after the darkness of the crucifixion, God knew we would need a lighter moment in the story. So go ahead and chuckle. I did.

There is no doubt in the disciples' minds that Jesus of Nazareth in Galilee was an exceptional Prophet. He was "powerful in word and deed before God and all the people" (v. 19). Thousands upon thousands experienced God's power working through him as he taught God's message with authority, healed the sick, drove out demons, and even raised the dead. But in time Jesus claimed to be more than a prophet. And that was the problem.

Gradually many came to believe he was the promised Son of David, the Messiah whom God had sent to establish his kingdom of righteousness, justice, and peace. In fact, when Jesus recently entered Jerusalem, many of the people praised God and welcomed Jesus as the promised Messiah-King who would at last fulfill the Scriptures. These two disciples express this same yearning when they say to Jesus, "We had hoped that he was the one who was going to redeem Israel" (v. 21). That was *their* problem.

Instead of establishing a kingdom, Jesus was handed over by the leaders of Israel to be crucified. A crucified Messiah? That's not possible. When God had sent his prophets to Israel to preach against their idolatry and injustice towards the poor, many were rejected and killed in Jerusalem. But Jesus? He was supposed to be the promised Messiah. Yet he was rejected and killed.

Despite the perplexity, we see a glimmer of hope in the two despondent disciples. As they walk and talk they remember that Jesus often said he would die. And they remember that he said he would also be raised from the dead. Is it possible he wasn't speaking in riddles? Is it possible that the report of the women may have been true? Perhaps angels really did appear to them saying that Jesus was alive. Yet in spite of all this, the disciples still do not believe God has raised Jesus back to life. What will it take? It will take the risen Jesus himself appearing to them. He must explain how everything that has happened to him was predicted in the Scriptures.

Jesus has listened; now he speaks. He rebukes the two disciples, saying they are foolish and slow to believe what God has spoken through the prophets. They have read the Scriptures selectively. If they had read all the prophets had said in all of the Scriptures, and read it with an open mind, they would have understood that Jesus, as the Messiah, had "to suffer these things and then enter glory" (v. 26). The disciples failed to see the places where the prophets say that the Messiah must first suffer and die, and only then be exalted by God to rule over his kingdom. So "beginning with Moses and all the Prophets, he explained to them what was said in all the Scriptures concerning himself" (v. 27).

If Moses and the other prophets had so clearly predicted the sufferings and death of the Messiah, how did the disciples fail to see it? While there are passages that speak of this, they could easily be overshadowed by the many places where the Scriptures speak of the Messiah coming to defeat Israel's enemies and rule over God's kingdom on earth. Still, if the people of Israel had read all that was predicted of the Messiah, they would have known that he must suffer before he would be exalted as King.

Besides their selective reading of the Prophets, there is another possible reason the disciples did not believe that Jesus, as the Messiah, must first suffer and die. The closest disciples gradually became so focused on their perception of Jesus as the Messiah that they minimized his identity as a Prophet. At the beginning of Jesus' ministry, many people recognized him as a great Prophet sent by God. But in time God revealed to Jesus' closest disciples that he was also the Messiah. Then they began to interpret the mission of Jesus primarily through their lens of him as a Messiah-King who would conquer their enemies and reign with power and great glory in Jerusalem.

Even though Jesus was first and foremost God's Messiah, he never ceased to live as and be treated as a prophet. In his earthly ministry Jesus "lived the life of a prophet, and prophets are regularly rejected, persecuted, and even killed"[155] (see 4:24; 6:22–23; 11:47–51). That's the point the disciples missed. The history of Israel showed that prophets invariably suffer—most of them at the hands of the leaders of Israel, right in Jerusalem.

The point is, there is "a presumed pattern of prophetic destiny that includes suffering" in all the Scriptures.[156] If Israel had rejected and killed the previous prophets God had sent them, how much more should the disciples have expected God's Messiah, his Prophet, to also be rejected, suffer, and be put to death. Because the disciples had come to minimize Jesus' identity as a prophet, they forgot the fate of prophets. They ended up creating the Messiah they wished for, just as people today create the Jesus they want.

We are not told how long Jesus walks with the two disciples on their journey. Surely it takes some time for him to explain what is said "in all the Scriptures concerning himself" (v. 27). What is strange is that even as Jesus explains the Scriptures to the two disciples, they still do not recognize him! Perhaps they believe he is an angel who has appeared to help them understand the events of the past few days. So as they approach the village of Emmaus, they invite the stranger to join them for a meal (vv. 28–29). They seem eager to learn more from the stranger, whoever he is. It is much too late in the day for him to continue his journey, so with good Middle Eastern hospitality they insist he stay with them.

The disciples prepare the evening meal and sit down to eat. We read that Jesus "took bread, gave thanks, broke it and began to give it to them"—and in that moment they see that it is Jesus! It is only now, while eating with Jesus, that their eyes are opened by God to recognize who this stranger is. He is alive! The disciples have shared many meals with Jesus

---

155. Tannehill, *Luke*, 356.
156. Ibid.

and often seen him take the bread, give thanks, and pass it to them. And it was often at such meals that Jesus revealed to them more of who he was and more of God's will for him. As the readers, perhaps we are meant to understand that we only recognize Jesus as he is, as the Messiah who dies and is raised to life, when he reveals himself to us.

As soon as the disciples recognize Jesus, "he disappeared from their sight" (v. 31). With this we understand that God transformed Jesus' body when he raised him from the dead, so that Jesus is now able to move in time and space in a way ordinary humans can't.

After Jesus vanishes, the two disciples ask each other, "Were not our hearts burning within us while he talked with us on the road and opened the Scriptures to us?" (v. 32). They are no longer downcast and confused. Jesus himself has appeared to them and brought clarity, joy, and hope. Jesus was the Messiah after all. He wasn't a well-meaning but mistaken prophet. And their decision to leave everything to follow him was the right decision all along!

Even though it is late in the day, the two disciples rush out the door in their excitement and hurriedly walk the ten kilometers back to Jerusalem. The other disciples must learn that the women's report was true; their words were not nonsense. They must continue as a community of disciples who follow Jesus.

When the two disciples return to the others in Jerusalem, they learn that while they were gone Jesus also appeared to Peter. (Perhaps Jesus appeared to Peter while he was alone because Jesus knew his sorrow from having denied him three times.)

Why does Jesus appear and then leave? What has happened to his body?

Jesus Appears to All the Disciples (24:36–49)

Living as we do in our limited world, with our limited understanding of God and his invisible workings, this final part of the Gospel can seem extraordinary, even strange. The focus of the story now becomes the nature of Jesus' resurrected body—a body unlike anything ever known to man— and how Jesus convinces the remaining disciples that he has risen from the dead, fulfilling what the prophets said of him as the Messiah. Of all the disciples in Jerusalem, only two understand how Jesus has completed the Scriptures by dying and being raised on the third day. The women, who went to Jesus' tomb to anoint his body, know he is alive, but Jesus has not yet appeared to them to explain everything. When Jesus is exalted to God's presence in heaven, the disciples will continue his mission of proclaiming the good news of the kingdom of God, a mission that has culminated in Jesus' death and resurrection. But how can they be witnesses of these things if they still don't believe and understand them?

That night, as the disciples are gathered discussing the report of the two disciples to whom Jesus appeared on the way to Emmaus, Jesus himself suddenly stands among them all. "Peace be with you," he says. Jesus' greeting is more than the traditional Middle Eastern greeting—in the Gospel, peace (shalom) is the result of the salvation God provides through Jesus. With his greeting of peace, Jesus thus implies that the leaders of Israel have not thwarted God's plan to bring peace to the world through his Messiah. To their surprise, the leaders of Israel will learn that God in his great wisdom and power has outwitted them and provided the means of salvation through the death of his Servant Jesus. By greeting the disciples with peace, Jesus offers them the fullness of peace they can now possess by believing in him.

But instead of receiving his peace, the disciples "were startled and frightened, thinking they saw a ghost" (24:37). Why would the disciples think they are seeing a ghost when it is Jesus standing before them in his resurrected body? One scholar offers this insight: "Apparently they recognize the one before them as Jesus, but are not yet ready to accept that he could have any other form than an intangible one."[157] Dead people have been brought back to life before. The disciples have seen Jesus raise people from the dead. But this is different. This is the Jesus they know in a different kind of body. The startled, frightened disciples find it hard not only to believe that Jesus is alive but also to understand the *way* he is alive. Who is this they see before them? It looks like Jesus—but what has happened to him?

Jesus must show the disciples that it is he, the very same Jesus they have walked, talked, and eaten with, but now in a transformed, resurrected body. First he shows them his hands and feet. Why would he point their gaze here rather than to the features of his face? Because the Roman soldiers drove large nails through his hands and feet to hold him on the

---

157.   Green, *Gospel of Luke*, 854.

cross, and the scars from those nails remain on his body. It is the very same Jesus who died only a few days ago, but now he is alive.

To further convince the disciples that it is he, Jesus also has them touch his body. It is indeed his body, a body with flesh and bones. It is not the intangible form of a ghost. Seven times in this story the disciples are told to see that it really is Jesus.[158] Finally, Jesus eats some broiled fish with the disciples to help them see that he is not appear ing in a non-bodily existence. They not only see Jesus eat as people do but also saw the manner in which he eats. They recognize the way he positions his arms and legs at the table and reaches for the food. It is the same way he has eaten with them many times.

It is safe to assume that all the disciples now believe that this is Jesus talking and eating with them, the same Jesus they followed from the beginning of his mission in Galilee, the same Jesus they saw arrested and put to death on a Roman cross. But they still do not understand how his dying—and now being raised to life—is God's plan.

Jesus then explains to all the disciples what he explained to the two disciples whom he joined on the walk from Jerusalem to Emmaus. He often told the disciples that he would suffer and die, but then be raised from the dead on the third day. Now he explains how his death and resurrection fulfill what was predicted about the Messiah. Jesus says to them, "Everything must be fulfilled that is written about me in the Law of Moses, the Prophets and the Psalms." Then we read that Jesus "opened their minds so they could understand the Scriptures." He says, "This is what is written: The Christ will suffer and rise from the dead on the third day" (vv. 44–46).

Jesus fulfilled the prophecies concerning the Messiah not only by proclaiming the arrival of the kingdom of God, healing the sick, and raising the dead, but also in suffering for proclaiming God's word, and above all in obeying God to the point of shameful, painful crucifixion.

Like previous prophets, Jesus suffered because he insisted on obedience to God's command to show mercy, loving from the heart, and expressing mercy in practical deeds for all, rather than on practicing the external rituals of religion. He suffered like previous prophets because he

---

158.   Ibid., 852.

exposed the hypocrisy of the leaders of Israel and of the rich, who failed to show compassion and execute justice toward the poor.

At the same time, Jesus suffered in his death like no other prophet, like no other spokesman for God—like no one either before or since. He suffered and died as God's Messiah, the Holy One of God. Jesus died *for* our sin and *to deliver us* from sin, to deliver us from the fear of punishment for our misdeeds, to deliver us from our powerlessness from sin our master. This was a deliverance much grander than conquering the Romans with the sword so that the people of Israel could live freely in the land.

Now that all the disciples believe—finally! —That it is truly Jesus in their midst and that everything has happened according to God's plan, they are ready to be witnesses of all he has said and done. They have been with him from the very beginning of his mission and can now verify that though he was put to death, God raised him from the dead. Most importantly, they can explain from the Scriptures why it was necessary for him to die and be raised.

Jesus tells the disciples that they, like John and himself, are to preach "repentance and forgiveness of sin" (v. 47). But unlike John and Jesus, they will preach repentance and forgiveness of sins *in the name of Jesus*. What can this mean? Repentance in the name of Jesus- in light of all we have read in the gospel- appears to mean to turn from a self-oriented life to live according to the kingdom of God embodied by Jesus in all he said and did; to obey Jesus in losing one's life by pouring it out for the good of others. We repent by believing who Jesus is, what he has done, and committing ourselves to living according to the way he has taught. By doing so a person receives the full forgiveness of their sins.

To preach the forgiveness of sins in the name of Jesus means that sins are forgiven based on his death on the cross as the Messiah. While Jesus died for the sins of all mankind, forgiveness is only procured when a person hears and embraces the salvation Jesus has achieved on the cross. Such people, by turning to the way of Jesus, can have the assurance and peace of a complete cleansing from the stain of sin, of a full forgiveness of sins, because God provided Jesus the Messiah as the one to take the punishment of our sins upon himself.

The people of Israel at this time believe Jerusalem is the center of the world, and they generally expect the nations to come to them to learn the ways of God as revealed in the Scriptures. But Jesus now instructs his disciples to proclaim the good news of God's offer of salvation "to all the nations, beginning at Jerusalem" (v. 47). In other words, they will start in Jerusalem, giving the leaders and the people of Israel another chance to understand that Jesus really is the Messiah, but in time they will go to all the peoples of the world to share the good news.

The mission will not be easy. The disciples will face opposition and suffer; some, like Jesus, will even die. Just as Jesus needed God's Spirit, God's enabling presence with him (3:21–22) to live and speak the message of God with power and authority, so will his disciples. John prophesied that Jesus would one day baptize with the Spirit those who turned to God in repentance (3:16). Speaking of God's Spirit, Jesus now says, "I am going to send you what my Father has promised; but stay in the city until you have been clothed with power from on high" (24:49).

Jesus has both taught and demonstrated that the powerful Spirit of God present in him is the way to advance the righteous kingdom of God against the evil rule of Satan. He said, "If I drive out demons by the finger of God [i.e., by God's Spirit], then the kingdom of God has come to you" (11:20). So before the disciples begin to proclaim and manifest the breaking in of God's kingdom upon the world, they are to wait until Jesus is exalted to God's presence, where he will receive the authority to send God's Spirit to the disciples. Only then will they have the wisdom, love, and power they need to boldly face hostility from God's opponents.

Jesus Is Exalted by God to His Right Hand in Heaven (24:50–53)

We now read that Jesus leads the disciples (as he has always done) out of Jerusalem near the village of Bethany just east of Jerusalem on the Mount of Olives. Bethany is the village where Jesus was welcomed to Jerusalem as the messianic King as he rode in on a donkey (19:18–40). From here God will now exalt his victorious, obedient Servant to his presence in heaven. Jesus will sit at God's right hand as King over his kingdom.

As Jesus lifts up his hands to bless the disciples, God lifts him up to be with him in heaven.

The kingdom of God that Jesus brought to earth still looks like a mustard seed, or leaven only partially kneaded into the dough. But Jesus promised that it would grow and grow among the nations and one day fill the earth. How this will happen through these simple laborers from the countryside of Galilee remains to be seen.

After God raises Jesus to his presence in heaven, the disciples respond by praising God and worshipping Jesus as the exalted King in heaven. The disciples finally understand that Jesus is more than the Messiah sent to rule on earth. Because of his humble obedience, God has exalted Jesus to rule as Lord from his very presence. From now on the disciples will address Jesus as Lord with this full new meaning. The disciples have only gradually understood the meaning of Jesus' lordship. Only now do they worship him as the exalted Lord (Luke 24:52).

The disciples no longer doubt that Jesus has risen from the dead as God's Messiah. Their joy is no longer mixed with disbelief (24:41), but is the pure joy of receiving, of experiencing the love and peace of God. In obedience to Jesus they do not return to their homes in Galilee but instead walk back to Jerusalem, where they continually meet at the temple, praising God for his great wisdom and love in sending Jesus. Here they wait for Jesus to send the Spirit as God promised.

CONCLUSION

This is the end of the Gospel of Luke, but it is not the end of the Gospel story. As readers we are eager to get the answers to our lingering questions. We may wonder, for example, when Jesus will send the disciples God's Spirit so that they have power to continue his mission. We may wonder how the leaders and the people of Israel will respond when the disciples of Jesus begin to preach that God has raised him from the dead. We may wonder how Jesus can be a King and bring peace on earth when he is in heaven. How can he rule on earth from heaven? And we may wonder how this ragtag community of disciples, who seem so slow to understand God's ways, can ever succeed in continuing to spread the kingdom God when Jesus is not with them. To discover the answers to these questions and many more, we will need to read the next part of the story, the part of Scriptures called Acts.

ACKNOWLEDGMENTS

I was a young lecturer in religious studies in Uppsala, Sweden, when the Gospel of Luke changed my world for the first time. For a year, several hours each day, I pored over the meaning and pondered the significance of Jesus' words and way of living. I still remember the rush of inspiration as I filled page after page with notes on the implications of Jesus' command to actively do good and to pray for those we consider our enemies.

After that initial immersion I continued reading and teaching the Gospel of Luke from time to time. Then, ten years ago, I began to see how many young people were eager to read the stories of Jesus and discuss the significance of his teaching about the kingdom of God. This led to a new immersion in Luke for six years with the intent of making the mission and message of Jesus readable for those with different religious backgrounds. I am grateful to my many Muslim and Christian friends who have been willing to read and discuss "the stories of Jesus" with me.

I am grateful to Steve, a friend and careful scholar, for his words of encouragement throughout this project. His expertise in understanding the titles used for Jesus in the Gospel was especially helpful. I am indebted to Pat for his enthusiasm for this book and his initial helpful editorial comments. Many thanks especially to Aidan for his care and skill in editing the manuscript. He added the right words in the right places when I had grown weary of looking. Many thanks also to Josie for her fine work in formatting the cover and the interior of the book.

I am especially grateful to my Finnish wife, Eeva, whom I met in my youth while living in Sweden. She models the life Jesus teaches about to the international students who come through our home. The first question they often ask me when they return from their English classes is, "Where's Miss Eeva?" Our students like me; they love her. Thanks, Eeva, for your patience these past six years when I have often been deep in thought.

Most of all, I cannot adequately express my thanks to you, my God, for helping me to continue writing year after year when I was often fatigued and frustrated. So many times I wondered how I kept going. I now know it was you who gave me endurance. May you be pleased with the words I have written and gracious where I may have misunderstood your words, and may you use this book to welcome many into your kingdom of love.

WORKS CITED

Barker, Kenneth L, ed. *The NIV Study Bible.* Grand Rapids, MI: Zondervan, 1995.

Bailey, Kenneth E. *Jesus through Middle Eastern Eyes: Cultural Studies in the Gospels.* Downers Grove, IL: IVP Academic, 2008.

Blomberg, Craig L. *Interpreting the Parables.* Leicester, UK: Apollos, 1990.

Bock, Darrell L. *Luke.* The NIV Application Commentary. Grand Rapids, MI: Zondervan, 1996.

Gorman, Michael J. *The Death of the Messiah and the Birth of the New Covenant: A (Not So) New Model of the Atonement.* Eugene, OR: Cascade Books, 2014.

Green, Joel B. *The Gospel of Luke.* Grand Rapids, MI: Eerdmans, 1997.

Green, Joel B., Scot McKnight, and I. Howard Marshall. *Dictionary of Jesus and the Gospels: A Compendium of Contemporary Biblical Scholarship.* Downers Grove, IL: InterVarsity Press, 1992.

Horsley, Richard A. *Galilee: History, Politics, People.* Valley Forge, PA: Trinity Press International, 1995.

Marshall, I. Howard. *The Gospel of Luke.* The New International Greek Testament Commentary: A Commentary on the Greek Text. Grand Rapids, MI: Eerdmans, 1978.

McKnight, Scot. *The King Jesus Gospel.* Grand Rapids, MI: Zondervan, 2011.

Porter, J. R. *Jesus Christ: The Jesus of History, the Christ of Faith.* New York: Barnes & Noble Books, 2004.

Tannehill, Robert C. *Luke.* Abingdon New Testament Commentaries. Nashville, TN: Abingdon Press, 1996.

Witherington, Ben, III. *New Testament History: A Narrative Account.* Grand Rapids, MI: Baker Academic, 2001.

Wright, Tom. *Luke for Everyone.* 2nd ed. Louisville, KY: Westminster John Knox Press, 2004.

Made in the USA
Middletown, DE
08 March 2017